THE
ANTIQUITIES
OF
CAMBRIDGESHIRE

by

Charles Lingard Bell
(1854 - 1941)

Vol. 2.

Transcribed from the original Bell manuscripts
by
Mike and Val Cowham

Cambridge 2013

First Published in Great Britain by M. J. and V. Cowham

Cambridge, 2013

Printed by

Henry Ling Limited
The Dorset Press, Dorchester, Dorset DT1 1HD

ISBN 978-0-9551155-4-7

THE

ANTIQUITIES

OF

CAMBRIDGESHIRE.

VOLUME II.

MAP OF CAMBRIDGESHIRE SHOWING THE VILLAGES COVERED IN THESE VOLUMES

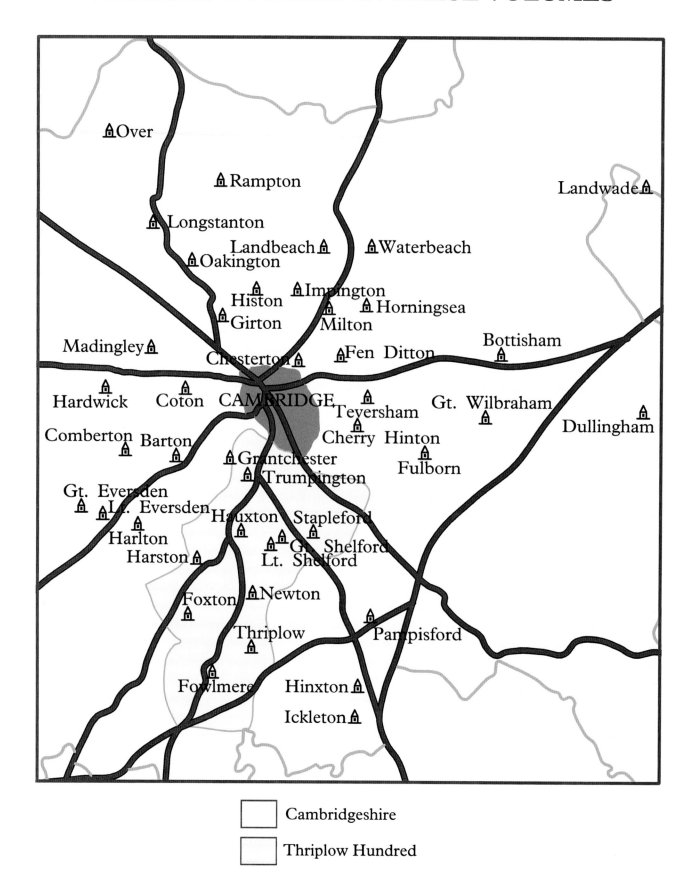

CONTENTS

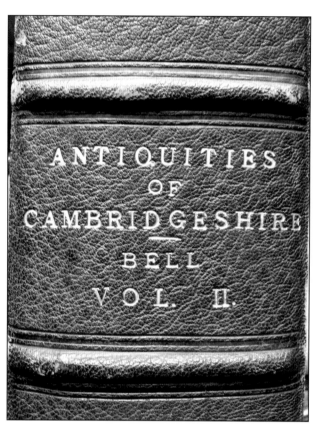

ANTIQUITIES
OF
CAMBRIDGESHIRE
—
BELL
VOL. II.

BARTON CHURCH

BRASS OF JOHN MARTIN & WIFE 1593

FULL SIZE.

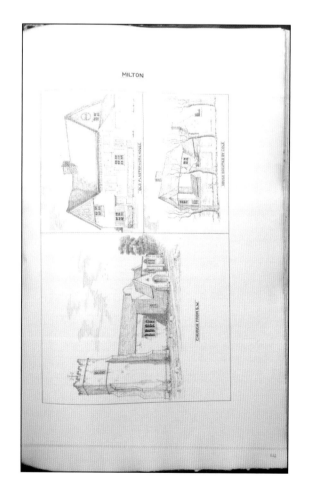

MILTON

OLD PARTERSHALL HOUSE

HOUSE OCCUPIED BY COLE

CHURCH FROM S.W.

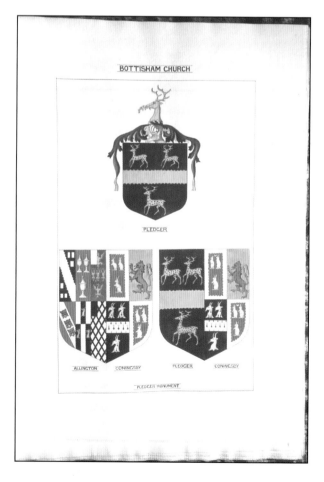

BOTTISHAM CHURCH

PLEDGER

ALLINGTON   CONINGSBY   PLEDGER   CONINGSBY

PLEDGER MONUMENT

INTRODUCTION TO VOLUME 2

In this second volume of the manuscripts of Charles Lingard Bell he covers 32 villages in the remaining part of Cambridgeshire. (The first volume covered the 10 villages of the Thriplow Hundred.) His entries for each village are not generally as detailed as in the first volume due to the number covered. In many, his notes and sketches are few in number. Therefore we have endeavoured to fill in some of the missing and more interesting features of each with modern photographs.

His coverage of Cambridgeshire is not complete and there are still many very interesting churches and other buildings that he has not described. No attempt has been made to redress this problem. However, for a fuller coverage the reader is directed to the book 'The County Churches of Cambridgeshire and the Isle of Ely' by C. H. Evelyn-White, F.S.A. written in 1911. For further details of Charles Lingard Bell reference may be made to 'The Sketchbooks and Diaries of Charles Lingard Bell (1854 - 1941)' by Janet Morris in the *Review of the Cambridge Association for local History,* 2010, Pages 30 - 35.

As with the first volume we have endeavoured to check many of the details and in the process found a few errors; or at least, changes since his time. The church with the most remaining questions is Chesterton. Here Charles Bell mentions several monuments but only one has been found. This may be due to the fact that they were lost during rebuilding as some of these missing monuments are listed by other authors. The other large puzzle is the church of St. Mary in Longstanton. Such a church does not exist. However, we believe that his sketch may be of the church of St. Mary and All Saints, in the same Parish, in the nearby village of Willingham. The Nave arches, pillars and mouldings there are certainly of the form that he shows in his drawing.

The church layout drawings done by Bell are in colour. He has colour coded the various architectural periods which we have decided are as shown below.

■ **Norman 1066 - 1189**

▨ **Early English 1189 - 1280**

▨ **Decorated 1280 - 1377**

▨ **Perpendicular 1377 - 1547**

☐ **Modern**

This chart has therefore been added, as a key, in one corner of each of his drawings. It may be noticed that there is some colour variation between them but it

should still be possible to ascertain which architectural period the various parts of each building belong to. If there is any doubt, the text usually clarifies this.

Any notes that we have added in this book are in the sans serif font that we have used here, whilst Bell's notes have been transcribed and have been printed in this serif font (M Plantin). We have also added a few photographs, particularly where Bell did not show a complete drawing of a particular church, or to illustrate some of the fine armorials on memorials that he describes in detail.

Some of the churches did not have any notes so we have added brief details from the book 'The Churches of Cambridgeshire and the Isle of Ely' by C. H. Evelyn-White, F.S.A. of 1911.

The two volumes of Antiquities of Cambridgeshire are rather large and heavy, the first on the Thriplow Hundred weighs 9kg and the Second Volume weighs 12½kg. They are bound between two rigid covers, probably of plywood, covered in a green cloth and have leather corners and spines. Inside the covers are End Papers that are attractively marbled

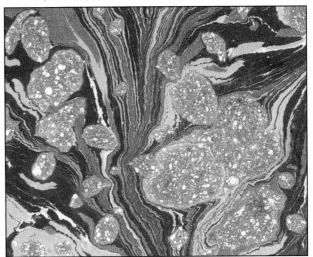

Due to the the weight of the books it was not easy to place them on a scanner for fear of crushing it, so the digital scanner was used inverted on each image. Standard photography had been ruled out due to the problems with getting even illumination and a perfectly flat image without distortion.

The A4 scanner used would not function inverted, so some modifications were necessary to keep it from jamming. As the scanner was made for use on A4 size sheets most images were scanned in several sections, sometimes as many as five scans being required, the results being reassembled by using a computer.

The Diaries of Charles Lingard Bell

In the Cambridgeshire Collection at the Central Library in Cambridge there are preserved, 31 of Bell's diaries, covering the years from 1871 to 1938 and two of his sketchbooks. The sketches (in ink) shown below have been taken from his diaries that were written around the period that his manuscripts for the 'Antiquities of Cambridgeshire' were being produced.

It is interesting to compare the sketch of Cole's House in Milton, as shown on the right, with his finished drawing on Page 208.

Cole's House in Milton (March 1883)

Aberdovey Quayside

Trinity Bridge from St. John's (September 10, 1880)

A sketch of Charles Bell's Study from one of his diaries
The above sketches are reproduced with the kind permission of The Cambridgeshire Collection

BARTON

The Church.

The Church is dedicated to St. Peter and consists of Chancel, Nave, West Tower and South Porch.

The Chancel is of Decorated date and in fairly original condition, the windows of two lights. There is a Priests Door on the south. The East Window is Perpendicular of poor character. The original pitch of the roof has been lowered.

The Nave is of the same period as the Chancel, c.1310, it has good two-light windows and a doorway on the north side and a Porch with two plain Nitches on the south.

The Tower is plain finished with battlemented parapet, the Belfry windows of two lights much decayed, the West Window blocked with brickwork, in the south west angle is a staircase.

The Interior presents few features of interest. The Chancel has a rude Piscina on the south side and there are three basins let into the sill of the adjacent window, on the north is a small Aumbry. The choir stalls are modern of good design finished with poppy heads and at the ends within a sunk quatrefoil are the arms of King's College. The roof is mean and boarded above the rafters. The Nave roof is of similar construction to that of

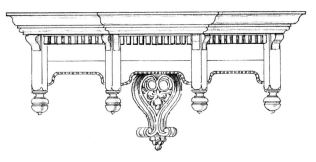

Canopy of the Pulpit

the Chancel but has tie beams in addition. There is a good Chancel Screen of Perpendicular work with small shields carved in the spandrils of the arches, eleven in all, three on the west side and eight on the east. There is also a good Jacobean Pulpit with canopy. On a panel is carved the date 1635 and beneath it is painted 1827. The lower panels are poor and the work shallow. Beneath a semicircular arch cut on the front panel are the letters I.H.S. painted in yellow with rays above and below. In the wall east of the South Door is a Stoup. A string of bold scroll moulding runs along both sides of the Nave beneath the sills of the windows and carried over north and south doorways.

Barton Church as it is today

BARTON

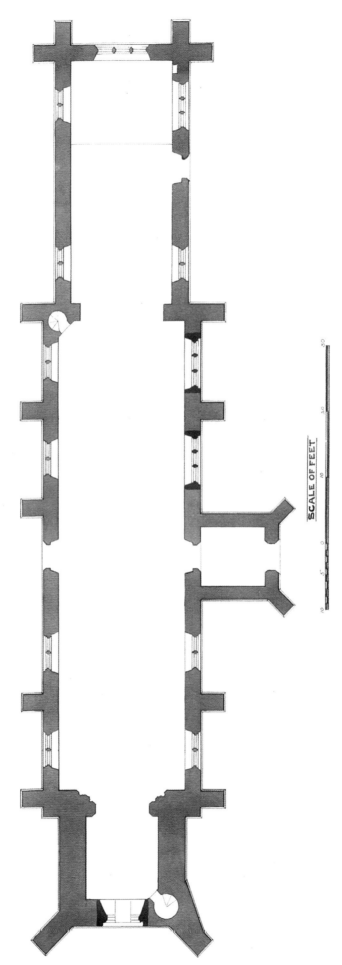

Norman 1066 - 1189

Early English 1189 - 1280

Decorated 1280 - 1377

Perpendicular 1377 - 1547

Modern

SCALE OF FEET

Formerly in Chancel Window　　*Formerly in Nave Window*

Monumental Inscriptions.

On the floor of the Chancel is a small late brass of man and wife with this inscription.

IVSTOR̃V ANIMÆ IN MANV D̃NISVNT
CONDVNTVR IN HOC TVMVLO CORPORA
IOHANNIS MARTIN ET MARGARETÆ VX
ORIS EIVS QVI CIRCITER ANÑV DÑĬ 1593
IN CHRISTO OBDORMIVERVNT.
MORI LVCRVM.

Stained Glass. The only fragment is a coat in the East Window which is much worn, the blazonry is false and on the sinister side is with difficulty to be made out. I give it as taken by Layer in the 17th century, from the Cole M.S.S.

Argent two bars gules between three martlets or within a bordure engrailed sable. Impaling quarterly 1st Argent on a chevron gules three lions passant sable. 2nd sable three covered cups or within a bordure argent. 3rd as 2nd 4th argent a chevron between three leopards faces or. He also gives the following coats now disappeared. Gules a cross argent. Vert a fess indented ermine (Somers). Or a fess between two chevrons sable.

On another slab of black marble with this coat. On a bend three fleurs de lis, a chief charged with two eagles displayed.

TOWER FROM WEST

EAST END.

BRASS OF JOHN MARTIN & WIFE c.1593.

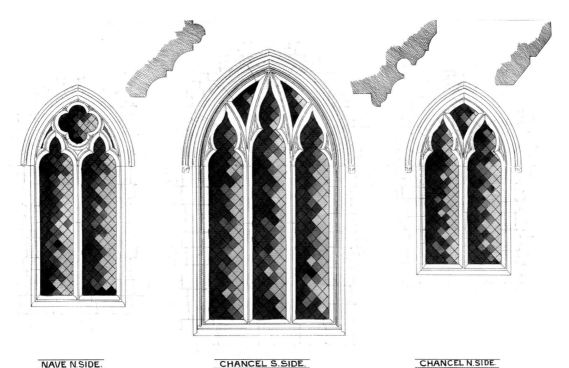

NAVE N.SIDE.

CHANCEL S.SIDE.

CHANCEL N.SIDE.

BARTON CHURCH

HERE LYETH THE BODIE OF MATHYAS MARTINE OF BARTON IN THE COVNTY OF CAMBRIDGE ESQR. WHO DIED THE 28TH OF NOVEMBER 1613:

On another slab.

SACRED
TO THE MEMORY OF
PHOEBE-ANN, WIFE OF
THE REVD DERISLEY HARDING, M.A.
VICAR OF THIS PARISH;
WHO DIED MAY 18, 1859,
Aged 69 Years
ALSO,
HENRY JOHN HARDING, B.A.
SECOND SON OF THE ABOVE;
DIED DECR 26, 1845,
Aged 27 Years.
ALSO
REVD DERISLEY HARDING,
35 YEARS VICAR OF BARTON
DIED DECR 30TH 1870, AGED 79.

On a tablet beneath a florid Gothic canopy on the north wall is the following.

To
the Memory of
Wilson Holben who died
Jany 16th 1861 Aged
Seventy five years
Also
In Memory of
Sanders Holben
Brother to the above

Who died May 5th 1862
Aged Seventy five
years
Also of Anne Holben, Widow
of the above Sanders Holben;
Who died Jany 28th 1877
Aged 73.

In the Nave are ten slabs with the following inscriptions.

1
In Memory of
MARY, the wife of
Sanders Holben
Who Died Feb. 1st 1814
Aged 59 Years.

Also of
MARY Holben
who died March 4th 1838
in the 58th year
of her Age.

2
In Memory of
SANDERS HOLBEN
who Died March 25th 1787
Aged 34 Years

Also of
JOHN HOLBEN
eldest son of Sanders
& Mary Holben
who Died Nov. 30th 1815
In the 34th year
of his Age.

PISCINA IN CHANCEL.

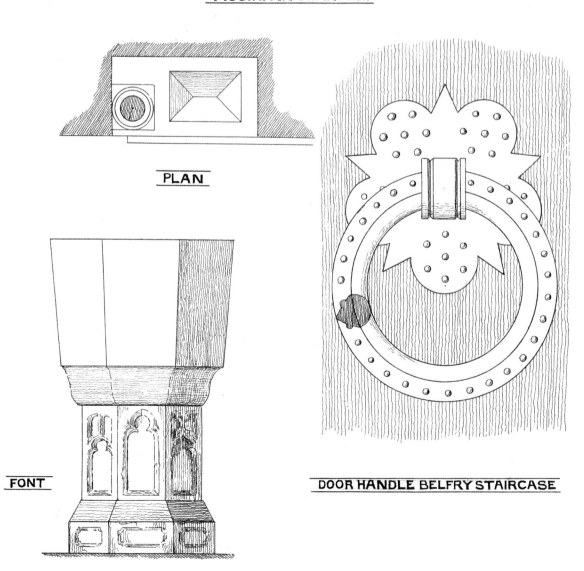

PLAN

FONT

DOOR HANDLE BELFRY STAIRCASE

3
IN MEMORY OF
ANNE WILSON
WHO DIED
AUGUST 24TH 1845
AGED 89 YEARS

———

ALSO OF
MARY DAUGHTER OF THE ABOVE
WHO DIED
FEB. 16TH 1868
AGED 84 YEARS.

4 Henry Page died July 29th 1713 aged 67 years.

5
Here lieth yᵉ body of
Ann
the Wife of
Henry Page
who died April
the 11th 1722 aged 33 years.

6
In Memory of
HENRY PAGE
who died Nov. 22nd
1788
Aged 65 Years.

7
ANN
the Wife of
HENRY PAGE
died Sep. 1. 1789
Aged 72 Years.

8
In Memory of
JOHN PAGE
who died May 3rd 1799
Aged 39 Years.

9
In memory of
Susannah the wife of
John Page
who died June 12th 1794
aged 35 years.

10
Sacred to the memory
of WILLIAM son of
HENRY and ANN PAGE
who died Febry 11th 1818
aged 64 years
also
of ANN the wife of
WILLIAM PAGE
who died May 3rd 1844
aged 86 years
also of
WILLIAM son of the above
WILLIAM and ANN PAGE
who died January 12th 1863
aged 61 years.

Pigeon house St. Catherine's Farm. 1914.

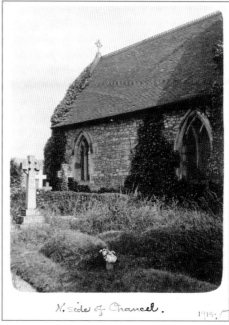

N. side of Chancel. 1914.

Other Buildings.

The old house of the Martins, now a farm house, stands on the north side of the church surrounded by a moat. The exterior is practically modernised but presents a picturesque appearance with its numerous gables and chimney stacks. The interior contains some slight remnants of old wood and plaster work.

In the farmyard of the farm formerly belonging to St. Catherines College Cambridge is an ancient dove cot probably of early 18th or late 17th century date, of brickwork in English bond with a steep hipped roof surmounted by a cupola. This was fast falling to ruins but in 1915 the College was persuaded to undertake some repairs when the roof was renewed and the thatch substituted for tiles.

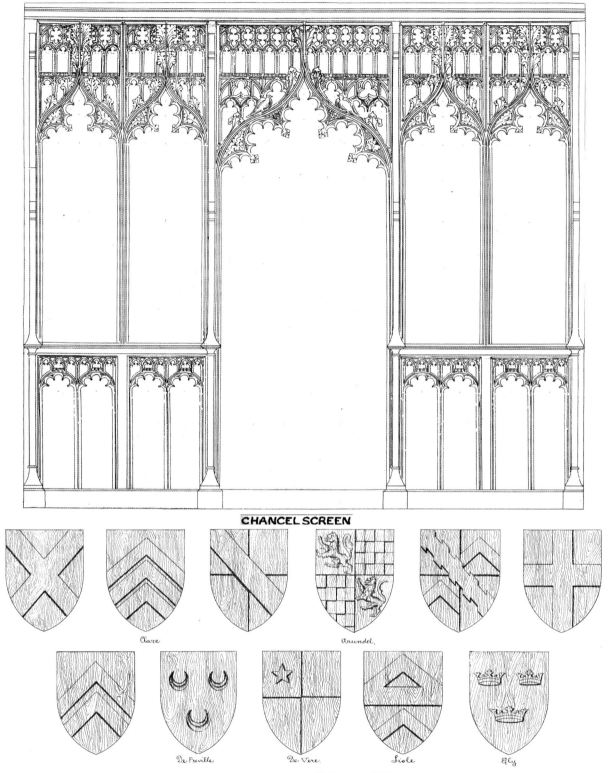

CHANCEL SCREEN

SHIELDS ON THE CHANCEL SCREEN

The coats carved in the spandrels of the Chancel Screen are as follows, eleven in all.

On the west side.
1. A saltire.
2. Three chevronels (Clare)
3. Quarterly, over all a bend.

On the east side.
1. Quarterly 1 and 4 a lion rampant, 2 and 3 Chequy (Arundel).

2. Quarterly. 1 and 4 the field, 2 and 3 a chevron, over all a bend raguly.
3. A cross.
4. Two chevrons.
5. Three crescents, 2 and 1 (De Freville).
6. Quarterly an etoile in the first quarter (De Vere).
7. A fess between two chevrons (Lisle).
8. Three ducal crowns 2 and 1, (Ely).

OLD FARM HOUSE

DOVE COT MANOR FARM

Pedigree of Martyn

John Martyn of Barton Cambridgeshire ┬ Margaret . . . . died c.1593.
died c.1593, buried in Barton Church. │ see the brass in Barton Church.

Elizabeth dau. of . . . . Knightley = Matthew Martyn of Barton ┬ . . . . dau. of Throgmorton
of Fawsley in Co. North'ton. 2.   ob. 28ᵗʰ Nov. 1613 bur. in   1 wife.
Barton Church, see inscription.

Sir Thomas Martyn of Barton ┬ Elizabeth dau. of Prisley of . . . .   Robert Martyn of Lye (Leigh)
ob. 1650 æt. 40. Knighted by │ in Co. Hertford. = 2ⁿᵈ husband   Courtin Co. Worcester. ┬
Charles 1ˢᵗ at Whitehall   Walter Devereux,
6 Jan. 1641-2.   5ᵗʰ ViscountHereford.

Leicester Devereux 6ᵗʰ Viscount. ┬

Anne sist. & heiress of Edward 8ᵗʰ Viscount. ┬ Leicester Martyn of
Leigh Court 1729.

Elizabeth = Drice Devereux 10ᵗʰ Viscount mar. 1721, her cousin.
sole dau. & heir.

Devereux Martyn of Barton = Dorothy dau. of Sir John   Lucy first married to Edward Hanbury
Esq. æt. 50, 1684. Sold the   Ashfield of Acton Knight   of Kelmarsh in North'tonshire after
Manor of Burghurst in   and Baronet.   Sutton Ashfield 2ⁿᵈ son of Sir John
Barton to the University of   Ashfield of Acton Co. Middlesex.
Cambridge 1680.

BOTTISHAM

The Church.

The Church is dedicated to the Holy Trinity and consists of Chancel, Nave, North and South Aisles, North and South Porches, West Tower and West Porch.

The Chancel is Early English with Perpendicular insertions. There are two three-light windows on the south and two on the north of two lights and three lights respectively. In 1875 or later, the East Window was also Perpendicular, but has since been rebuilt in the Early English style, a triplet, richly ornamented with tooth ornament and Purbeck marble shafts. The Priests Door is Early English of plain design with double chamfered jambs and arch. In the south wall is a Sedilia and double Piscina of Early English work but the easternmost arch of the former has been replaced by a round chamfered head. The Chancel Arch is Early English, well moulded and supported on corbelled caps. There is one step at the Chancel Arch and one at the Sacrarium and two at the Altar. The floor of the Chancel is formed with stone slabs, that of the Sacrarium is elaborately tiled, the roof is poor of flat pitch. The Reredos is modern painted stonework of poor design. The choir stalls are good, carved by Rattee and Kett. The eastern triplet is filled with modern stained glass the subjects being:

The North Window, above, The Resurrection,
   below, Christ bearing the cross.
Central window, above, The Ascension,
   below, The Crucifixion.
The South Window, above, Pentecost,
   below, Burial of Christ.

The drawing of these is good but the colouring somewhat opaque. On each side of the Altar are placed the Creed and Ten Commandments, painted. The Chancel is of fine proportions, lofty and wide.

The Nave is Decorated. The pier arches are well moulded, the columns clustered. The Clerestory consists of single light windows with mouldings of unusual richness. Between the Nave and Chancel is a fine stone Screen of three arches of Perpendicular work. Above the Chancel Arch are two windows of late character. The west end is blocked by a gallery. The seats and reading desk are of modern (1839) and poor design. The lectern is of oak, the

Bottisham Church as it is today.

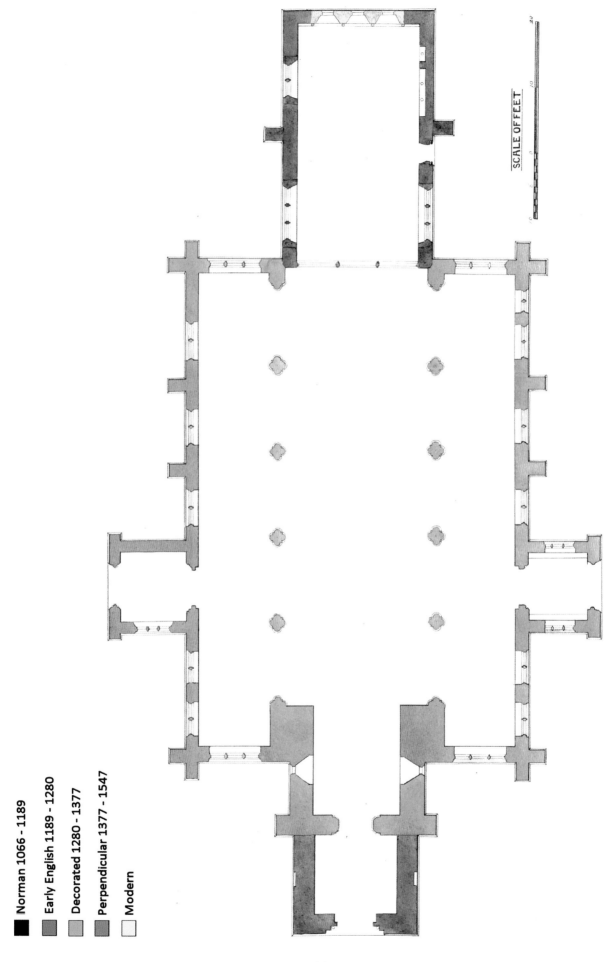

Norman 1066 - 1189
Early English 1189 - 1280
Decorated 1280 - 1377
Perpendicular 1377 - 1547
Modern

SCALE OF FEET

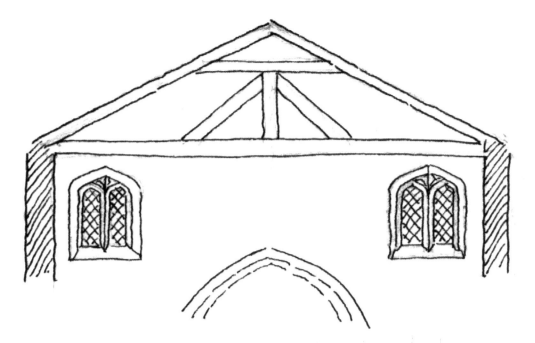

design adopted being an eagle with extended wings. The roof is of flat pitch and simply constructional shewing no artistic design.

<u>The Aisles</u> are Decorated, the windows being richly moulded both externally and internally. They are of two lights and all of similar design excepting the windows at the east and west ends which are of three lights. The easternmost windows both on the north and south are square headed with transoms, beneath that in the South Aisle is a well moulded Sedilia and Piscina. The easternmost bays of both aisles were formerly Chantries and are raised one step above the level of the Aisle floors. These Chantries are separated from the Nave and Aisles by richly traceried screens, these however are "made up" and do not stand as originally planned, they are coeval with the Nave.

The Font is of the same date of poor design, a hexagonal basin on a square base.

<u>The Tower</u> is Decorated with embattled parapet and furnished with low pinnacles at the angles, it opens into the Nave by a low segmental arch not much larger than a doorway. Above this is an archway looking into the Tower.

The Belfry windows are of two lights with a quatrefoil in the head. The West Door has plain chamfered jambs and arch. It leads into the West Porch or Galilee. This is coeval with the Chancel and it has been suggested that this was the lower stage of an earlier tower and the thickness of the walls 3ft. 3in. rather favour the theory. Above the west doorway is a recess for an image. There is a good cross on the gable.

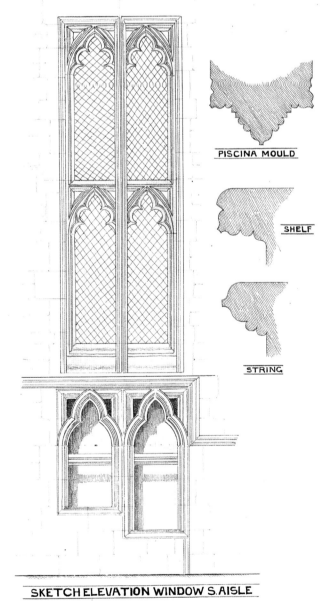

PISCINA MOULD

SHELF

STRING

SKETCH ELEVATION WINDOW S. AISLE

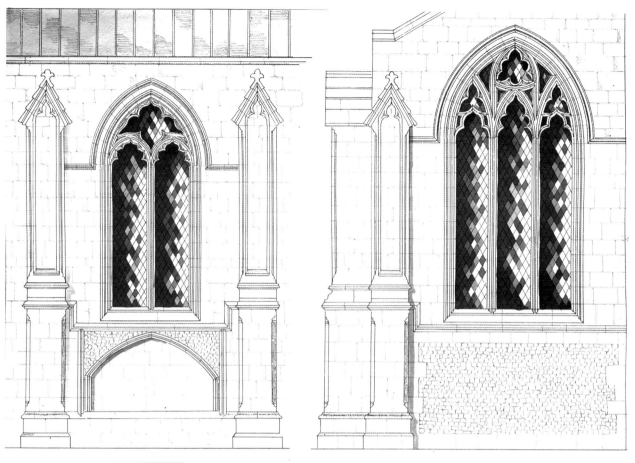

SOUTH AISLE

E.END S.AISLE.

The Bells.
In the Belfry are five bells with these inscriptions.
1. Thos.Newman and Henry King
   Churchwardens. Wm. Dobson founder 1829.
2. John Draper made me 1606.
3 and 5. John Draper made me 1626. H.C.
4. Ricardus Nicholson me fecit, with the heads
   of a king and queen as shewn.

The Porches are Decorated with well moulded arches. The north is blocked and used as a vestry, the south has been considerably restored. On each side of the doorway are two tablets of Renaissance character but without inscriptions.

The elevation of the aisles on the exterior is very fine. The windows are richly moulded with the hood moulds returning along the wall stopping at the buttresses. These are terminated in gable heads and the angles are moulded. In the upper part is a sunk panel with cusped head. Beneath the windows are arcades in square panelled recesses, these are richly moulded (the moulding is the same as that to the Sedilia in the South Aisle) and of segmental form, the spandrils are filled with flint work, each arcade encloses a stone coffin.

The exterior walls of the Chancel are covered with cement, the east end now presents three simple lancets. Formerly it had a Perpendicular window of similar character to those on the north and south.

The roofs of the whole church are covered with lead.

Inscriptions.
The monumental inscriptions are fairly numerous.
In the Chancel are the following.
On a marble tablet south wall.

NEAR THIS PLACE
ARE DEPOSITED THE REMAINS OF
THE REVEREND WILLIAM PUGH M.A.
A SENIOR
FELLOW OF TRINITY COLLEGE CAMBRIDGE

AND VICAR OF BOTTISHAM IN THE COUNTY OF
CAMBRIDGE
WHO DEPARTED THIS LIFE
ON THE 19TH DAY OF APRIL 1825
AGED 57 YEARS.

On the north side on a brass plate.

TO : THE : GLORY : OF : GOD
THE · EAST · WINDOW · AND · REREDOS
IN · THIS · CHURCH · WERE · ERECTED
BY · RELATIONS · FRIENDS · AND
BROTHER · OFFICERS · IN · MEMORY · OF
COLONEL : SOAME : GAMBIER : JENYNS : C : B
ASSISTANT · ADJUTANT · GENERAL
AT · HEAD · QUARTERS · AND · LATE
OF · THE · 13TH · HUSSARS · ELDEST
SURVIVING · SON · OF · GEORGE · JENYNS
ESQUIRE · OF · BOTTISHAM · HALL
HE · SERVED · IN · THE · ARMY · FOR
28 · YEARS ·INCLUDING · THE · CRIMEAN
WAR · AND · WAS · ONE · OF · THE · SURVIVORS
OF · THE · BALAKLAVA · CHARGE · IN · 1854
BORN · FEB : 4 : 1826 ❖ DIED · NOV : 26 : 1873 :
BURIED · IN · THE · FAMILY · VAULT
BY · HIS · DEATH · A · MOST · VALUABLE
OFFICER · WAS · LOST · TO · HIS · COUNTRY

On the north east respond of the Nave Arcade is
this inscription on a tablet.

To the memory of HESTHER
PAULINA LUSHINGTON
who died July 24th *1795*
aged eighteen.

As purity of heart will be accepted at the
day of Resurrection through the merits
of her Saviour Jesus Christ,
She has not lived in vain.
Her Parents have erected this Memorial
as a testimony of her virtues
and of their affection.

Near the Chancel Arch a little to the south is the
matrix of a brass but no inscription remains.

At the east end of the North Aisle is an old altar
tomb with the matrix of a brass. On the north side
were formerly three coats of arms, probably for
William Allington, Speaker to the House of
Commons 1472, died 1479.

Against the east wall of this aisle is a monument
of white marble sculptured with reclining figures
of a boy and girl.

STAY PASSENGERS AND WONDER WHOM THESE
STONES
HAVE LEARND TO SPEAKE : TWO INFANTS
ALINGTONS
THESE Y^E WORLDS STRANGERS CAME NOT
HEERE TO DWELL
THEY TASTED, LIKE IT NOT AND BAD
FAREWELL :
NATVRE HATH GRANTED WHAT THEY BEGD
W^TH TEARES.
AS SOONE AS THEY BEGVN TO END THEYRE
YEARS
IACEMVS HIC LEONELLVS ET DOROTHEA
EXIMIORVM GVLIELMI ET
ELIZABETÆ ALI^NGTONVM, FILIVS FILIALQVÆ.
FATO SVCCVBVIM̃ ANNO SAL : 1638

Against the north wall is an elaborate monument
of Elizabethan date representing a man in armour
kneeling before a faldstool and behind him his
wife. Above them are two coats of arms and the
monument surmounted by a third. The upper one
is, sable a fess engrailed between three bucks
trippant or, spotted of the field. Crest. A bucks
head erased holding an oak branch with acorns or,
leaves proper.

NAVE ARCADE

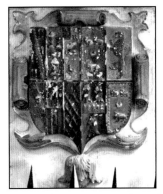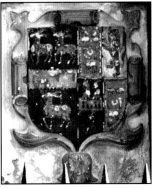

Over the womans head a shield Allington with quarterings impaling Coningsby.
1. Sable a bend engrailled between six billets argent (Allington)
2. Gules, three covered cups argent (Argentein)
3. Azure five eagles or displayed 1.3.1 a canton ermine (Fitz Tek)
4. Gules on a bend argent three leopards faces sable (Burgh)
5. Per fess argent and sable a pale counterchanged, three griffins heads erased or. (Gardner)
6. Argent fretty sable and a canton of the last. (Middleton)
1 and 4. Gules three conies sejant within a bordure engrailed argent, a crescent of the last. (Coningsby)
2. Or a lion rampant gules. (Streche?)
3. Sable a fess ermine between three goats heads erased of the second. (Feriby)

Over the man's head a shield with the arms of Pledger impaling Coningsby quarterly as above. Beneath is this inscription now getting rather illegible.

HERE LYETH MARGARET THE DAUGHTER
OF WILLIAM CONINGSBYE OF KINGES
LYN, ONE OF THE IUSTICES OF THE
COMMON PLEES AT WESTMINSTER WHO
MARRIED ROBERT ALLINGTON
ESQUIRE SONNE AND HEIR OF SYR
GILES ALLINGTON OF HORSEHEATH
KNIGHT BY WHOM SHE HAD FIVE SONNES
AND SIX DAUGHTERS, THAT IS TO SAYE
WILLIAM, JOHN, GILES, JAMES AND
GEORGE, ALICE, ANN, MARGARET, ELI
ZABETH, FRANCES AND BEATRICE
AND AFTER SHE MARRIED WITH THOMAS
PLEDGER GENT. WITH WHOM
SHE LIVED HIS WIFE FOUR YEARS
AND DIED THE 16 DAYE OF MAYE ANNO
DNI 1598 ANNO ÆTATIS SUÆ 78 AND THE
SAYDE THOMAS PLEDGER DYED THE 13
DAY OF MARCH ANNO DNI 1599 AND IN
THE THREE SCORE AND TENTH YEAR

OF HIS AGE WHO LYETH HERE BURYED.
WHO BY HIS LAST WILL AND TESTAMENT
DID GIVE FORTYE POUNDS TO BE
STOWED IN FREEHOLD LANDS AND THE
YEARLY RENT OF THE SAYD LANDS TO
BE EMPLOYED AND BESTOWED UPON
EIGHT OF THE POOR PEOPLE AND AN
CIENT INHABITANTS DWELLING IN THIS
PARISH OF BOTTISHAM FOREVER.

On the north wall is a monument with this inscription.

In hope of ✝ eternal life
Maria Jane, wife of George Jenyns Esq
Of Bottisham Hall;
who died at Alverstoke Hants, March 13, 1867 Aged 68
lies buried in the family vault in this church
Also, in St. James' churchyard Dover.
George Gambier, the then eldest son of the above
George Jenyns Esq, and Maria Jane his wife
Aged 15 Years
Also in the family vault,
Jemima Maria Hicks, eldest daughter of the same,
who died at Ryde Isle of Wight,
January 9, 1858, Aged 28 Years
And
Roger Leonard Gambier, youngest son of the same,
who died at Culford Hall, Suffolk,
February 12, 1853, Aged 13 Years
Also buried elsewhere, three Infants of the same,
Soame, died March 10, 1821, Aged 11 days.
Leonard, died August 28, 1823, Aged 7 months.
And a son born and died May 1824.
Also George Jenyns Esq.
born March 18, 1795, died April 13, 1878.

South Aisle. On the south wall with these arms on a hatchment close by. Argent on a fess gules three bezants. (Jenyns) impaling Erminois a fess of four lozenges vert, on a chief azure an annulet between two suns or. (Heberden).

THOMAS PLEDGER. 1599.

SIR ROGER JENYNS. 1740.

IN A VAULT BENEATH IS DEPOSITED THE BODY OF
MARY, WIFE OF
THE REV^D GEORGE LEONARD JENYNS,
THE MOTHER OF TWELVE CHILDREN, SIX OF WHOM
ONLY SURVIVED HER.
SHE DIED THE 18TH DAY OF AUGUST 1832, AGED 69.

———◆———

IN THE SAME PLACE HAS BEEN LAID THE BODY OF
SOAME, ELDEST SON OF THE ABOVE
GEORGE LEONARD & MARY JENYNS,
WHO DIED AT HARROW SCHOOL,
TO THE INEXPRESSIBLE GRIEF OF HIS PARENTS,
AFTER A FEW DAYS ILLNESS, ON THE 27TH OF
OCTOBER 1803
AGED 14.
HIS AMIABLE DISPOSITION HAD INTIMATELY
ENDEARED HIM
TO HIS RELATIONS AND COMPANIONS,
AND HIS DISTINGUISHED ABILITIES,
AND EAGER INQUIRY AFTER KNOWLEDGE, HAD RAISED

THE FLATTERING HOPE OF A VALUABLE LIFE HAD
IT PLEASED GOD
TO PROLONG IT.
The Lord gave & the Lord hath taken away ; blessed
be the name
of the Lord.

———◆———

IN THE SAME VAULT ARE DEPOSITED,
THE REMAINS OF HER HUSBAND
THE REV^D GEORGE LEONARD JENYNS
OF BOTTISHAM HALL, CANON OF ELY
AND VICAR OF SWAFFHAM PRYOR
IN THIS COUNTY.
HE WAS DESCENDED BY A COLLATERAL BRANCH
FROM THE FAMILY OF SOAME JENYNS ESQ. TO WHOSE
ESTATES HE SUCCEEDED
FOR MANY YEARS HE SAT AS CHAIRMAN AT
THE BOARD OF THE HON^{LE} BEDFORD LEVEL
CORPORATION
OF WHOSE INTERESTS HE WAS ON ALL OCCASIONS A
ZEALOUS SUPPORTER.

HE DIED ON THE 25TH DAY OF FEBRUARY 1848,
IN THE 85TH YEAR OF HIS AGE,
LEAVING THREE SONS AND THREE DAUGHTERS.

———◆———

On a tablet close by surmounted by sculpture, a cherub wreathing an urn signed "J. Bacon" R.A.

Near this place are interr'd the Remains of
SOAME JENYNS Esqʳ the only Son of
Sir ROGER JENYNS Knᵗ. and DAME ELIZABETH
his Wife, one of the Daughters
of Sir PETER SOAME Barᵗ. of *Haydon* in the
County of Essex. He ſat in *Parliament*
38 years and as one of the *Lords* Commiſſioners
of the Board of *Trade* 25 years
He was twice married, first to MARY the ſole
Daughter of Colˡ. SOAME of *Dereham*
in the County of Norfolk, afterwards to
ELIZABETH the Daughter of HENRY GREY Esqʳᵉ
of *Hackney* in the County of Middlesex: ſhe
ſurvived him.
He was born the 31ˢᵗ December 1703, and died
leaving no Iſſue on the 10ᵗʰ of December 1787.

His amiable and benevolent temper,
The ſuperior powers of his underſtanding,

Accompany'd with an uncommon brilliancy of
the trueſt and chaſteſt wit
His exemplary moral Character, his able defence
of CHRISTIANITY, whoſe rules he uniformly practic'd:
Were all ſuch excellency's in him, as will ſurvive,
with an affectionate
And deep regret for his loſs, in the remembrance
of thoſe with whom he liv'd :
When they are no more, POSTERITY will know
from his writings,
The juſtneſs of the Sketch here drawn of his Character.
This memorial was erected by his afflicted
Widow, who, having paſſed her life in the exerciſe
of all thoſe virtues which render her sex amiable.
died July 25ᵗʰ. 1796 Aged 94.

At the east end of the South Aisle is a large monument of white marble with figures of a man and wife joining hands seated on a massive base. Above is this coat. Argent on a fess gules three bezants on a canton azure, a crescent or, impaling Gules a chevron between three mallets or. (Soame) Crest. A demi lion rampant affronté or holding a spear of the last tipped Azure. Motto "IGNAVIS NUNQUAM". Above this inscription:

Jenyns.   Heberden.
Hatchment S. Aisle
1832

Jenyns.   Soame.
Mon. Sir Roger Jenyns
1740

Jenyns.   Harvey.
Hatchment. Roger Jenyns.
1753 (Cole M.S.)

In this Vault
lyeth the Body of Sr Roger Ienyns Kn^t
Lord of the Manor's of Allington and Vauxes in this Parish
Who defcended from Sr Iohn Ienyns of Churchill
In Somerfettfheire. Hee Marryed Elizabeth Daughter
Of Sr Peter Soame of Heydon of Efsex Barr^t. By whom
He had onely One Sonn Soame Ienyns who Marryed
Mary Soame of Deereham Grange in Norfolke.
Hee dyed the 22 day of Septr. 1740
Ætatis 77.

Below is this inscription.

In this Vault lyeth the Body of Dame
Elizabeth Ienyns Wife to Sr Roger Ienyns
Who dyed the firft of May
1728 Ætatis 62 :
She was a Lady of great Virtue and piety
And thro the whole Courfe of her life of
An Unbleamish'd Reputation, A conftant
Attendant of Public as Well as a Strict
Obferver of Stated hours of her private
Devotion. Her piety as Well as her Uncommon
Tendernefs and compafsion of Nature
Engag'd her to daily Acts of Charity
As Well in her life as at her Death, She was
Of a Mild Temper, a Graceful and Winning
Prefence, an Eafey and engageing
Converfation, 'tho her own infirmityes
Often interrupted the naturall
Cherefullnefs of her difpofition, She was
An affectionate Wife, an Indulgeing Mother
A Sinceer Friend, and a good Chriftian,
Att her Death Sr Roger Ienyns by her defire
Setled the Schooleing of 20 poor Children;
And as his addition the Cloathing of them
And a Schoole to teach them and others
in for ever.

In the Nave is the matrix of a large brass with a foliated canopy, an angel on each side and beneath the figure of an ecclesiastic. Round the edge is this inscription in Lombardic letters.

HIC : IACET : ELIAS : DE : BECKINGHAM :
QVONDAM : IVSTICARIVS : DOMINI :
REGIS : ANGLIE : CVIVS : ANIME :
PROPICIETVR : DEVS.

On a large board in the North Aisle is this painted.

𝒢iles Bream Efq. Son of Arthur
Breame of Eaftham in the
County of Effex & Ann Allington
daughter of Robt. Allington of
Horfe heath in the County of Cambridge
Efq. who married the daughter of Thomas
Edwards of Swafham in ye faid County
wch Giles Bream difpofed of his greatest
part of his Eftate to ye building of alms
houfes did build fix alms houfes in East
ham & endued them wth forty pounds a year
for fix poor men three in Bottisham in
Cambridgefhire & three in Eastham in Effex by
the payment of 20 nobles a year to each of y^e
the f^d Giles Bream died March ye 31st 1621.
and made Sr Giles Allington of Horfe heath
aforefaid & others his Executors to perform
this trust.

the Estate wch was first fettled is fold & another
fettled for the fame ufe at Braintree in Effex
and now in occupation of Edward Horton.

This put up by   Gilbert Miffen
                  Matthias Dofiter.
                  Churchwardens 1728.

Above the North Door is a small board with this.

John Salisbury of Bottisham who died in the year of our Lord God 1639 did some time before his death give ten pounds to the town of Bottisham forever. The use whereof to be paid quarterly and disposed of by the minister and Churchwardens of the said parish for ye teaching of three poor children in ye said parish.

On a board on the north-west respond surmounted by the arms of Jenyns and Allington empaled is this.

S͏ʳ ROGER IENYNS KN͏ᵀ
Built a Free School in this Parish
and endowed it with Twenty
Pounds a year for the Schooling
and Cloathing of Twenty Children
to be paid out of his Farm, in this
Town Street.

Below this Inscription are listed the names of the first 20 children, followed by :

DANIEL WOOLARD, SCHOOL MASTER.
The succeeding Children and Schoolmaster to be put in or removed by the owner of Bottisham Hall for ever.

Formerly on Jenyns Free School.

Mary Jenyns, d.1832

Rev'd George Leonard Jenyns, d.1848

Boards mounted high on the wall of the South Aisle

PLEDGER

ALLINGTON   CONINGSBY   PLEDGER   CONINGSBY

PLEDGER MONUMENT

CHERRYHINTON

3 March 1883.

The Church.

The Church is dedicated to St. Andrew and consists of Chancel, Nave, North and South Aisles, South Porch, West Tower and Vestry on the north side of the Chancel.

The Chancel is Early English of very good design and is perfect with the exception of the East Window. On the south are eight lancet windows arranged in couples between bold original buttresses and a Priests Door richly moulded with shafts in the jambs. On the north is the same arrangement but the windows are blocked and a Perpendicular Vestry built up against the eastern end of the wall. The jambs of the windows are moulded thus externally. The East Window  is a Perpendicular insertion of very poor character. The roof is of flat pitch. There are no Clerestory windows and those of the aisles are all of Perpendicular character of three lights and similar in design. These insertions for the walls are of 13th century date coeval with the Chancel and the original South Door remains richly moulded, there is also an Early English doorway on the north. The South Porch is modern. The roof is tiled and finished with a moulded parapet.

The Tower is poor of late Perpendicular date with mean Belfry windows and a battlemented parapet.

Notes.

In 1879 the Nave and Aisles were pulled down and rebuilt, the old walls and window tracery were for the most part built of clunch. In the rebuilding hardly an old stone remains; although decayed in some parts the work was not so dilapidated as to warrant such ruthless destruction of old work. It was rebuilt in yellow Ketton stone. The interior work, I was assured by the Vicar, was original, all the stones of the Nave arcades having been numbered, but whether this was so or not they have been so scraped and shaved that the original contours of the old mouldings have been quite destroyed. The bases of the pier arcades are new and of stone (the rest are clunch). The old iron escutcheon on the south door was removed at this time and a new one substituted of similar design. The Chancel Screen of late Perpendicular date also disappeared, likewise a mural tablet to Ann Cromwell 1556. So much for the "restoration". The Architect was J. O. Scott.

Cherry Hinton Church as it is today.

23

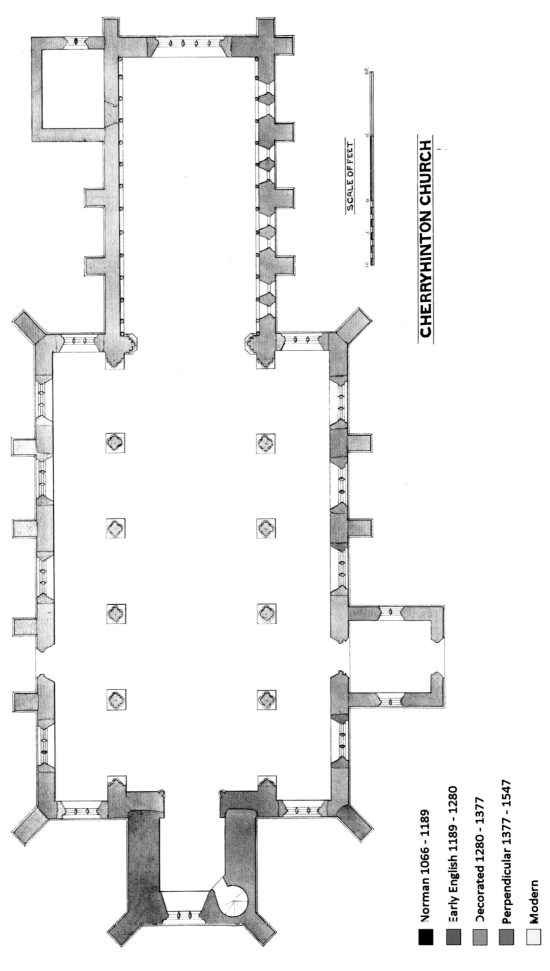

CHERRYHINTON CHURCH

SCALE OF FEET

Norman 1066 - 1189

Early English 1189 - 1280

Decorated 1280 - 1377

Perpendicular 1377 - 1547

Modern

The interior of the Church is very fine but of one level throughout and is temporally paved with wooden bricks. The Chancel is whitewashed and unrestored. On the south side are 13 Early English cusped arcades, eight enclosing lancets, the others being blank. The arrangement is the same on the north side but all the windows are blocked. In the south wall is a fine double Piscina and Sedilia of three arches all decorated with tooth ornament. The Priests Door has a well moulded segmental arch cutting into the splayed sill of the lancets above it which are consequently slightly raised. On the north is a four centred moulded doorway leading to the Vestry. The East Window is of five lights devoid of tracery the lights finishing with cusped heads beneath a flat arch thus.

The Chancel Arch is broad moulded with a triple hollow. Altogether the Chancel presents an example of Early English work equal to any in the Eastern Counties. The Nave Arcade is very fine consisting of five richly  moulded Early English arches on clustered columns. The roof is modern framed with hammer beams and wall posts resting on stone angels holding shields, the cornice is decorated with quatrefoils and panels. At the intersection of the purlins and principals are carved bosses. In Cole's time there was a Clerestory of plain Tudor windows of three lights, this fell or was removed c.1792. The Pulpit is small of Jacobean date the upper panels cut in shallow patterns of poor design.

The aisle windows are of late Perpendicular date but immediately below the sills is a good Early English string running the whole length of the aisles shewing that the walls up to this level at least are coeval with the Arcade and Chancel. The roof of the North Aisle is original with plain rafters resting on embattled corbels which are supported by angels bearing shields on which are the following charges.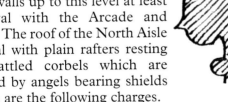

1. The cross of St. George.
2. Three crowns (Ely).
3. A fess between two chevrons (probably for Lisle).
4. A fess between six annulets (probably for Avenell).

5. Three escallops within a bordure engrailed.
6. Three palets (St. Peters College).

The roof of the South Aisle is of plainer character. At the east end of both aisles were formerly Chantries, the parcloses of which existed in Cole's time; the lower panels of these were painted with saints and other figures. On that to the south were portraitures of a man and woman in prayer with this inscription running partly around the chapel.

Orate pro animaƀ Johis Thryplawe (or Thenplew) et Margarete Uxoris ejus.

A Piscina was discovered in the South Chapel during the recent restoration. In the North Aisle are five very good benches with carved poppy heads on one of which is the fragment of an inscription ". . . ea i Deo".

The Font consists of a circular bowl perfectly plain supported by a single cylindrical shaft, this was substituted in 1811. The following entry in the Parish Books alludes to it "Aug 13. 1811. Item. A stone pedestal to support the Font at the Church 3.4.6. making a hole through do. for pipe 0.5.6. bringing it in a cart 0.18.3."

The jambs of the Tower Arch are of Norman date proving the existence of an earlier church, they are square with a nook shaft on either side of the eastern face, the Arch itself is four centred coeval with the Tower.

In the Belfry are five bells with inscriptions as follow.
1. Walter Serocold Esqre. Fra. Ellard C. W. 1727.
2. . . . magn Ave Maria in Lombardic capitals with cross and crowned head.

3. Jubilate Deo omnis populus terre.
4. John Taylor and son founders Loughborough 1853.
5. T.Mears London fecit 1828. Revd Stephen Davis curate.

CAP & MOULDING CHANCEL ARCH

NAVE ARCADE

The beading on the treble resembles that on Penns little peal in Ely Cathedral. The words Fra. Ellard are rudely incised.

The ancient altar slab still remains inscribed with five crosses which are still visible although nearly effaced by the constant tread of feet. The dimensions are 6ft. 3in. by 2ft. 8in. and formerly formed a portion of the pavement in the centre of the Nave.

There is not a remnant of stained glass throughout the Church ancient or modern. The communion plate is modern with the exception of a silver chalice ornamented with bands of Arabesque foliage worked in gold. It bears the inscription: "For the Towne of Hintown in Cambrygesher" of the date 1569. There is a brass almsdish embossed with an inscription on the rim.

Inscriptions.
The monuments are fairly numerous but not of great interest. On the north wall of the Tower surmounted by this coat. The inscription nearly illegible is quoted from Cole.

Party per pale gules and sable three chevronelles ermine impaling argent on three hurts as many choughs or within a bordure engrailed gules, on a chief vert and eagle displayed argent. (Hutton). Crest. A rams head argent pellety issuing from a ducal coronet or.

FRANCISCVS WISVS NVPTIS MIHI CROMWELL
ET HVTTON
SEPTENAQVE OLIM PROLE BEATVS ERAM.
ADDICTVS LEGVM STVDIIS VITÆ QVE PROBATÆ,
POST ANNOS MORIOR SEPTVAGINTA SENEX
OBIIT 5 IVNI 1589.

Another tablet of 16th century date removed at the restoration bore this inscription:

Hic jacet Anna suo, Cromwell vicina marito
nunc consors tumuli quæ fuit anti tori
Conjugium duplici detabat pigorore Wisi
Concedens fatis mater honesta suis 1556.

On the north side of the Chancel are six marble tablets. Commencing from the east.

1. IN THE VAULT BENEATH LIE THE REMAINS OF
THE REV.D BEWICK BRIDGE BD. F.R.S.
LATE FELLOW OF S.T PETERS COLLEGE
CAMBRIDGE & VICAR OF THIS PARISH.

HE WAS A NATIVE OF LINTON IN THIS COUNTY;
BECAME SENIOR WRANGLER IN THE YEAR 1790;
& WAS LONG A DISTINGUISHED
RESIDENT MEMBER OF THE UNIVERSITY OF
CAMBRIDGE.
BEING SELECTED BY THE EAST INDIA COMPANY
TO BE ONE OF THE PROFESSORS
IN THEIR COLLEGE AT HAILEYBURY, HE WAS
FOR MANY YEARS ACTIVELY ENGAGED
THERE, & ON HIS RETIREMENT WAS HONOURED
WITH A SPECIAL TESTIMONY TO THE
IMPORTANCE OF HIS SERVICES.
HE WAS AUTHOR OF SEVERAL POPULAR &
VALUABLE TREATISES IN THE
MATHEMATICS, AND WAS EMINENT FOR HIS
BENEVOLENCE, CHEERFULNESS, KIND
AFFECTIONS AND FERVENT PIETY.
TO THIS PARISH HE WAS A MUNIFICENT
BENEFACTOR,
WHERE AFTER A LONG ILLNESS, HUMBLY
TRUSTING IN THE MERITS OF HIS REDEEMER,
AND FROM THE FIRST ENTIRELY RESIGNED TO
THE WILL OF HIS CREATOR,
HE DIED IN THE 67.TH YEAR OF HIS AGE,
MAY 15: 1833.

The Master and Fellows of his College have erected this monument
in memory of his distinguished talents, amiable qualities and useful virtues.

2. On a white marble tablet surmounted by this coat. Quarterly 1 & 4 Party per chevron argent and sable in chief two fleurs de lis azure in base a tower embattled or (Serocold). 2 & 3 Barry wavy of 6 argent and azure on a chief of the last three pellets.

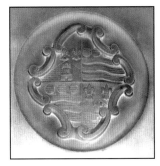

IN MEMORY OF
M.RS MARY SEROCOLD
SECOND DAUGHTER OF
THE REV.D WALTER SEROCOLD
WHO DIED ON
THE 13.TH DAY OF JANUARY 1837,
AGED 81 YEARS.

EXTERIOR   INTERIOR   CAP

PRIESTS DOOR

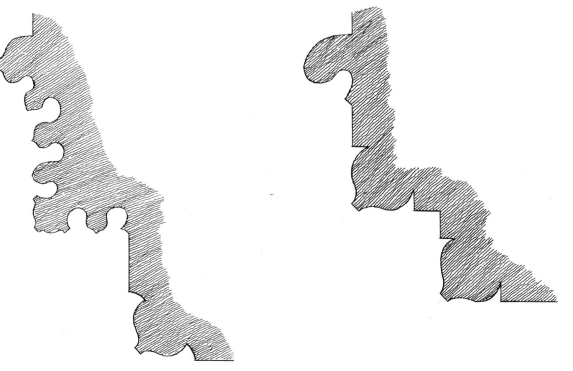

S. DOOR   N. DOOR

3. Surmounted by the same arms with crest. On the top of a tower or a fleur de lis azure (Serocold).

TO THE MEMORY
OF WALTER SEROCOLD ESQ:
ONLY SON OF THE LATE REV. WALTER SEROCOLD :
CAPTAIN IN HIS MAJESTY'S NAVY
SLAIN AT THE SIEGE OF CALVI IN CORSICA IULY VIII,
M.DCC.XCIV
AGED XXXVII.
HIS THREE SURVIVING SISTERS ERECTED THIS
MONUMENT,
AS A TOKEN OF AFFECTION FOR THE BEST OF
BROTHERS :
THE PUBLIC LOSS MAY BE ESTIMATED FROM THE
FOLLOWING
EXTRACT OF ADMIRAL LORD HOOD'S OFFICIAL LETTER.

"BUT I HAVE TO LAMENT, AND WHICH I DO MOST
SINCERELY,
THE LOSS OF A VERY ABLE AND VALUABLE OFFICER,
CAPTAIN SEROCOLD;
WHO WAS KILLED BY GRAPE SHOT
WHILST GETTING THE LAST GUN IN ITS PLACE,
SOON AFTER THE ENEMY HAD DISCOVER'D OUR
BATTERY.
THE KING HAS NOT A MORE MERITORIOUS YOUNG
CAPTAIN
IN HIS MAJESTY'S NAVY:
HE COMMANDED THE FLOATING BATTERY,
WHICH WAS BURNT BY RED-HOT-SHOT BEFORE BASTIA;
AND AFTERWARDS SERV'D WITH INFINITE REPUTATION
AT THE BATTERIES ON SHORE.
INDEPENDENT OF MY REGARD AND ESTEEM FOR HIM,
I FEEL HIS LOSS A PUBLIC ONE"

4. With these arms. Party per chevron embattled, in chief two Cornish choughs, close, from a mount in base three dasies (Pierce). An escutcheon of pretence for Serocold.

ANN
ELDEST DAUGHTER OF
THE REVᴰ WALTER SEROCOLD
AND WIDOW OF
WILLIAM PEARCE D. D.
DEAN OF ELY
BORN MARCH 12. 1754
DIED MAY 29. 1835.

5. Surmounted by this coat. Quarterly 1 & 4. Pierce. 2 & 3 Serocold, as above, impaling or a chevron coticed, sable between three demi dragons rampant, a mullet for difference. (Smith).

GEORGIANA • ELIZABETH,
DAUGHTER OF GEORGE SMITH, ESQUIRE, M.P.
NIECE OF ROBERT LORD CARRINGTON,
AND WIFE OF THE REVEREND
EDWARD • SEROCOLD • PEARCE,
BORN JUNE VII. MDCCCI,
DIED IN CHILDBED DECEMBER XVII.
MDCCCXXVIII.

FAREWELL, BELOVED GEORGIANA!

AS LONG AS I LIVE,
I SHALL REMEMBER WITH THE TENDEREST
AFFECTION
THY MEEK AND GENTLE SPIRIT ;
AND REVERE THE STRENGTH OF MIND AND
ENERGIES
WHICH IT CONCEALED.

IN THEE
THE NATURAL FEELINGS
OF THE DAUGHTER, WIFE, AND MOTHER,
WERE HEIGHTENED INTO VIRTUES
BY PRINCIPLE AND RELIGION :
AND, THANKS BE TO GOD,
THE RECOLLECTION OF WHAT THOU WERT,
THY GOODNESS, THY PIETY,
FORBIDS US TO MOURN, EXCEPT FOR OURSELVES,
THAT THOU WERT TAKEN FROM US SO SOON.

E.S.P.

6. With this coat. Quarerly 1 & 4 Serocold & Pierce quarterly as above. 2 Barry wavy of six azure and argent on a chief of the last three pellets. 3 argent, on a fess sable between three mascles gules three crescents or. Impaling. Ermine an eagle displayed, on a chief gules a crown between two crosses pattée. (Vansittart).

S. SIDE OF CHANCEL.

SACRED
TO THE MEMORY OF
THE REV^D EDWARD PEARCE SEROCOLD
OF CHERRYHINTON, CAMBRIDGESHIRE,
ONLY SON OF THE LATE DR PEARCE, DEAN OF ELY,
BORN 20TH APRIL 1796,
DIED 21ST NOVEMBER 1849.

The arms of Pierce as here blazoned appears to have been made up from a quartered coat which according to Berry was borne by "the late Dr

William Pierce Dean of Ely and Master of Jesus College Cambridge 1824". viz. Quarterly 1 & 4 Argent on a mount vert three heraldic roses gules stalked and leaved ppr. 2 & 3 Argent three Cornish choughs sable, beaked and membered gules. Crest. A Cornish chough as in the arms. The name also on the monuments is differently spelt.

On a brass plate on the south wall of South Aisle with these arms.

1 Gules on a cross ermine between four lions passant gardant or, a bible lying fessways of the field clasped and garnished of the third (Cambridge University).
2 Or four pallets gules (St. Peters College).
3 Gules two keys in saltire argent.
4 Per pale argent and gules two legs in armour couped counterchanged (Cookson).

AD HONOREM DEI
HANC ALAM ECCLESIAE MEMOREM
VIRI REVERENDI ET DOCTI
HENRICI WILKINSON COOKSON S.T.P.
COLLEGII SANCTI PETRI PER XXIX ANNOS MAGISTRI
ACADEMIAE CANTABRIDGIENSIS QUINQUIENS
PROCANCELLARII
QUI COLLEGIO JUSTE REGENDO
IN ACADEMIA PRUDENTER ADMINISTRANDA
IN MUNERIBUS STRENUE OBEUNDIS
IN OMNIBUS QUI ADIBANT CONSILIO ADJUVANDIS
PRAECLARAS ANIMI DOTES EXCERCEBAT
QUIQUE ERGA DEUM PIUS ERGA HOMINES COMIS
IN AMICOS FIDELIS IN SUOS AMANTISSIMUS
DIGNITATEM AC SIMPLICITATEM PRAE SE FEREBAT
REFICIENDAM CURVERUNT
PLURIMI MAERENTES COGNATI AFFINES AMICI
A.S. MDCCCLXXX.

NATUS EST IN MUNICIPIO WESTMERIENSI KENDAL
DIE X^{MO} APRILIS A.S. MDCCCLXXVI
CINERES HABET HUJUS ECCLESIAE SEPULCRUM.

In the north wall of the Tower is a good coffin slab with sculptured head and indications of elaborate scroll work all greatly defaced. There is no inscription the date probably early 13th century. In the floor is another slab with indications of a matrix. In the churchyard near the South Porch is the mutilated stem of a large cross of plain character.

The Parish Register dates as far back as 1538. The Parish Accounts do not extend beyond the middle of the 18th century.

Additional information taken from the Cole M.S.S. 1773-1774.

"There is a screen of partition between the Nave and Chancel the lower parts of which being large panels are still very perfect. Several curious figures of Saints men and women are painted but chiefly decaying. However, on that to the east end of South Aisle the figures are well preserved of a man and his wife on their knees in the habit of Henry 6th time and on a rim of wainscoat which runs round the Chapel was this inscription partly obliterated the mans name unluckily more particularly.

Orate pro animat Johis Threnpoll et Marie uxoris ejus."

"Before the Altar to the north touching the rails lie three black marble slabs, the first exactly in the middle of the Chancel with these arms. On a chevron Inter 3 martlets^ 3 crescents (Watson).

Here Lyeth the Body of
Mr William Watſon, born
at Hull in the County of
York; in Teſtimony of his
Love to Religion and the
decency of Gods Worſhip
he Beautified this Chancel
and Erected this Altar and
in Gratitude to the place
of his Nativity Endow'd
the Hoſpitall there built by
his Brother Thomas Lord
Biſhop of S^t. Davids;

He died ⎫ Decemb^r. 2^d
A: D: ⎬ 1721
Aged ⎭ 84.

---

* Although described by Charles Bell as martlets, the birds on the slab appear to be ducks.

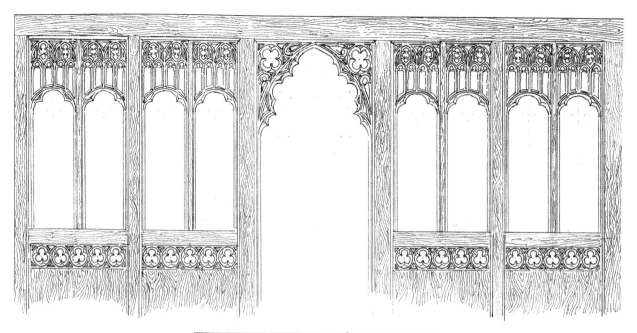

CHANCEL SCREEN (DESTROYED)

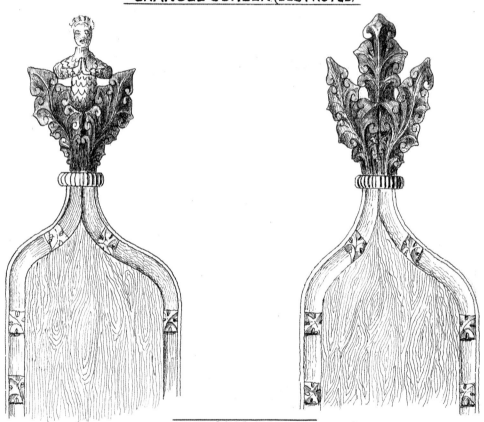

BENCH ENDS

Close to this lies the second slab with these arms.
Serocold impaling Watson & crest of Serocold.

Here lieth the Body of Abigail
(fifteen Years and fifteen Days)
Wife of Walter Serocold of
Hinton Efq: & youngest Daughter
of William Watſon of Hull Gent;
Who was only Brother and ſole
Heir to Thomas Watſon late Biſhop
of Sᵗ. Davids; She died Aug: 13ᵗʰ 1734
Ætatis 49.

On the third slab.

In Memory of Walter Serocold Eſqʳ
one of his Majeſtys Juſtices
of the Peace for this County
Ob : 11 of August 1747
Ætat : 63.

He lived Belov'd
And died Lamented.

On a freestone lozenge fashion.

In memory of Elizabeth Serocold an infant ob.
27 Dec. 1760.

A little higher up and near the south door into the Chancel lies an old stone with the half figure of a priest in his mass habit and hands conjoined in brass but no inscription on it, and under the south stalls lies another large old stone which has had on it in brass a large curious cross the bottom of it supported by some animal the head sumptuously ornamented and in one corner of it a crescent."  This was the matrix of a fine cross of early Decorated date between a crescent and a star supported by a lion. The slab measured 9 feet in length by 3 feet nine inches in breadth. It was in the Church up to the time of its restoration when with the other slabs mentioned by Cole was demolished or carted elsewhere.

Cole mentions remains of stained glass in the Clerestory windows. "In the upper window of the Nave on the north side are three or four coats of France and England quarterly. In the North Aisle the arms of the See of Ely and the following inscriptions.

In the first window on the north side

Orate pro ai~abus Rob. Cannewelle et benefactor~ suor~.

In the fourth window on the same side

Orate pro aiabus Johannis Wryht et Rob. Pursere.

Blomefield has preserved the devices and inscriptions carved on the bench ends.

On the north side.

1.   Ave Maria gracia plena.

6.   Grace folwyth Governaunce.

8.   A sow gelder blowing his horn.
            Or you be wo Wethe be war.

9.   A fool in hood with pipe and bell.
      Wyt my pype I wel play and wyt my Bal yf I may.

10.   A Harpey.
            Manerys makyth Man

On the south side

3.   A man playing on a rebeck.
            Herte be trewe, herte be trewe.

7.   A man bidding his beads.
            Evyl getyn good, geryt yt ageyn.

10.   A pelican in her piety.
            Sic et Christus dilexit.

11.   Ecce Ancilla Domini fiat michi
            secundum verbum tuum.

On the seats of the south sides.

1.   Delectavi in Domino.

2.   A man only.
            Timor mortis conturbat me.

3.   Gloria in excelsis Deo.

Church Furniture.

The following inventory of Church furniture is taken from a M.S. volume in the Library of Caius College compiled for the use of the Archdeacon of Ely. The document is considered by Blomefield to date from 1276 during Bishop Balshams Episcopate, additions not later than 1349.

"Ecclia de Hinton. Nõ app'ata est ibi Vicar' et Rector, et taxatur ad XXX marc' et solvit p Synod ijs iiijd p den. Beati Petri Vs p procuri' xviijd. et s̃t ejus ornamñta haec. Duo missal bona j legendi duobus voluibus, iij Antiph' cũ psaltris, et aliud antiph' vetus, iij gradal' cum trop'us et ij t'pia per se, 1 manual, j martilog' et j ordinall' vi pia vestimentorum nova cũ ptinenciis ij ferialia vestimenta, tres cappe chori et 2 palle, j frontal' tunica et dalmatica iij cruces enee, vj phiole, et ij phiole vitree ij Turibula cum Lanterna, et patella ad ignem, iiij calices, pix enea, viij vexilla fons cum s'ur', velum templi. c'smator (bonum cu s'ur). (There is a line through these last words and added in a later hand "debile deficiunt candelabra") una Casula, tunica dalmatica iij tuale unum cum pne ex dono Magri Johis Yaleby, amiche et pa' amic', et duo suppell, unum pannũ deauro ex dono ejustem."

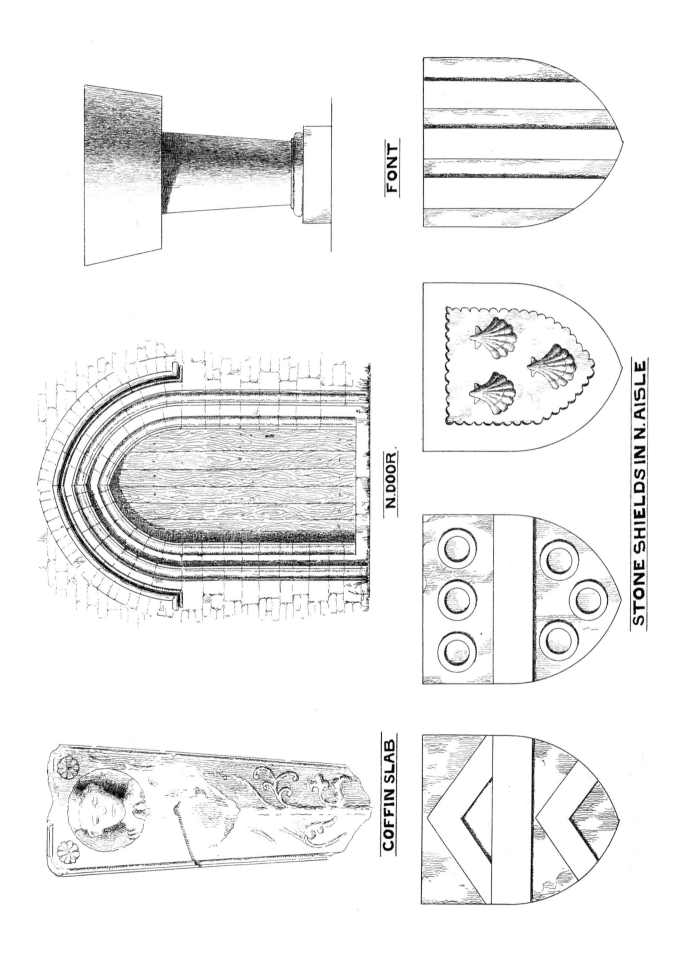

FONT

N.DOOR.

COFFIN SLAB

STONE SHIELDS IN N. AISLE

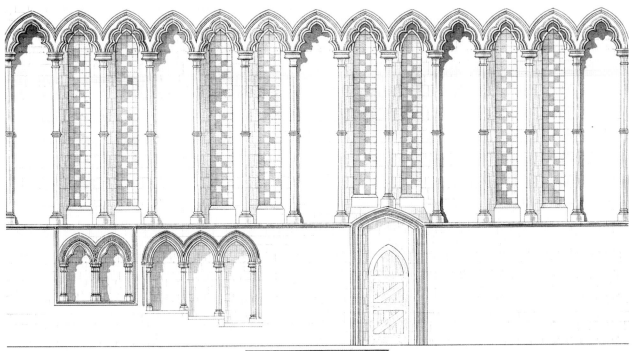

SOUTH SIDE OF CHANCEL

PISCINA & SEDILIA

Serocold-Pierce 1801.

Serocold-Pierce Serocold 1849.

Walter Serocold 1794.

Pierce 1835.

From the monuments of the Serocold family.

Wise 1589.

Serocold (Watson 1734.

Watson 1721.

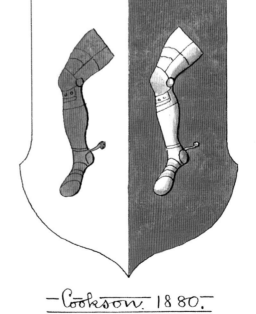

Cookson. 1880.

From monuments in the Church.

Pedigree of Wysse

William Wysse of Hinton. = Agnes d. of . . . Wilcocks.

. . . dau. of Hutton = Francis Wysse of Hinton ob. 1589 æt 76 = Anna d. of . . .Cromwell 1 wife
of Drayton.   Bur. Hinton church, vide Epitaph.   Bur. Hinton Ch. vide Epitaph
ob. 1556.

Alice dau. of = John Wise = Joane d. of   Allice   Francis   Gilbert Wisse. = Maryan d. of Browne.
Dreyner of   of Hinton.   . . . Cooke   (son of William?)
Foulborne.   of Cheshire.

Edward Wysse. = Francis d. of . . . Meade of Ebdem in Essex.

Mary ux . . .   Mary ux William   Francis ux   Anne ux   Elizabeth ux
         Oneley of Co. Suff.   Hugh White.   Frances Collins.   Edward Newman.

1. Dryver Wysse = Anne d. of   2. Thomas.   Catherine ux   Frances ux   Mary ux Robert
of Hinton 1619.   Francis Brakin.   3. John.   Thom. Docwra   Tho. . . . of   Killingworth
                                         of Fulborne.   Cambridge.   of Hinton.
Francis.   Hamon.   Dryver.   James.   Allice.

CHESTERTON

The Church.

The Church is dedicated to St. Andrew and consists of Chancel, Nave, North and South Aisles, North Porch, West Tower and Spire.

The Chancel is of 15th century date, the exterior coated with cement and all the windows renewed. These are of good design but rather late in character, the East Window is of five lights. There is a good plain Perpendicular Sedilia in the south wall. At the Chancel Arch is a Screen of poor design. In the south wall are four corbels above the Sedilia. On north and south sides two three-light windows. Between Sacristy and Chancel a small square opening, the inner side forming a quatrefoil. The Chancel was restored 1844.

The Nave has seven bays on each side of Decorated date, c.1330, having octagonal piers and well moulded caps and bases. The arches display the double wave moulding, the clerestory windows are of late Perpendicular character, the roof probably of the same date is supported on small corbels of stone carved with angels hearts. These are of the same date as the arcade, two of these bear shields with these arms.
1. A pale between two lions rampant.
2. A fess between three martlets.

The Tower is of the same date as the Nave and Aisles, c.1330. It is battlemented and finished with a well proportioned Spire. The arrangement of the staircase to the Belfry floor is unique being an addition of Perpendicular date corbelled from the inside of the west wall terminating in good mouldings and a lion's head about three feet from the ground. This alteration necessitated blocking up the West Window, the outline of which on the exterior face is clearly visible. This mars considerably the west front for with the exception of a few slits to light the staircase there are no openings below the Belfry windows to break the monotony of a blank wall. The Belfry windows and spire lights are of good design the former with traceried gablets crocketted.

Bells. In the Belfry are five bells with these inscriptions.
1. Sonoro sono meo sono Deo 1612. Ricardus Holdfeld me fecit.
2. God save thy church 1612. Ricardus Holdfeld me fecit.
3. Cantabo laudes tuas Domine. 1606. Ricardus Covington.
4. Christopher Graye made me 166..

5. Willm. and John Taylor Oxford founders. Febry, 9th 1825. John Brigham Wiles & Willm Johnson Churchwardens.

The third and fourth are said to have come from Jesus College. The former is said to be a very fine specimen of sharp lettering. (Raven)

The North Porch is of good Perpendicular work but the gable has fallen away. A corbel remains over the arch which probably had a canopy above. The top is now patched up with brickwork. The angle buttresses probably ended in pinnacles, the bases of which remain. The moulding to the doorway is much decayed and also the side windows but the fabric of the porch is sound and good. (See drawing.)

Notes.

In 1880 the Church was thoroughly restored under the superintendence of William Smith, architect. During the restorations these discoveries were made.

In the South Aisle an original Decorated window was opened with an ogee headed arch and tracery of lowing character. (See drawing.)

A doorway beneath the second window from the east in the North Aisle with shafts in the jambs, also portions of Early English mouldings with tooth ornament, the remains of a Church of earlier foundation. This Church was probably cruciform, the Early English remains occurring in both North and South Aisles, the original north and south walls of the Transepts, these probably were prolonged (and the nave arcade raised), c.1330, forming the present aisles. The West Window of the North Aisle was opened. Over the Chancel Arch is a large wall painting representing The Judgement completed before the Clerestory windows were inserted, also in the spandrils of the Nave Arcades are paintings but too faint to distinguish the subjects. On the jamb of the eastern window of the North Aisle are portions of a painting with figures. On the opposite jamb the subject seems to represent a feast, a crowned head being visible among the figures, but all very faint and confused. These paintings are on the jambs of the original 14th century windows and may be of that date. The Porch was rebuilt during the restorations but needlessly, the ornamental portions only requiring repair and the gable pinnacles adding.

Cole under the date June 8th 1748 has these notes on the Church. "There are two Porches, the north is leaded the south tiled as is the Vestry on the

S.W. VIEW.

north side of the Chancel. The whole of the Church is paved with free stone very handsomely. The Altar is on one step railed in with handsome carved rails. There are twelve handsome old stalls on each side of the Chancel which is divided from the Nave by a neat and elegant Screen on which are the arms of King James II."

Inscriptions.

At the foot of the step on the south side touching the stalls lies a very handsome black marble slab with these arms. Three bars gemelles wavy in chief three sprigs of flowers slipped (Burton) impaling. A chevron between three wolves heads erased.

Beatam in Christo lætiss imamque
ressurrectionem expectans
Hic jacet
Samuel Burton L.L. Baccalaureus
Filius et hæres Zachariæ Burton
de Sibsey in Com. Lincoln armigeri
vir doctus et liberis perpolitus eximia in
Deum pietate Indigis
beneficus, integutate vitæ
morumque tum probitabe tum etiam comitate gratus
omnibus et æceptissimus qui postquam 22~ et
quod excurrit ætatis complasset annum in ipsis
pene sponsalibus raptus placide tamen obdormivit
30mo die Nov. A.D. 1752. Flebilis omnibus multi
autem flebilior quam afflictissimæ conjugi Susannæ
quæ dilectes simo suo suique plusquam dimidio
hunc lapidem posiut memorialem.

Over the cap of the first pillar on the south side hangs an achievement with these arms in a lozenge. Argent a lion rampant gules (Storey) and on a gold ground this is written.

Neare this place lieth the body of
Anne Storey daughter of Thomas
Storey Esqre of Beach in this County.
She died the 7th day of May Ano. Dom. 1669.

On the south wall of the Chancel a small black marble.

WILLIAM CLAPHAM Gent, died
the 12th Novr 1766 Aged 51 Years.
Interr'd clofe to this wall.
Alfo Mrs JANE CLAPHAM
his Wife who died 21st Jan^{ry}
1779, Aged 58.

In the South Aisle on a free stone is this inscription.

Here lieth the body of John Johnson who died
Febry. 14th
1762 aged 43 years, also Tabitha his daughter who died July 10th 1756 aged 5 years and six months.

On another free stone is this "anxious inscription".

Here lyeth in hope of a joyful resurrection Wm Perry late husband of Grace Perry at the Castle in the Butcher Market in Cambridge which house he kept upwards of 40 years and maltster in Chesterton upwards of 30 years. He was born at Morpeth Cheshire and died March 1. 1762 aged 70.

On another free stone near the North Porch.

Here lieth the body of William Dowse
schoolmaster of this
town 28 years. He died May 8. 1757 aged 52 years.

At the upper end of the same South Aisle on another free stone.

Here lieth the body of Stephen Danby who died
May 28. 1762 aged 62 years.

List of Vicars.
The Church was granted to the Abbey of Vercelli in 1217 in whose possession it remained until 1440 when it was annexed to King's Hall.

1217 Laurence (de Sancto Nicolas) rector appointed by the King on Cardinal Gualas nomination. (Pat. Rolls. 29 June 1217)

1218 Nov. 16th Adam of Wissenbeach (Wisbech) priest chaplain appointed perpetual Vicar by Guala.
Stephen Rampton "noster primarius" Vicarius, the first vicar appointed by the Abbey.

1258 Ricardus.

1290 - 97 Bartholomew

1311 - 26 Henricus de Maddingle

1333 - 50 Simon or Symon

1350 Richard de Westelee otherwise Kertelyng (per Petrum procuratorem Abb et Com. Mon. Sti Andreu. Entered Gild of Corpus Christi Cambridge 1351 (Cole)

1359 - 65 Galfridus Andrew.

1369 - 74 Wills. de Borwell, resigned 1390 (Fordhams Reg.)

1390 - 99 John Granby, alias Loret presented by Andrew de Alice canon and proctor of the Abbey (Ford. Reg.)

1399 - 1408 John Merchaunt rector of Swafeld exchanges with John Granby July 3, 1399 (Ford. Reg.)

1408 John Wolston rector of Thurgarton exchanges with John Merchaunt Mar. 23. the Prior of Barnwell being patron. (Fordhams Reg.)

1450 Ecclesia appropriata Aulæ Regis.

- - - - John Goold.

1468 Thomas Baro L.L.B. presented by John Gunthorpe, Master of King's Hall.

1472 Thomas Turpyn. Jan 18.

EAST END

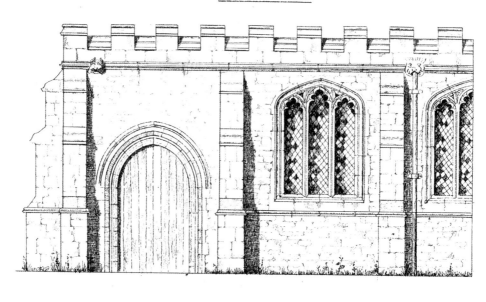

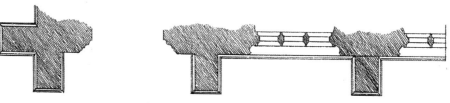

SOUTH AISLE

1491 Robert Frank. Jan. 25.
1518 Jacob Nicholson.
1528 Jeffry Blith, Master of King's Hall.
1534 Thomas Blith S.J.B. July 21.
1557 John Moody.
1561 William Greene, 9 June.
1564 John Todd, Feb. 6.
1566 Robert West, Oct. 28.
1571 Lucian Gylpin, Aug. 21.
1573 John Hanson, Mar. 24.
1579 Mart. Williams, Mar. 11.
1587 - - - - Hamton.
1592 Edmund Battie S.J.P. 1595. 3 Nov. and 2 March. Mr Batty for his vicarage was rated to find one culiver furnished.
1596 Samuel Heron.
1599 Francis Savage.
1601 Thomas Furth, Nov. 14th. . 4. April 1609. Mr Furth was rated with the Vicar of Barrington to raise a pair of curols with a pike furnished.
- - - - John Chapman.
1627 Dr Topham. Dean of Lincoln 1630.

- - - - Richard Watts, ob. 4th Sept. 1661.
1661 Theodosius Crossland S.J.B.
1665 William Lynnet S.J.B. 22nd July. on the death of Theodosius Crossland. Idem Guls Lynnet S.J.B. fuit vicarius ibm et unus commissioni epi Laney ad visitandu dioc 29 Aug. 1674.
1679 Thomas Bainbrigg. July 25. Cedente Gulo Lynnet.
1687 Patrick Cock, 16 Feb. Resignante Tho. Bainbrigg.
1689 George Modd, resigned 1693. Feb. 14. (geo Trumpington).
1693 Edward Bathurst. resigned.
1696 Thomas Smith S.T.P. Aug. 10 resigned.
1711 Matthew Barwell. 9. April. Dns. Johes Episcorum confert Mattheo Barwell Cl. A. M. ad vicariam de Chesterton ad dona coem suam plapsus hac vice p̃tinentem.
1722 John Craister S.J.P. 2 Aug. Mortus Mattheo Barwell. Eodem die concessa est eidem Johi lycentia non residendi.

NORTH PORCH   INTERIOR OF TOWER

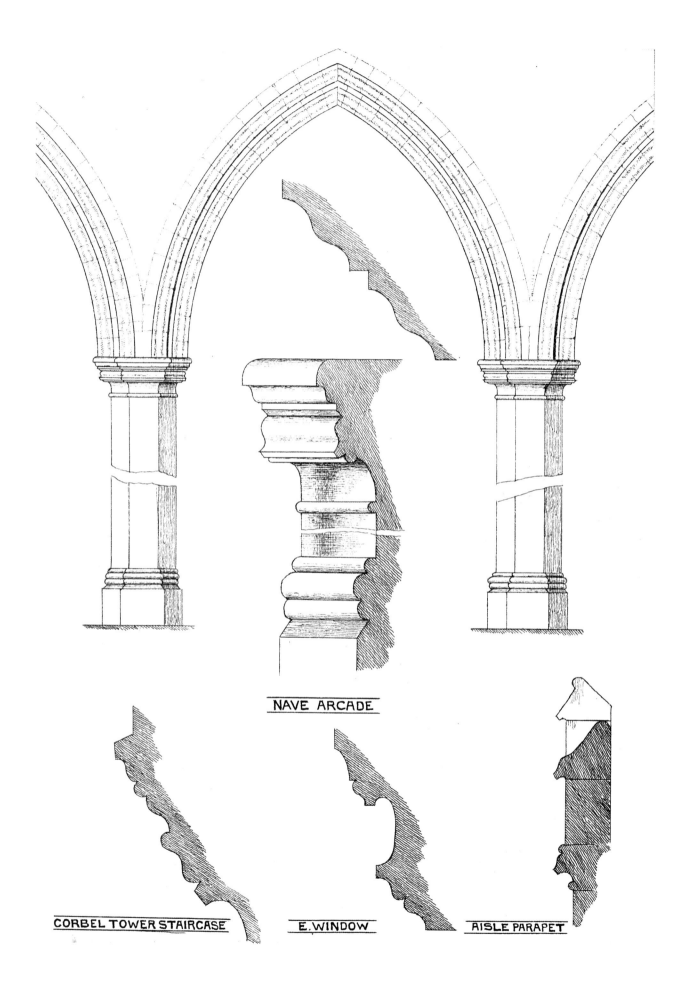

NAVE ARCADE

CORBEL TOWER STAIRCASE

E. WINDOW

AISLE PARAPET

ORIGINAL WINDOW S. AISLE

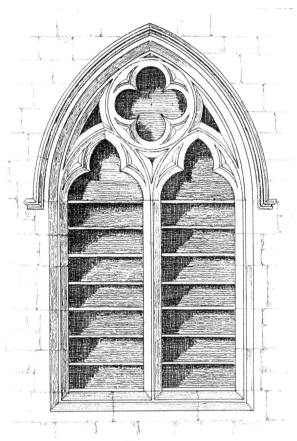

BELFRY WINDOW

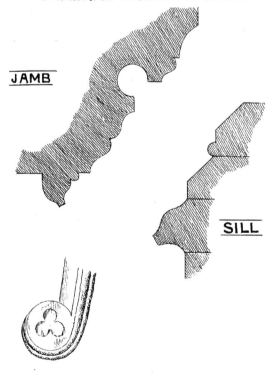

JAMB

SILL

CHESTERTON CHURCH

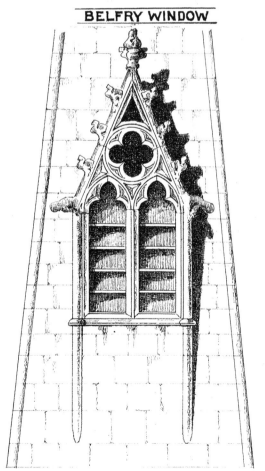

SPIRE LIGHT

Memorial Stone to Anna Maria Vassa on the outside wall to the East of the North Porch

Near this Place lies Interred
ANNA MARIA VASSA
Daughter of GUSTAVUS VASSA the AFRICAN.
She died July 21. 1797
Aged 4 Years.
Should simple village rhymes attract thine eye,
Stranger, as thoughtfully thou pafest by,
Know that there lies beside this humble stone
A child of colour haply not thine own.
Her father born of Afric's sun-burnt race,
Torn from his native fields, ah foul disgrace;
Through various toils, at length to Britain came,
Espous'd, so Heaven ordain'd, an English dame,
And followed Christ: their hope two infants dear,
But one, a hapless Orphan, slumbers here,
To bury her the village children came,
And dropp'd choice flowers and lisped her early fame:
And some that lov'd her most, as if unblest
Bedew'd with tears the white wreath on their breast;
But she is gone and dwells in that abode,
Where some of every clime shall joy in God.

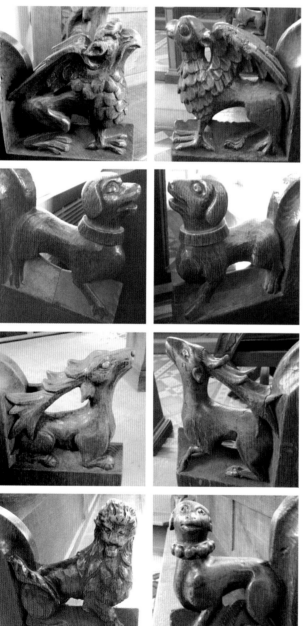

Animal Carvings on the Chancel Pews

Carved Fisherman near Chancel Arch

CHESTERTON

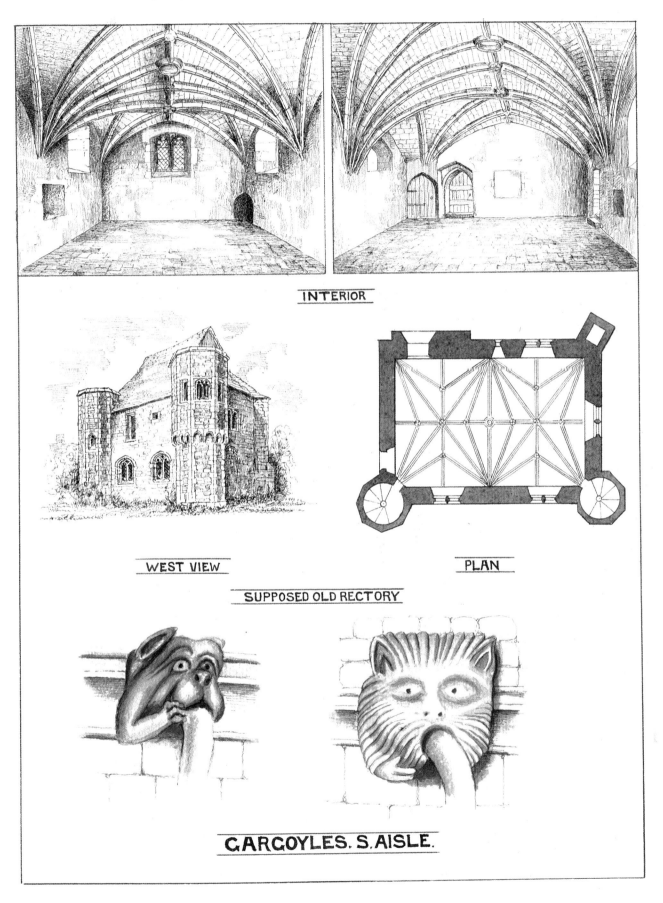

INTERIOR

WEST VIEW

PLAN

SUPPOSED OLD RECTORY

GARGOYLES. S. AISLE.

Pedigree of Battisford

Edward Battisford of Chesterton = Margaret d. of Sʳ Rob. Chamberlayne   Battisford Chastlett of
descended of the families of the   of Kingston in Com. Cambridge.   Cambridgeshire.
Battisford of Battisford in
Com. Suffolk.

John Battisford. = Catherin d. of John Starges of Norf. and Jane his wife d. and heir of
Jeffery Ratcliff of Framsden in Com. Suffolk.

John Battisford = Elizabeth d. of	Phillip ux. John	Sible ux. George	Jane ux.	Catherine ux. John
of Chesterton	John Whiting	Tawyer of	Houghe of	Michell	Barnard of Com.
1619.	of Devonshire.	Com. North'ton.	Norfolk.	Hall of . . .	Cambridge.

John Battisford = Margerett d. of   John Battisford. = Elizabeth d. of   2 Robert.   Margerett ux.
of Chesterton.   Thomas Stotevile   Willm. Thurston   Tho. Gee of
Brinkley Hall.   of Colchester.   Isleham.
Edward.

Elizabeth ux. Roger   Barba ux. Ric Lawsonn   Catherine ux. Lawrance Beresford of
Hutton of Dry Drayton.   of London.   Staffordshire and hath John and Catherin.

48

Pedigree of Brakin of Chesterton

Arms. In the Visitation of Cambridgeshire 1575 the arms of Brakin of Ely are given as above with crest, a hawks head erased argent ducally gorged or quartering Arras or Okesley. (Cole M.S.)
In the Visitation of Cambridgeshire 1619 the arms of Brakin of Chesterton are given as above quartering the same but no crest. This branch is also entitled to quarter Taverner.

John Brakin. ⊤   John Tavernor of Spalding in Holland. ⊤

Thomas Brakin of Chesterton Co. Cambridge. ⊤ Lucy dau. and heir.   William Tavernor ob. s.p.

Elizabeth dau. of Thomas Wrenn of ⊤ Richard Brakin of Chesterton = Alice dau. of . . . .
Haddenham Isle of Ely 1 wife.   Co. Cantabr.   Hutton 2 wife.

Thomas Brakin   Francis Brakin Esq. Recorder of Cambridge J.P. ⊤ Barbara dau. of Thomas
1 son and heir.   for the County of Cambridge 2 son.   Goodrich of Ely.
            (Resigned Recordership 1624).

Mary mar. to Dryver Wise   Rose mar. to Fuller Mead   Edmund 2.   Thomas 3.   Mary ux. Rich
of Linton.   of Foxton.   Parnham Clerk.

Elizabeth. ⊤ Sir James Wingfield of   John Brakin 1 son and heir ⊤ Elizabeth dau. of Sir John Cutts
     Kimbolton Hunts.   Knighted at Whitehall   of Childerley Knt. by the sister
                    22nd Jan. 1628.   of Sir Henry D'Arcy of Hunts.

Edward 1 son   Lucy.   Anne.   Mary.   John Brakin 1 son and heir æt 12. 1619 ⊤
æt. 8. 1619.   ob. 2nd of . . . 1669, bur. in the
                      Chancel of Lolwoth Church Cambs.

Thos. Brakin Mayor of Cambridge 1523, 1528, 1542. Burgess in Parliament for the Town 1536, bur. St. Clements, Cambridge.

49

Pedigree of Thorold

Arms as above in the visitation of Cambs. 1613.

Note. In the 9th quarter the lozenges should be in fess. 1 Thorold. 2. Hough. 3. Brerehaugh. 4. Burnell. 5. Hussey. 6. Neasfeld. 7. Hussey. 8. Say. 9. Denham. 10. Audley. 11. Haugh.

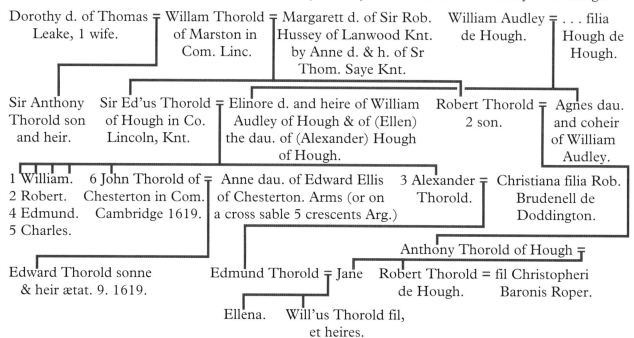

COMBERTON

The Church is dedicated to St. Mary and consists of Chancel, Clerestoried Nave, Aisles, South Porch, and Embattled Tower with four bells. The Chancel and Nave are from the Early English period with Decorated and Perpendicular windows. The Priest's Door is Decorated, S. W. Window is Decorated, of two cinquefoil lights, with flowing tracery above.

Details from County Churches by C. H. Evelyn-White.

Pew End

Fragment of Early Stained Glass

Comberton Church as it is today

51

COMBERTON

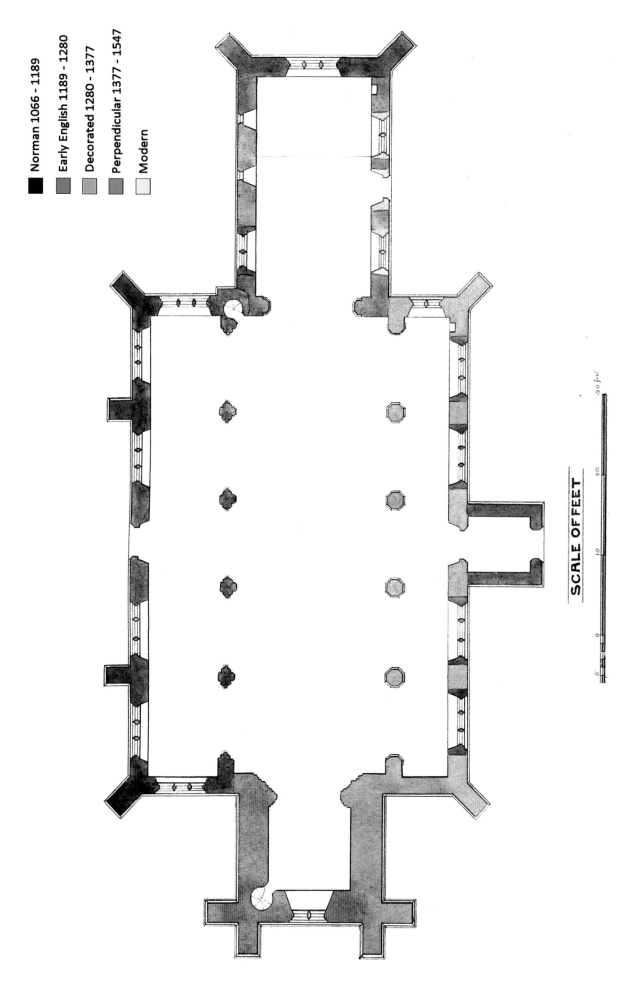

Norman 1066 - 1189
Early English 1189 - 1280
Decorated 1280 - 1377
Perpendicular 1377 - 1547
Modern

SCALE OF FEET

COMBERTON CHURCH

CHANCEL SCREEN AND NAVE SEATS.

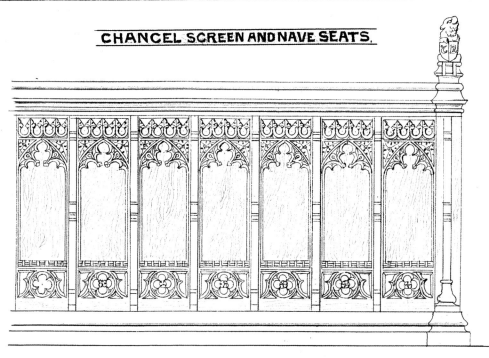

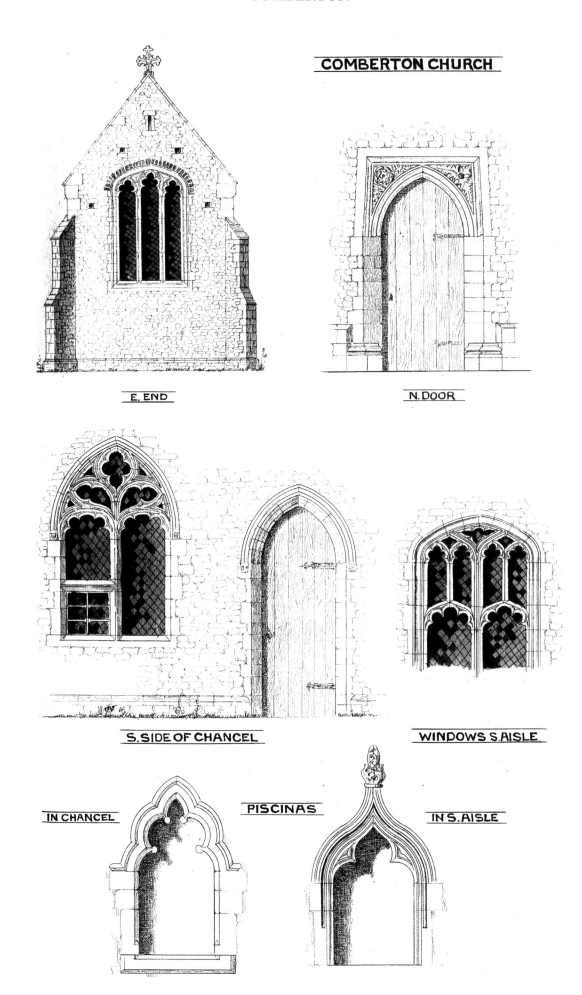

COMBERTON CHURCH

E. END

N. DOOR

S. SIDE OF CHANCEL

WINDOWS S. AISLE.

IN CHANCEL

PISCINAS

IN S. AISLE

COMBERTON CHURCH

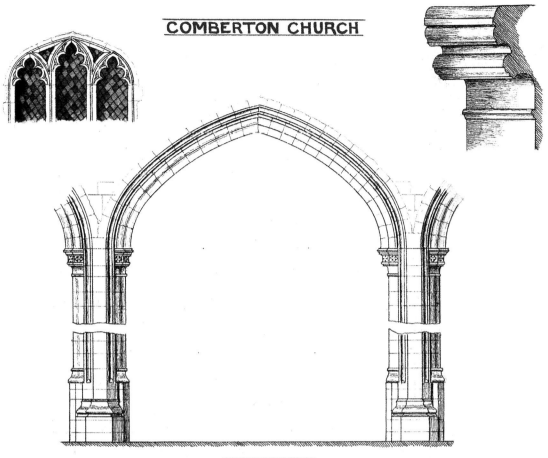

N. ARCADE.

S. ARCADE

Royal Arms of William III.

Carved Angels on Chancel Pews

COTON

The Church is dedicated to St. Peter and consists of Chancel, Nave, North and South Aisles, North and South Porches and Embattled Tower with Spire. The Church dates from the 12th century.

12th century Font.

Nave and Chancel.

Coton Church as it is today seen from the South East.

ANDREAS DOWNES SALOP COL D IOHAN APVD CANTABOLE
SOCI° GRÆCÆ LINGVÆ REGIVS PROFFSSOR: QVAM PROVINCIAM
SVMA CVM FIDELITATE ET EGREGIA IAVDE PER VNDEQ VADRAGINIA
ANNOS EXORNAVIT: VIR MOR VM CANDORE SPECTABILIS. IN RE
BVS DIVINIS PROBE EXERCIT VS. IOTIVS A HVMANIORI: LITE
RATVRÆ. AD STVPOREM VSQ CALLENTISSIM IAM SEPTVA
GENERI°: ET QVOD EXCVRRIT RVDE DONATVRAB ACADE:
MIA, RESERVATO TAMEN EI CONSVETO HONORARIO. AÑO Æ IA
TIS 77 SECESSIT HVC IN AGRVM SVBVRBANVM. VBI ANTE ANVM EX
ACTVM POSTRIDIE CAL FEB 1627 MORTALITATEM DEPOSVIT°

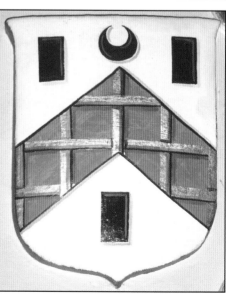

Monument with its Coats to Andreas Downes, February 1627.

Coat of Arms from the tomb of Richard Hatley (1707) and his wife Mary Hatley (1699)

Above left. Stained glass in the window on the North side of the Chancel.

Above. Outside of window on North side of the Chancel.

Left. Painted figures from stained glass windows either side of the Chancel.

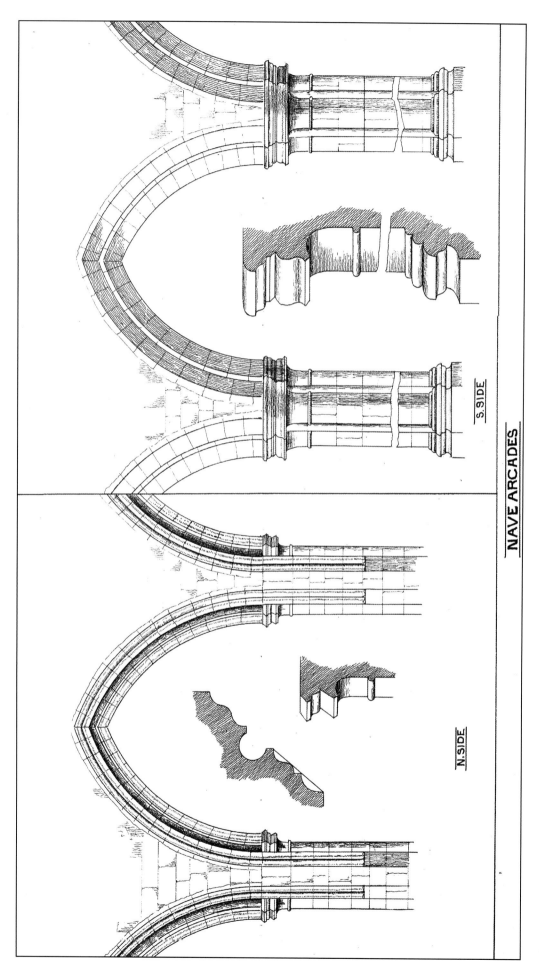

NAVE ARCADES

S.SIDE

N.SIDE

INNER DOOR S. PORCH

FONT

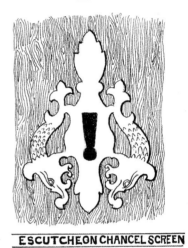

ESCUTCHEON CHANCEL SCREEN

N. SIDE OF CHANCEL

COTON CHURCH

- Downes.

- Delves.

- Greek Professor

- Hatley. 1707.

Stained Glass.

COTON CHURCH

62

DULLINGHAM

27 May 1883.

The Church.

The Church is dedicated to St. Mary the Virgin and consists of Chancel, Nave, North & South Aisles, South Chapel, North Porch and West Tower.

The Chancel has two windows to the south of poor Perpendicular character with square heads. The East Window is of three lights Perpendicular but the lower portion of it is built up. On the north are two windows and a Priests Door all blocked, the easternmost window on this side is of 14th century date. The floor is laid with slabs, the seats are old high deal pews, the ceiling plastered, the Chancel Arch Perpendicular. There is a double Piscina.

The Nave consists of four bays all of Perpendicular date with good mouldings. The Clerestory windows are poor of two lights, square headed. The roof is good framed with moulded tie beams and wall posts on corbels, braced with curved braces, the spandrils are pierced with tracery. The seating and Pulpit are poor, the floor tiled. The Font is of good Perpendicular work, octagonal with cusped panels containing shields, the stem is also panelled, the base well moulded: the shields were painted in the 17th century (Evelyn White in "The Churches of Cambridgeshire" gives the date of the font 1625 a

manifest inaccuracy, but the painting on the panels might be of this date) and bear the following devices.

1. J.R. crowned.
2. Three leopards.
3. Three lillies (fleurs de lis).
4. St. Georges Cross.
5. Prince of Wales feathers.
6. Harp of Ireland.
7. St. Andrews Cross.
8. A lion rampant.

The North Aisle is of the same date as the Nave. It has three windows and a door to the north and windows to the east and west, the latter half blocked by the Tower buttress. There was formerly a Chapel at the east end, a cusped Piscina remains in the adjoining respond of Nave Arcade. The roof is flat framed with wall posts resting on stone carved heads and braced with moulded braces

The South Aisle has one window in the south wall and one to the east and west, part of the latter being blocked by the Tower buttress. There was formerly a Chapel at the east end and a cusped Piscina

S.E. VIEW.

63

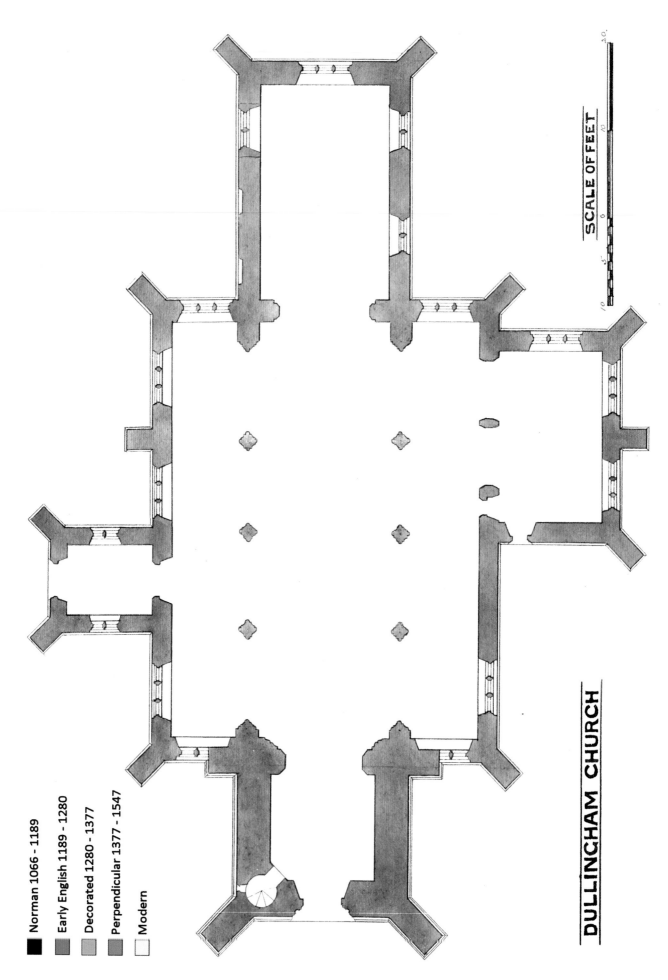

SCALE OF FEET

Norman 1066 - 1189

Early English 1189 - 1280

Decorated 1280 - 1377

Perpendicular 1377 - 1547

Modern

DULLINGHAM CHURCH

NAVE ARCADE

DULLINGHAM CHURCH

FONT

remains in the south wall but mutilated. The doorway leading to former Rood Loft is in the respond opposite. At the south of this aisle eastward is a Chapel with two arches and a small doorway opening into the aisle. There are two three-light Perpendicular windows with good tracery in the south wall, to the east a window of poorer character and to the west a small doorway.

The North Porch is good Perpendicular with traceried side windows, there is a Stoup by the inner door.

The Tower is lofty in three stages of good proportions, the parapet embattled from within. It uses a low square cupola of metal bearing the weathercock. The West Door is well moulded and the window above has good Perpendicular tracery. The tracery of the two-light Belfry windows is also good. The buttresses adjoining the aisles partly block the windows as noted above. Although no difference can be discerned in the character of the work it is probable that the portion of the buttresses below the second set off was added after the Tower was built although not many years subsequently.

In the Belfry are five bells and a clock bell with the following inscriptions.

1. John Briant Hartford fecit 1784.
   J. Haylock and W. Frost C.W.
2. T. Mears of London fecit 1828.
3. John Draper made me 1627.
4. John Draper made me 1626.
5. Miles Graye made me 1660.

Clockbell. J. Mears of London Fecit 1828.

Inscriptions.

These are fairly numerous.

On a slab south side of the Sanctuary.

HERE • LIETH • THE • BODY • OF•
WILLIAM • NORTON • WHO •
DEPARTED • THIS • LIFE • THE • VI •
DAY • OF • SEPT • AD • 1681 •
ANNO • ETATIS • 77 •
VIA • LETHI • OMNIBY • EST •
CALCANDA •

In the centre of the Sanctuary is a stone with the matrix of a cross and inscription below illegible.

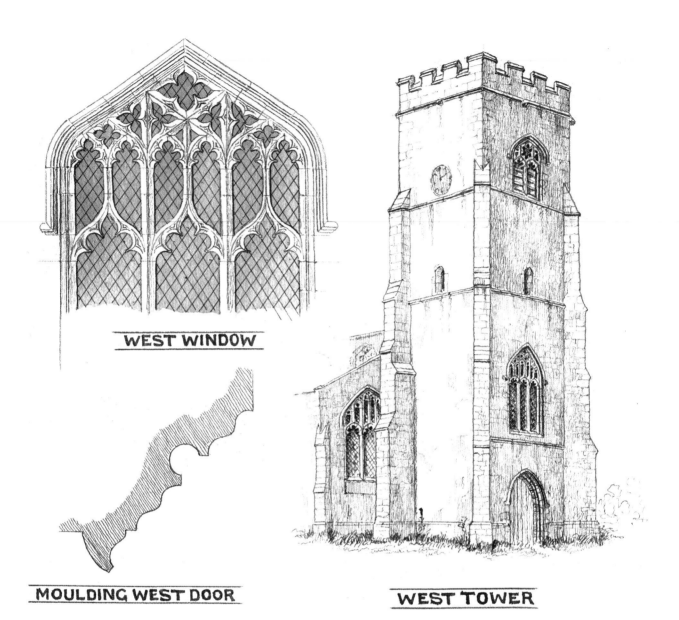

WEST WINDOW

MOULDING WEST DOOR

WEST TOWER

On the south wall a marble tablet surmounted by this coat. Ermine three lozenges in fess sable (Pigott) with an escutcheon of pretence. Azure a fret argent on a chief of the last three leopards faces gules (Jeffreson). Crest. A wolf's head (Pigott).

IN THIS CHANCEL ARE INTERRED THE REMAINS
OF
HARRIET PIGOTT,
WHO DIED IN PARIS MARCH 12TH 1838.
SHE WAS THE ONLY CHILD OF
LIEUT. GENERAL CHRISTOPHER JEAFFRESON,
AND HENRIETTA, VISCOUNTESS GORMANSTON,
AND WIFE OF WILLIAM,
SON OF SIR GEORGE PIGOTT, BART.

*HER HUSBAND CAUSED THIS MONUMENT
AS A LAST SAD TESTIMONIAL OF HIS AFFECTION
TO BE ERECTED IN HER MEMORY.*

On the north wall are four tablets.

1. Surmounted by this coat. Azure a fret argent on a chief of the last 3 leopards faces gules (Jeffreson) impaling Sable a chevron between 3 astroits argent. Crest. A talbots head erased argent eared and langued gules (Jeffreson).

Sacred
To the Memory of
Mrs ELIZABETH JEAFFRESON
Wife of CHRISTOPHER JEAFFRESON Efq
Of this Parifh.
And Daughter of Sir JOHN SHUCKBURG Bart.
Of Shuckburgh in the County of Warwick.
She died the 12th of July 1778.
Aged 78 Years.

2. A tablet with bas relief signed R. W. Westmacott R.A. 14 Great Audley Street London.

Above is a lozenge with these arms. In chief or on a chief sable three crescents argent (Preston) in base Jeffreson as above impaling Vert a chevron or charged with three roses gules between 3 stags trippant of the second (Robinson). Supporters. Dexter. A fox ppr. Sinister. A lion rampant or. "Sans Tache"

IN MEMORY OF
HENRIETTA VISCOUNTESS GORMANSTON
DAUGHTER OF JOHN ROBINSON, OF DENSTON HALL,
IN THE COUNTY OF SUFFOLK, ESQUIRE.
SHE MARRIED FIRST, ANTHONY 11TH VISCOUNT
GORMANSTON,
AND HAD ISSUE JENICO, THE PRESENT VISCOUNT ;
SECONDLY, MAJOR GENERAL CHRISTOPHER
JEAFFRESON, OF THIS PLACE,

BY WHOM SHE HAD AN ONLY DAUGHTER HENRIETTA,
WHO IN TESTIMONY OF HER DUTY AND AFFECTION
HAS CAUSED THIS MONUMENT TO BE ERECTED.
SHE DIED 29TH JANUARY 1826.

3. A tablet with Jeffreson impaling Shuckburgh as above. Crest. A talbots head argent eared and langued gules.

Near this place lyeth the Body of
CHRISTOPHER JEAFFRESON Efq.
Several years one of His Majefty's Juftices of the Peace
For the Counties of Cambridge and Suffolk.
And twice Elected to ferve in Parliament
For the Town of Cambridge.

He marry'd ELIZABETH the Daughter of
Sir JOHN SHUCKBURGH Bart. of Shuckburgh in
Warwickfhire,
By whom he had two Sons and two Daughters;
ELIZABETH, who dyed Auguft 1733,
CHRISTOPHER, SHUCKBURGH, and
ELIZABETH.

This worthy Gentleman was born July the 12th, 1699.
He dyed the 18th of January 1748.

He wrongs the Dead, who thinks this Marble Frame
Was ſet to be the Guardian of his Name:
Whereas, twas for the Aſhes only meant
His Name was ſet to guard the Monument.

4. With arms on a lozenge much worn. Azure a chough argent (Cross) impaling a lion rampant.

Sacred to the Memory of
MARY, Widow of RICHARD CROP Esqr
of Westloe Lodge, in this County,
but late of Taplow, in the County of Bucks.

Her Nephew Colonel JEAFFRESON,
caused to this Monument to be erected
in grateful Remembrance of his
lamented Relative, endeared to him by
inceſsant Proofs of kindest Affection;
to her Friends by the undeviating Sincerity
of her Attachment, and to all who knew her
by the elegant Politeneſs of her Manners,
and the amiable benevolence of her Conduct
through Life protracted to the venerable
Period of Fourscore Years.
She died at Dullingham House,
August 26th 1808.

On the north side of the Chancel is a full length marble effigy signed "Richard Westmacott R.A. invt et sculpt. London" and this coat. Jeffreson as above impaling Robinson.

NEAR THIS PLACE ARE DEPOSITED THE
REMAINS OF
LIEUT. GENERAL CHRISTOPHER
JEAFFRESON,
WHO DIED ON THE 22ND OCTOBER 1824 AGED 63 YEARS.
HE MARRIED HENRIETTA, DAUGHTER OF JOHN
ROBINSON, OF
DENSTON HALL, IN THE COUNTY OF SUFFOLK, ESQUIRE
AND WIDOW OF ANTHONY 11TH VISCOUNT
GORMANSTON, LEAVING AN ONLY DAUGHTER.
TO PERPETUATE THE MEMORY OF A TRULY
JUST AND LIBERAL MAN, WHOSE HEART
TEEMED WITH KINDNESS AND BENEVOLENCE.
THIS MONUMENT IS ERECTED BY HER WHO
TENDERLY LOVED HIM, AND MOST DEEPLY
LAMENTS HIS LOSS.

On the south wall of the Chancel are two tablets.

1. With this coat. Jeffreson as above impaling. Azure a lion rampant crowned argent (Dayrell). Crest for Jeffreson as above.

In a Vault near this Place are depofited the Remains
of CHRISTOPHER JEAFFRESON Efqʳ.
The Tenor of whofe Life difplayed
All that could conciliate Regard, or command Refpect.
As a *Hufband* and a *Parent* He was kind and affectionate
As a *Friend*, zealous and fincere;
As a *Magiftrate*, judicious and impartial.
He fuftained a long and painful Illnefs with exemplary
Fortitude,
And died full of Chriftian Hope on the 26th Day of
September 1789,
Aged 55 years.
He married SARAH the Daughter of FRANCIS
DAYRELL Efqʳ.
of *Shudy Camps* in this County,
by whom he had four Children, but left only two to
lament his Lofs.
CHRISTOPHER and SARAH ELIZABETH.

———————

In the same Vault have fince been depofited the Remains
of
SARAH, Widow of CHRISTOPHER JEAFFRESON Efqʳ.
who died June 10th 1792, Aged 62 Years.

2.   MARY daughter of
CHRISTOPHER JEAFFRESON ESQᴿ.
by SARAH his wife
was baptized Oct: 28: 1764
and buried Oct: 31: 1764.

JOHN fon of
CHRISTOPHER JEAFFRASON ESQᴿ.
by SARAH his wife
was baptised Oct: 10: 1768
and buried February 20: 1769.

On the north-east respond of the Nave this tablet.

This Monument
the last sad tribute of fraternal affection,
is erected to the Memory of
SARAH ELIZABETH, Daughter of
CHRISTOPHER JEAFFRESON Esqʳ.
and SARAH his Wife
who died the 11th of May, 1804,
Aged 40 Years.
Elegant by nature, accomplished by education,

and good by principle,
she attracted the regard of all who knew her,
and having lived most affectionately beloved,
she died most sincerely lamented.

On the opposite respond is a tablet surmounted
by the coat of Jeffreson.

Near this place
lyes Interred in hopes of
a bleffed Refurrection ẙ body
of CHRISTOPHER IEAFFRESON of
this County Efqʳ. Son of Colonell
IOHN IEAFFRESON of Sᵗ. Andrews
Holbourn in ẙ County of Middlefex
and of MARY his Wife Daughter of
ADEN PARKINS Efqʳ. of ẙ County
of Nottingham. He Departed this
Life ẙ 1ˢᵗ of Auguft 1725 in ẙ
75th year of his Age.

His Eminent good Qualities were
fo many, and his Impartiality in
Adminiftering Iuftice in his Country
fo Confpicuous, that he died
Greatly lamented by all
who had ẙ happinefs
to know him.

By the North Door surmounted by this coat. Barry
of 6 or and sable a pile counterchanged.

✠ JOHN CROWSE, ELDEST SON OF
WILLIAM & MARY CROWSE, OF COWLING,
BORN FEB. 6. 1653, DIED IN THE YEAR 1706
X HOBY CROWSE, SECOND SON OF
WILLIAM AND MARY CROWSE, OF COWLING
BORN FEB. 12. 1657, DIED OCT. 22. 1722.
✠ SARAH, THE WIFE OF HOBY CROWSE,
DIED OCT. 1. 1725, AGED 66 YEARS.
✠ HOBY, THE ONLY SON OF
HOBY AND SARAH CROWSE
BORN OCT. 1702, DIED DEC 22. 1738
✠ ANN, THE WIFE OF HOBY CROWSE,
DIED MAY 31. 1739, AGED 39 YEARS.
✠ SARAH, HOBY, AND HOBY, CHILDREN OF
HOBY AND ANN CROWSE,
DIED INFANTS
IN THE YEARS 1728, 1730, AND 1737.
THE
INSCRIPTIONS IN THIS CHURCH YARD
TO THE MEMORY OF THE ABOVE
HAVING BECOME DEFACED BY TIME
THIS TABLET HAS BEEN ERECTED BY
FREDERICK SALMON CROWSE, C.I.E.
BENGAL CIVIL SERVICE,
A GREAT-GREAT-GRANDSON
OF HOBY & ANN CROWSE.

On a slab north side of the Chancel.

Here was Buried
the Body of
ELIZ. SYMONDS Wid.
March 31st 1733:
Aged 76.

On a tablet on the south wall of Chancel exterior.

The Revd IOHN SYMONDS
M.A.
Vicar of this Parish
died June 4th
1778
Aged 85.
SARAH SYMONDS his Widow
died March 2nd
1780
Aged 84.

Above the North Door is a board with the Charities and Donations of the Parish of Dullingham.

On the south wall of the South Aisle are five hatchments.

1. Ermine 3 lozenges in fess sable (Pigott) with an escutcheon of pretence for Jeffreson.
2. Pigott with crescent for difference with escutcheon of pretence for Jeffreson impaling. Azure 3 bird bolts or (Boland). Crest. A wolfs head erased proper gorged or.
3. The arms of Jeaffreson.
4. Or on a chief sable 3 crescents of the field (Preston) impaling Vert on a chevron between three stags trippant or 3 roses gules (Robinson). Supporters. Dexter a lion rampant or, Sinister, a fox ppr.
5. Jeaffreson impaling Robinson. Crest. A talbots head erased argent langued and eared gules.

Boards below the Tower

Boards below the Tower

Pedigree of Jeffreson and Robinson

Colonel John Jeffreson of St. Andrews = Mary dau. of Adens Parkins Esq. of Co. Notts.
Holborn purchased Dullingham 1656.

Christopher Jeffreson of Dullingham ob. 1725 æt. 75. Bur at Dullingham. =

Christopher Jeffreson of Dullingham b. 1699. = Elizabeth 3rd dau. of Sir John Shuckburgh Bart.
M.P. for Cambridge. ob. 18 January 1748. of Shuckburgh Co. Warwick, ob. 1778.
Bur at Dullingham.

Shuckburgh. | Elizabetts. | Christopher Jeffreson = Sarah dau. of Francis Dayrell Esq.
Elizabeth | of Dullingham | of Shudy Camps Co. Cambs,
ob. 1733. | ob. 26th Sept. 1789, | ob. 10th June 1792 æt 62.
| bur. at Dullingham.

Sarah Elizabetts. | Christopher Jeffreson of Dullingham = Henrietta dau. of John Robinson Esq.
ob. unmar. 1804 | Lieut. Gen. and Col. Cambs | of Denston Hall Suff. and widow of
Two children | Militia, ob. 22nd Oct. 1824 æt. 63. | Anthony 11th Viscount Gormanston
died young. | | ob. 1826.

2nd wife Charlotte Maria = William Pigott Esq. J.P. = Harriet dau. and heir also eventual heiress
widow of General Lord | & D.L. 3rd son of Sir | of her maternal grandfather John Robinson
Keane. mar. 18. | George Pigott of Knapton | of Denston Hall, Suff.
Oct 1847. | Mar. 23rd June 1827. | ob. at Paris, March 12th 1838.

Harriet. | Ada = John Dunn Gardner Esq. = 1 wife Mary dau. of Andrew Lawson Esqre of
| 2 wife. of Chatteris Co. Cambs. | Bow Bridge Hall, Boroughbridge Co. Yorks.
| mar. 15 March 1853
| ob. 1903.

Mary Marianne Mariana = Christopher William Pigott b. 23 Jan. 1830. Assumed the arms and
mar. 1870, now of name of Jeffreson under the will of General Jeffreson of Dullingham
Dullingham House. House and in 1857 that of Robinson only by the testamentary
injunction of William Henry Robinson of Dunston. ob. 1889.

SANS TACHE

HERALDRY

GREAT EVERSDEN

20 May 1884.
The Church.
The Church is dedicated to St. Mary and consists of Chancel, Nave, West Tower and South Porch. The whole Church is of Perpendicular work.

<u>The Chancel</u> has an East Window of three lights. There are two three-light windows and a Priests Door on the south and one three-light window on the north. In the east wall is a Piscina on the south side and an Aumbry on the north. The Chancel Arch is good Perpendicular. The roof is old framed with tiebeams, moulded cornice and arched braces resting on corbels. The floor is covered with plain tiles, the seating poor, but there are two old stalls with elbows and misereries on which are carved these coats.
1. Three cinquefoils within a bordure engrailed.
2. A fess between six cross crosslets botony.

<u>The Nave</u> has two three-light windows on the south and a doorway (blocked). On the north a door and a three-light window. In the north east angle are the stairs leading to the former Rood Loft, the upper doorway remains. The Pulpit is of Jacobean date, a few old benches remain, the rest of the woodwork modern and poor. The Font is octagonal on an octagonal base perfectly plain. The roof is old framed with tie beams and braces.

Coats below the Misereries in the Chancel

S.E. VIEW

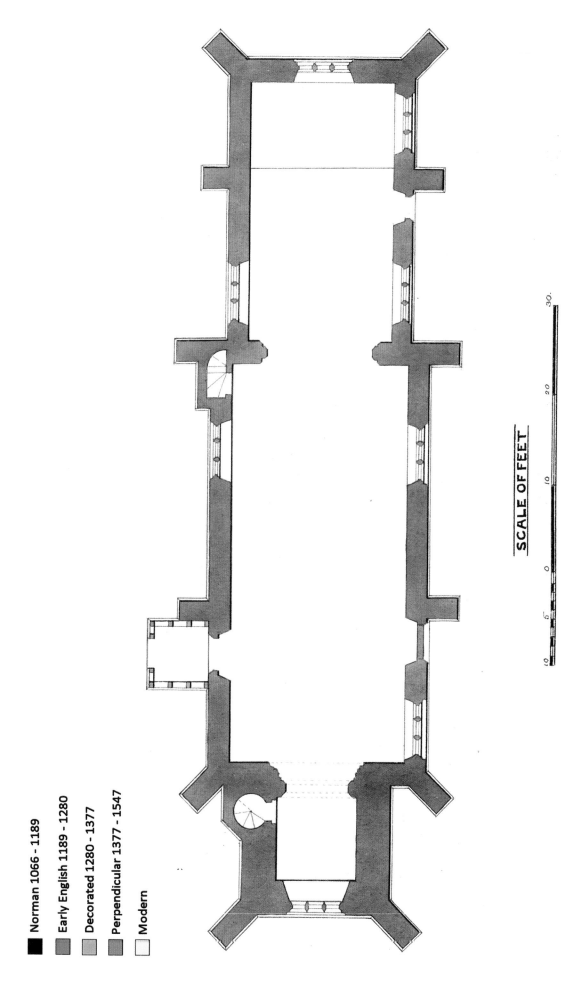

Norman 1066 - 1189

Early English 1189 - 1280

Decorated 1280 - 1377

Perpendicular 1377 - 1547

Modern

SCALE OF FEET

The Porch is of wood and plaster and it bears in the gable the date 1636.

The Tower is of poor design and in a dilapidated state. It has bold angle buttresses, a battlemented parapet and a small lead Spire. The West Window is of three lights. In the Belfry are three bells with these inscriptions.
1. John Butcher Churchwarden 1767.
2. (No inscription).
3. Miles Graie fecit 1639.
The treble and second are from the St. Neots foundry as the border at the end of the inscription is identical with that at Fulbourne.

Inscriptions.
In the Chancel on a slab with this coat. On a fess between three roundeles a lion passant (Rose).

Here lies Interr'd the body of
Richard Rofe
late of Everfden Gent.
who departed this life March 7th 1742
Etatis 38.
He married *Mary* the daughter of
John Day Gent.
by whom He had three Children
Thomas, Editha, & Richard.

On another slab half covered by seating.

In Memory of
RICHARD ROSE Esq.
who died Jany.3.1800
Aged 49 Years.

On the south wall is a tablet with this coat. Party per chevron or and azure three martlets* counterchanged.

In Memory of
JOHN DAY ESQR
who died July 30th 1751
Aged 57 years.
Alfo
ELIZABETH DAY his Wife
who died April 13th 1782
Aged 84 Years.

In the Nave a tablet on the north wall.
UNDERNEATH THIS PEW ARE DEPOSITED
THE REMAINS OF
MR ALFRED MEERES,
LATE OF MUSWELL HILL, NEAR LONDON
WHO DIED WHILE STAYING AT HIS BROTHERS,
IN THIS PARISH
DECEMBER 18TH 1854,
AGED 47.

———◆———

SO TRIALS AND SORROWS THE CHRISTIAN PREPARE
FOR THE REST THAT REMAINETH ABOVE ;
ON EARTH TRIBULATION AWAITS HIM, BUT THERE
THE SMILE OF UNCHANGEABLE LOVE.

———◆———

---

* On the tablet itself these are not martlets but mullets, as shown above.

WINDOW S. SIDE

EAST WINDOW

On the Misereries in the Chancel

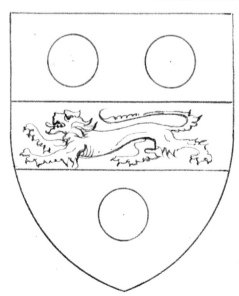

Slab to Richard Rose, ob. 1742

Tablet to John Day, ob. 1751

LITTLE EVERSDEN

4 June 1883.

The Church.

The Church is dedicated to St. Helen and consists of Chancel, Nave, South Porch and West Tower.

The Chancel is of Decorated date and much restored. The arch has been demolished and a sham plaster one substituted. There is one step to the Altar and the floor is paved with plain square tiles. The East Window is of three lights. On the south are two two-light windows, the westernmost of which is Decorated, the easternmost Perpendicular. On the north is a single light trefoiled lancet. For the south wall there are two arched openings, probably Sedilia and Piscina, nearly three feet from the floor which probably was originally higher, neither contain basins. The seating is of deal of poor character (since fitted up with oak stalls from Queens' College Chapel).

The Nave is of the same style and date as the Chancel. At the west end is a gallery. The floor is tiled with red and black tiles. There are two windows on the south, the westernmost of which is of peculiar design with well moulded jambs and label of two lights, the centre mullion continuing almost to the apex of the arch then forming a tiny quatrefoil; on the north side is one window of similar design to the easternmost on the south. The South Door is blocked, the north opens into a porch of good Decorated wood and plaster work but much dilapidated. It has traceried barge boards and an arched wooden head to the outer door. There is a stoup by the side of the inner door. The Font is plain octagonal, it stands on a square of black and white marble slabs.

The Tower is good Perpendicular, with a traceried window of three lights with grotesque dripstone finials to the label. It is finished with a battlemented parapet and a small lead Spire; the Belfry windows are of two lights with traceried heads, the staircase is in the north-west angle.

Bells. In the Belfry are four bells with inscriptions as follow.
1. No inscription.
2. Robert Leet Churchwarden.
   J. Eayre St. Neots fecit 1756.
3. Miles Graye made me 1629.
4. Christopher Gray made me 1666.

S.E. VIEW.

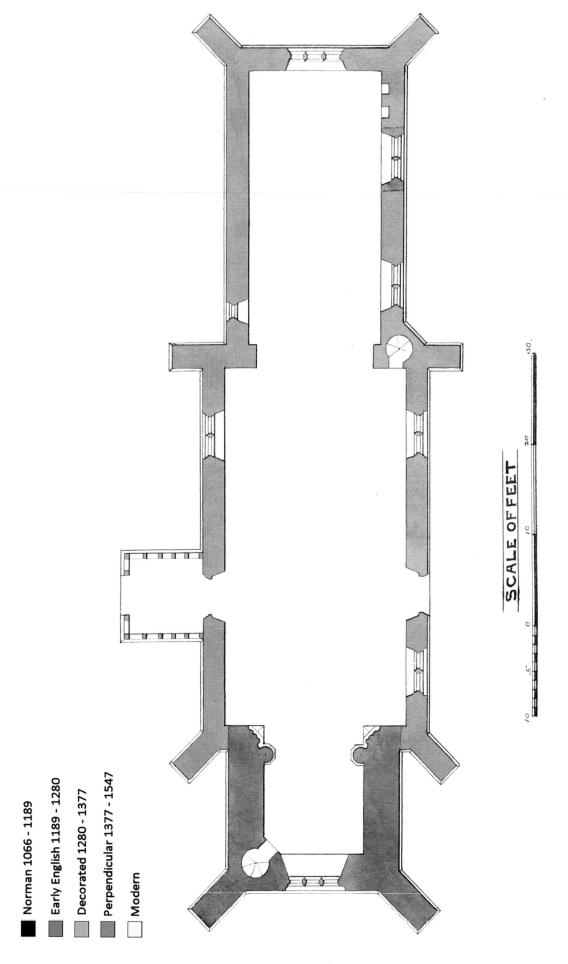

Norman 1066 - 1189
Early English 1189 - 1280
Decorated 1280 - 1377
Perpendicular 1377 - 1547
Modern

SCALE OF FEET

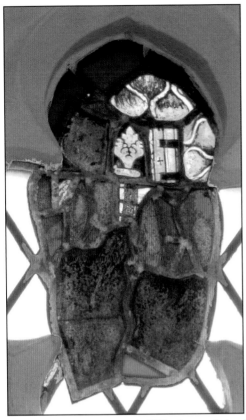

UNDERNEATH
REPOSE THE MORTAL REMAINS OF
RACHEL YORKE
THE BELOVED INFANT DAUGHTER OF
THE REV^D JOHN L. F. RUSSEL M.A.
CURATE OF THE PARISHES OF GREAT AND
LITTLE EVERSDEN

SHE DIED AT THE RECTORY HOUSE IN THIS PARISH
AFTER A SHORT ILLNESS, NOVEMBER 1ST 1854,
AGED 4 MONTHS.

CHE SARA SARA

On the north side of the Chancel.

In memory of
the Rev. Peter Heaton B. D.
Rector of this Parish
who died on the XIXth November
MDCCCXXIV
aged LXXV years.

There are no slabs in the Nave. On a board on the south wall is this.

CHARLES BARON DEER, Gent^n
gave by Will, One hundred Pounds to the
Parish of Little Eversden the Interest where-
-of is to be laid out annually towards repair-
-ing the CHURCH.
THE RECTOR, Churchwardens, Overseers,
and their Succeſſors are appointed Trustees for
this Legacy.
The said Sum of *L*.100, was placed in
Trust on the 30th day of Jany 1805, in the hand of
the Bursar of Queens College in Cambridge among
the College money, and the Bursar is to pay the Trust-
-ees the annual legal Interest for the same.

C.B.DEER also gave by Will, Fifty Pounds to
Addenbrokes Hospital, in CAMBRIDGE on condition,
that the Governors admit one Patient into the Hos-
-pital at a time for ever, belonging to the Parish
of Little Eversden, who shall be recommended by
the Rector, Churchwardens, and Overseers of
the Parish.
He gave a similar Legacy, to Adden-
-brokes Hospital, in favour of Great Eversden.
P. HEATON, Rector.
Wm RYCRAFT, Churchwarden
Wm RYCRAFT, and } Overseers.
T. CRISP }

Stained Glass. In the North Window of the Nave are two very good quarries of old stained glass, one on an elaborately designed crocket, there are also slight remains in the West Window.

The Church was restored 1891 - 92.

Inscriptions.
The monumental inscriptions are few.
On a tablet in the north wall of the Chancel.

SACRED
TO THE MEMORY OF
LYDIA LEETE
WHO WAS BORN AT QUARRY FARM
IN THIS PARISH
AND DIED AT BRIDGE STREET WESTMINSTER
AUGUST XXII, MDCCCLIV
AGED LXXVI YEARS.
BY HER WILL SHE GAVE TO THE POOR OF THIS PARISH
THREE HUNDRED POUNDS CONSOLS,
THE INTEREST OF WHICH
TO BE GIVEN AWAY AT CHRISTMAS IN CLOTHING
AND FUEL.
ALSO TO
ADDENBROKE'S HOSPITAL, CAMBRIDGE
ONE HUNDRED POUNDS CONSOLS,
ON CONDITION
THAT ONE PATIENT BE ADMITTED ANNUALLY
FROM THIS PARISH FREE OF EXPENCE.

On a tablet of white marble with crest. A goat trippant (Russel).

NAVE WINDOW

CHANCEL WINDOW

PORCH

FEN DITTON

March 29th 1883.

The Church.

The Church is dedicated to St. Mary the Virgin and consists of Chancel, Nave, North and South Aisles, South Porch and West Tower. There was formerly a Sacristy on the north side of the Chancel.

The Chancel was restored in 1881, the roof being removed and the East Window inserted. Beyond these changes the fabric suffered little damage. There are three good two-light windows with flowing tracery on the south side and one on the north, the sill of the easternmost window on the south continues to within a few inches of the floor forming a Sedilia. The westernmost window on the same side and the opposite one on the north have a low sill and transom above. A bold Decorated moulding runs along each side below the sills of the windows. There is a Priest's Door on the north. The East Window is modern of five lights with elaborate flowing tracery, on each side of it is a cusped Nitch. The roof is boarded, the rafters being visible, each one framed and braced. The floor is covered with glazed tiles and stone. The Chancel is of one date, c.1340. The buttresses shew supposed consecration crosses worked in flint.

The Nave is unrestored and is Perpendicular of four bays in extent. The Clerestory is poor of two-light windows. The roof is of a flat pitch framed with moulded tie-beams, wall posts and braces. On the south side on a level with the Clerestory windows is the doorway opening onto the former Rood Loft, this is rather an unusual height. On the north side is a doorway opening from the ground to the staircase. The seating is of oak, modern and of poor design. The Pulpit is modern set up in 1880. The Font stands at the west end before the Tower Arch, it is octagonal with cusped panels containing carved angels holding shields. These are much mutilated but among others are the following.

1. A bend between six lions rampant (de Bohun').
2. Quarterly 1 & 2 a lion rampant 3 & 4 chequy (Arundel).
3. Three ducal crowns (Ely).
4. An emblem of the Trinity.

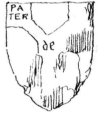

The other shields are defaced. Thomas Fitz Alan Bishop of Ely 1374 to 1388, this fairly fixes the date of the Font.

S.E. VIEW.

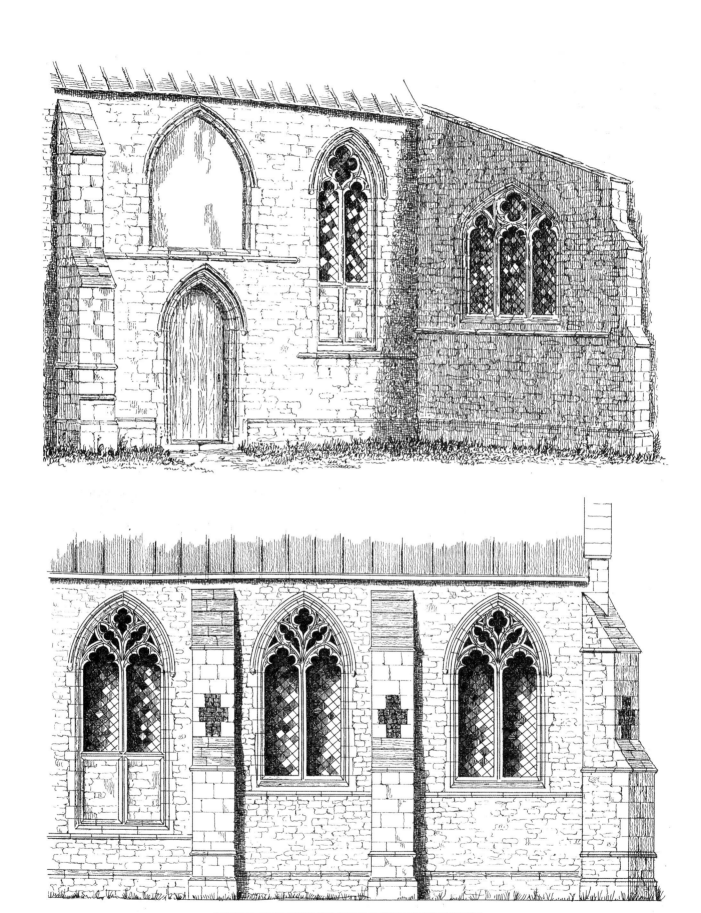

NORTH & SOUTH SIDES OF CHANCEL

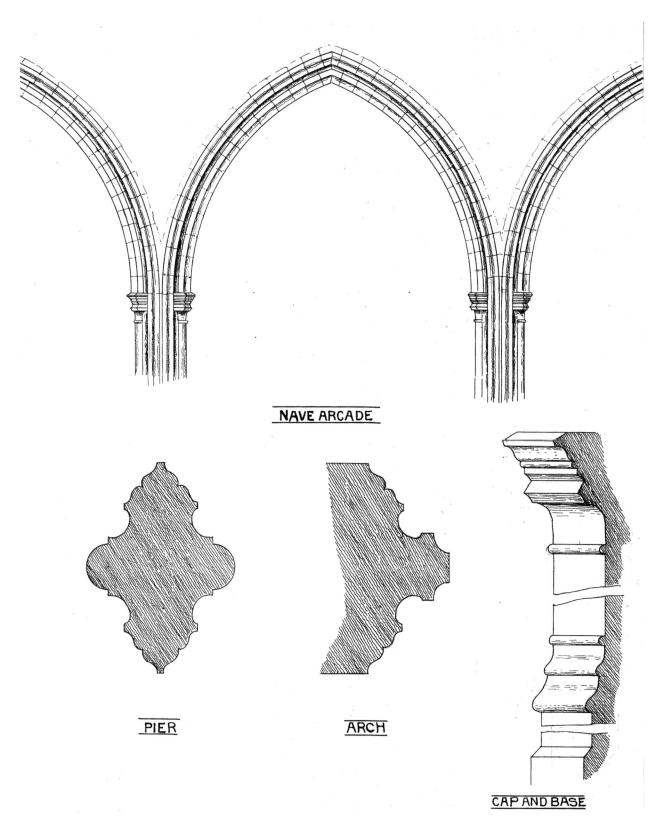

NAVE ARCADE

PIER

ARCH

CAP AND BASE

The South Aisle is unrestored, it has four windows to the south, two of three-lights, and two of two-lights. The east and west windows are of three-lights, all of early Perpendicular date, probably coeval with the font c.1380. The roof of the Aisle is good, formed in trusses with curved brace pieces and the spandrils filled with tracery. No perfect truss remains and only one spandril retains its tracery.

The North Aisle has been restored. There are four windows and a door on the north, the three easternmost are two-light Perpendicular, the

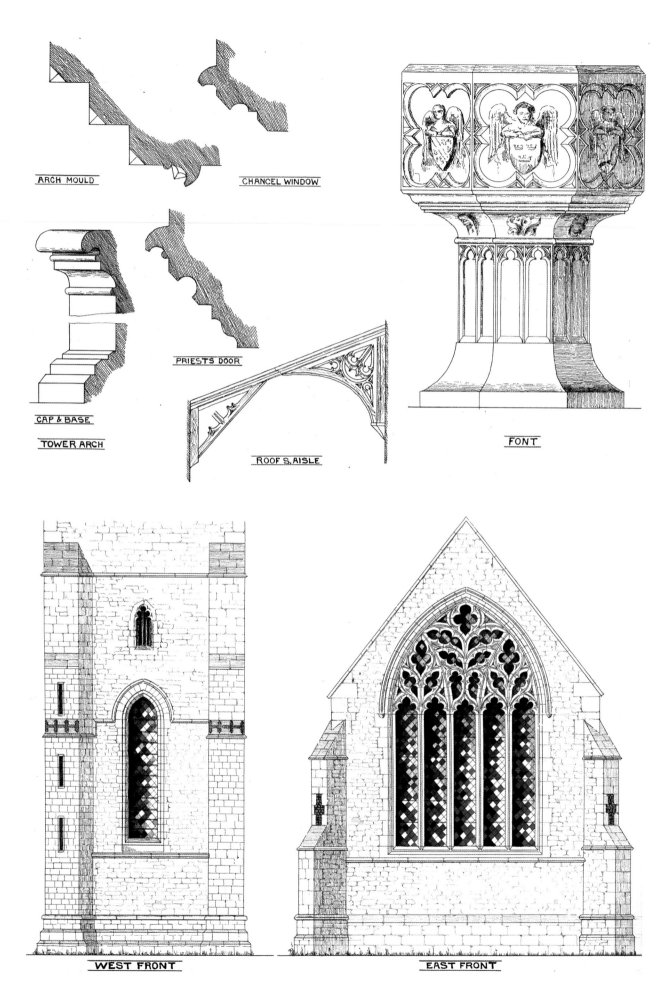

ARCH MOULD

CHANCEL WINDOW

CAP & BASE

TOWER ARCH

PRIESTS DOOR

ROOF S. AISLE

FONT

WEST FRONT

EAST FRONT

84

westernmost and that in the west wall are two-light Early English. (See sketch). The East Window is three light Perpendicular, beneath it is a second Altar. The roof is much restored, of poorer character than that of the South Aisle, although in all probability they were originally of the same design.

<u>The Tower</u> was restored in 1881. The arches are massive of good Early English character being a triple chamfer, the caps and bases are octagonal somewhat rudely worked. The east and west arches have the toothed ornament introduced in the hollows of the labels. The ceiling is framed with four beams well moulded with wall posts and curved brackets resting on stone corbels with shields of arms, two of which remain. viz. A fess between two chevrons (Lisle). A fess between five annulets (Avenell).

Inscriptions.
The monumental inscriptions are not of great interest. At the restoration, the sepulchral slabs in the Chancel floor were carefully removed from the centre and placed beneath the choir seats and organ, some being hidden and others rapidly becoming obliterated through the constant friction of feet.

On a large black marble tablet on the north side of Chancel.

Richard Willys of ẏ Inner Temple Londoⁿ
Esq, (eldest Son & Heir of Thomas Willys
of Horningsey in this County Esq:) &
Jane his Wife, sole Daughter & Heir
of William Henmarsh of Balls
in ẏ Parish of Sᵗ Johns neare Hartforᴰ
in ẏ County of Hartford Esq.
He dyed ẏ 16ᵗʰ of October 1625.
She dyed ẏ 12ᵗʰ of February 1628.
They left Issue Three Sons
and one Daughter.

With these arms, 1. Party per fess three lions rampant counterchanged within a bordure ermine (Willys). 2. Per pale 1 Willys as above, 2 A lion rampant gardant ducally crowned. (Henmarsh).

Here lyeth the Body of Damᵉ
Anne Willys late Wife of Sir
Thomas Willys Baronet, she waˢ
Eldest Daughter and Coheir of
Sir Iohn Wylde of ẏ City of
Canterbury Knight, she lived with
her said Husband 55 years
Wanting two months & had by him
Thirteen Children, 6 Sons & 7 Daugʰ
She dyed ẏ 20ᵗʰ of October in ẏ
yeare of our Lord 1685
in ẏ 75 year of her Age.

With these arms 1. Willys as above with Ulster badge. 2. A chevron, on a chief two martlets (Wilde).

Sir Thomas Willys Baronet
departed this life the 17ᵗʰ
of November 1701 in the
90ᵗʰ year of his Age.

with coat. Per pale Willys - six lions rampant 3. 2. 1.

Sir Iohn Willys Baronett
departed this life the 2ᵈ
of Aug. 1704 in the 69 year
of his Age.

Sir Thomas Willys Baronet
Son of the above sd Sir Iohn
Willys departed this life the
17ᵗʰ Iune 1705 in the 31ᵗʰ (sic) year
of his Age.
He left Issue Sir Thomas Willys
an Infant.

Underneath lie the Remains of Sʳ THO: WILLYS Baronett, the only Son and Heir of Sʳ THOˢ WILLYS Baronet, mentioned in ẙ preceeding Inscription.

He died on ẙ 30ᵗʰ of March, 1724 soon after ẙ Day which brought him into ẙ World was turn'd To him indeed it was a Ioyful Commencement of Immortality, but to his ever forrowing Mother a day of bitternefs & confummate affliction, and which together with Her, His Mourning Friends,

Semper acerbum
Semper honoratum (sic Di voluistis) habeunt.

with arms of Willys.

On a polished marble slab with a brass cross inlaid; in the centre of the Chancel.

MARY HAVILAND DIED JAN 30ᵀᴴ 1831 AGED 76.

LOUISA MARIA HAVILAND BORN FEB. 22ᴺᴰ 1823 DIED APRIL 30ᵀᴴ 1834.

ROBERT HAVILAND BORN FEB. 19ᵀᴴ 1827 DIED MAY 3ᴿᴰ 1834.

AUGUSTUS POLLEN HAVILAND BORN DEC 2ᴺᴰ 1833 DIED JUNE 19ᵀᴴ 1834.

JOHN HAVILAND M.D. REGIUS PROFFESOR OF PHYSIC IN THE UNIVERSITY OF CAMBRIDGE BORN FEB 2ᴺᴰ 1785 DIED JAN 8ᵀᴴ 1851.

ELIZABETH POLLEN DIED APRIL 7ᵀᴴ 1853 AGED 76.

LOUISA WIFE OF JOHN HAVILAND M.D. AND SISTER OF ELIZABETH POLLEN, BORN FEB 14ᵀᴴ 1791 DIED APRIL 7ᵀᴴ 1868.

On a black marble slab on the north side of Chancel, beneath the choir benches.

Sacred to
the memory of
the Revᵈ John Haggitt
many years Rector of this Parish
he died VII January M.DCCCXLIII
aged 81
We have an advocate with the father Jesus Christ the righteous.
In memory of Frances his wife
who died May 10ᵗʰ 1854 aged 81

and him that cometh to me I will in no wise cast out.
Also of Constance Mary Ann Ray
their beloved grandchild
who died Oct. 15ᵗʰ 1843 aged 6 years.

On an adjoining slab is the following with four lines of verse nearly obliterated.

Edward Curtis who departed this life May 23ʳᵈ 1765 aged 13 years.

On a slab on the south side of Chancel.

Sub Hoc Marmore
depositæ sunt Reliquæ Feminæ
non minus Caftæ quam Piæ,
Janæ Cornwall
uxoris Ioh. Cornwall S : T : P.
ac nepts Dⁿⁱ Tho : Malet in
agro Somerfettenfi Capitalis
dum vixit Angliæ Iufticiarii
Obiid 25 die Sept.
Anno { Ætatis 48
{ Salutis 1712

Arms. A lion rampant crowned within a bordure bezantée (Cornwall) impaling three escallops (Malet).

There is another slab beneath the organ, the inscription completely hidden. It is surmounted by a coat. The crest of which above an esquires helmet is alone visible. A wiverns head couped pierced by an arrow.

On three small square stones

P. C. T. ob June 1760.

P. T. ob July 1732.

A. S. ob . . . . 1748.

On the east wall of South Aisle a marble tablet.

IN MEMORY OF
JAMES BONES
WHO AFTER A LIFE SPENT IN
THE FAITH AND FEAR OF GOD,
DIED OCT^R THE 1ST 1766 AGED 66.

ALSO OF **MARY** HIS WIFE
WHOSE SINCERE AND UNIFORM PRACTICE
OF ALL RELIGIOUS DUTIES,
THE TENDER CARE OF HER CHILDREN,
AND READINESS TO RELIEVE THE POOR,
MADE HER LIFE TRULY EXEMPLARY,
AND HER DEATH SINCERELY LAMENTED
BY HER FAMILY AND FRIENDS.
OBIIT 15TH MARCH 1774 ÆT^S 67.

On the south wall, west of the Porch, is a large marble tablet with kneeling figures carved in high relief, also a medallion portrait of the deceased and these arms. Argent on a bend azure three fleurs de lis.

IN A VAULT BENEATH ARE DEPOSITED THE
REMAINS OF
JOHN BONES ESQ^RE
AN EMINENT SOLICITOR,
LATE OF GREAT SAINT ANDREWS STREET,
CAMBRIDGE, WHERE HE LIVED FORTY-TWO YEARS.
HE WAS THE YOUNGEST SON OF JAMES AND
MARY JONES, FORMERLY OF DITTON HALL.

POSSESSED OF A STRONG AND GOOD HEART, HE
WAS STRICTLY AN UPRIGHT HONEST MAN;
AND UNIVERSALLY RESPECTED FOR INTEGRITY
AND PUNCTUALITY IN THE DISCHARGE OF HIS
PROFESSIONAL DUTIES.
HE WAS A MOST AFFECTIONATE HUSBAND TO A
BELOVED WIFE, WHO DIED AT THE EARLY AGE
OF TWENTY-NINE,
LEAVING HIM TWO INFANT DAUGHTERS, TO
WHOM HE DEVOTED HIS WHOLE LIFE,
BEING TO THEM A TENDER AND INDULGENT
FATHER, WHO ALWAYS FELT MOST HAPPY IN
THEIR SOCIETY.

HIS GRATEFUL DAUGHTERS HAVE CAUSED THIS
MONUMENT TO BE ERECTED
TO THE MEMORY OF THEIR BELOVED FATHER,
WHO AFTER A WELL SPENT LIFE, DIED WITH
PIOUS RESIGNATION TO THE WILL OF HIS CREATOR,
NOVEMBER 21ST 1813, AGED 66 YEARS.

There is also a slab on the floor of the Porch to the same. A slab to "Humfrey Gardner Armiger" obiit 1691 with arms. Party p fess and pale counterchanged 3 griffins heads erased.

The only remnants of old stained glass are in the easternmost window south side of South Aisle. The East Window of the Chancel is modern, the subjects are the Crucifixion in the upper part and scenes from the New Testament below. Beneath is this inscription.

+ TO • THE • GLORY • OF • GOD
AND • IN • PIOUS • MEMORY • OF
JOHN • HAVILAND • M : D : 1851
AND • LOUISA • HIS • WIFE • 1868
DEDICATED • BY • THEIR • SONS

Window on the north. Subject Christ and St. Peter. Beneath

East Window of North Aisle has this inscription.

+ To · the · Glory · of · GOD +
In · remembrance · of · the · Reverend ·
Frederick · Cox · and · Matilda · his · Wife
This · Window · is · gratefully · dedicated · by
· their · sons · F.H.C. and · F.B.
A°. · Dni · MDCCCLXXXI.

Bells.

There are five bells but none of great antiquity.
Weight of Tenor 12cwt. Diameter 39½ inches.
Note G. The inscriptions as follows.
1. Robert Malton, William Pettet
   Churchwardens 1623.
2. Ring and fear not, but swear not. 1623.
3. John Hodson made me 1654.
4. Fear the Lord and on him caul,
   William Hursley made us all. 1623.
5. Edward Wrangell, John Curtice.
   Charles Newman made me 1692.

Bell with inscription to Robert Malton and
William Pettet preserved in the Church

List of Rectors.
1281 Theobald de Deyn.
1345 Elias Thoresby.
1349 William de Peeham May 28.
      Comis Eliens psent to Ditton.
.... Robert Seyr June 18.
1351 Nicholas de Bagford
      rector of Stretham Sept. 9. change.

1376 Roger de Wodnorton Nov. 16.
.... Stephen Atte Rothe. change.
1381 John Sundrash Oct. 4.
.... Dñs Johēs Canefeld de Ditton.
.... Simon Romayne of Grantesden Nov. 3.
      He purchases land to enlarge the
      mansion 1389.
1394 John Fendom Jan. 19.
1395 John de Repyndon, Nov. 23.
1396 Nicholas Mockyng, July 4.
1401 John Brigge, July 22.
1407 John Judde, Sept. 6.
1430 John Sudbury, D.D.
      Master of Pembroke Hall.
1441 Magr̃ Richard Scrope.
1468 Alexander Lye, May 22.
1473 Walter Buck, April 23.
1506 Edmund Norton.
1516 Radulph Hopwood, March 4.
1538 William Lorde, Oct. 2.
1544 Richard Wylkes, June 11.
1556 William Perpoint.
1557 John Fuller L.L.D.
1558 Henry Goodwin, Curate.
1565 John Parker.
1570 John Bell, S.T.B.
      (Rector of Fulbourne St. Vigors).
1588 Dr John Smith.
1614 John Macarnesse, Curate.
1645 William Retchford.
1661 John Worthington, Rector.
1664 William Davey, Curate.
1665 Thomas Stephens.
1677 Humphrey Gower.
1680 Richard Apleford, Curate.
1702 William Edmondson, Curate.
1707 Robert Lambert, Curate.
1711 John Sayer, Curate.
1721 Matthew Baines M.A.
1730 Dr John Davies.
1725 William Sedgwick, Curate.
1730 Mor̃ Unwin, Curate.
1732 Thomas Sturges.
1752 John Gooch, son of the Right Revd Sir
      Thomas Gooch Bart. Bishop of Ely. He
      was Rector till 1797 or probably after,
      there is no evidence of his death or
      resignation, but Curates has signed till
1804 John Haggit, signs.
      Died 1843, bur. at Ditton.
1843 John Turner.
1844 W. B. James. Died Aug. 1877.
1877 F. H. Cox, Oct. 18, died 1880.

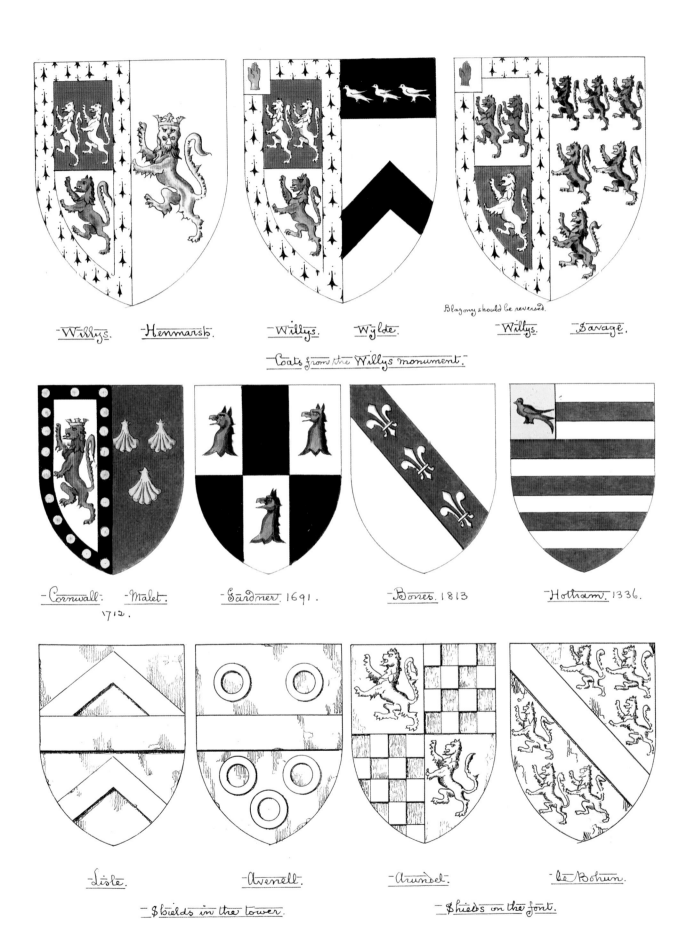

Blazonry should be reversed.

Willys. Hennmarsh.   Willys. Wylde.   Willys. Savage.

Coats from the Willys monument.

Cornwall. Malet. 1712.   Gardner. 1691.   Bones. 1813.   Hotham. 1336.

Lisle.   Avenell.   Arundel.   de Bohun.

Shields in the tower.   Shields on the font.

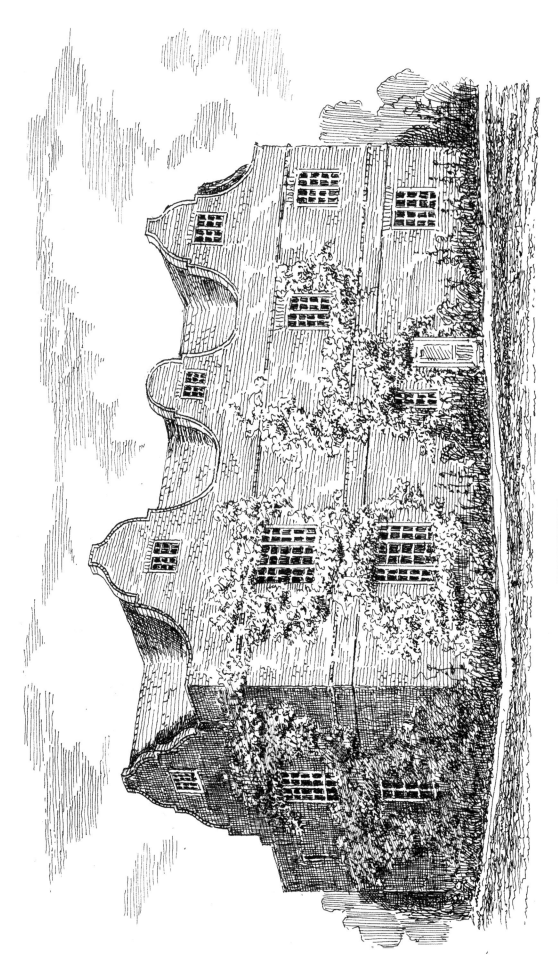

THE HALL.

FULBOURNE

The Church is dedicated to St. Vigor with All Saints. It consists of Chancel with a Sacristy on the north side, clerestoried Nave, South Transept, South Porch, and Embattled Tower with six bells.

Church Interior.

Fulbourne Church as it is today.

N.SIDE.

S.SIDE.

NAVE ARCADES　　FULBOURNE CHURCH

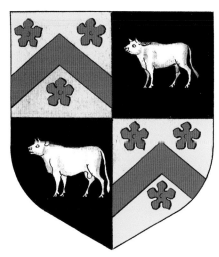

Chicheley quartering Wood

Tomb S. Transept 1633

Dalton ——— Goring

Tablet S. Transept 1682.

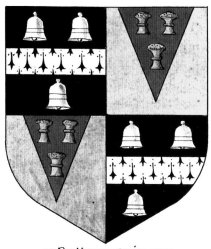

Bell quartering

Tablet S. Transept 1787.

Townley impaling Tate

Tablet S. Transept 1823.

Farmer impaling Aldham

Tablet S. Aisle 1712.

Monument to William Farmer, 1712

Early Pulpit, dating from 14th century

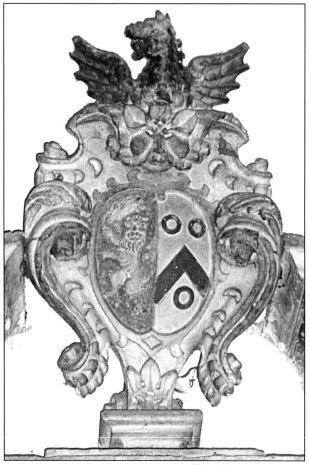

Crest on Monument to Tyrrelli Daltoni, 1682

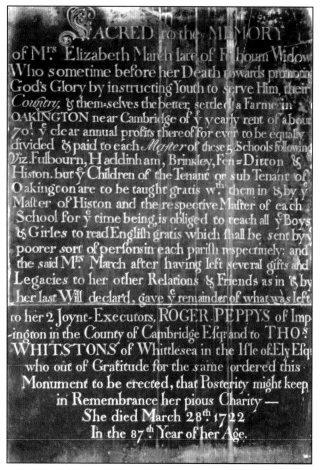

Benefaction of Mrs Elizabeth March, 1722

Pedigree of Wood

Arms. Quarterly.　1. Wood.　2. Clopton.　3.　　　4. Francis.　　Vis. Cambs 1619.

Thomas Wood of Fulborn in Com. Cantabr. ⊤ John Clopton of Kentwell ⊤ Alice d. of Rob. Darcye
Esqʳ Sergt. at Law temp Hen. 7.　　　　　in Com. Suff.　　　of Walden in Essex.

John Wood of ⊤ . . . d. of . . .　　Sʳ. Wm. Clopton　Edmond a knight　Edward Clopton ⊤
　Foulborne.　│　Hilton.　　of Kentwell.　　of Rhodes.

Nicholas Wood of Foulbourne. ⊤ Elizabeth d. and heire of Edw. Clopton.

Edward Wood of Foulbourne ⊤ Elizabeth d. of Thomas Chichley of
(ob.1633, bur. Fulbourn Ch.).　Wimple in Com. Cambridg.

1. Peter　　Anne d. of John ⊤ 3. Nicholas Wood　2. Sir John Wood　Elizabeth ux. John Smyth
　Wood.　Ferror of Gresnald │　of Sneterley　　　Knight.　　of Clare in com. Suff.
　　　　in Norff.　　│　in Norff.

　　　　　　　　　　　　　　　　　　　　　Mary ux. Tho. Wood of
1. Edward.　2. Nicholas.　3. Audley a daughter.　Elizebeth.　Anne.　Suffolk, Doctor of Phissick.

FULBOURNE

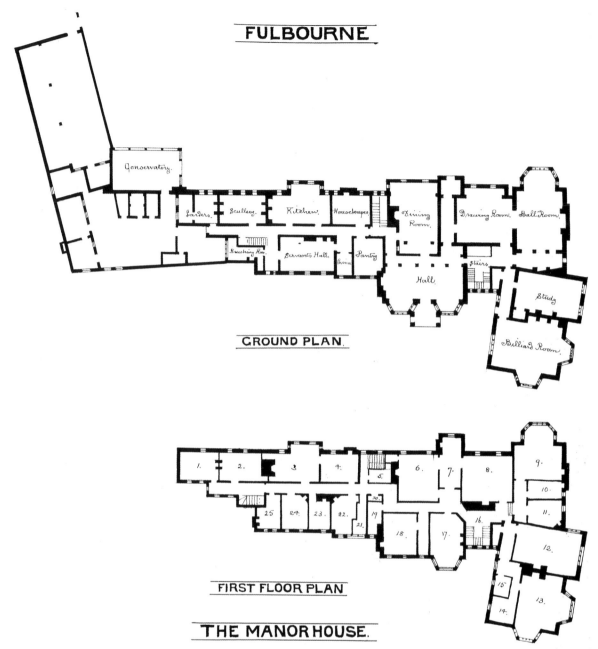

GROUND PLAN.

FIRST FLOOR PLAN

THE MANOR HOUSE.

Fulbourn Manor House

GIRTON

Feb. 23rd 1883.

The Church.

The Church is dedicated to St. Andrew and consists of Chancel, Nave, North and South Aisles, South Porch and West Tower. The style of architecture is Perpendicular of rather late character, considerably debased by subsequent alterations. All the windows excepting the West Window in the Tower and those of the Porch have had the tracery cut away and now display but simple cusped heads beneath a flat arch. The walls are built of rubble and pebble and the exterior covered with plaster.

The Chancel has an East Window of 5 lights similar in character to those in the body of the Church. There is a plain Priests Door on the south and two three-light windows and two similar windows on the north but blocked. The Vestry and door leading into it are modern. The roof is of a flat pitch with moulded principals and wallposts on wooden corbels. The choir stalls are of poor modern Gothic design probably dating from 1853 when the Church was restored. The Chancel Arch is of wide span and over it is still fixed a board on which are painted the Royal Arms. There is a Perpendicular Piscina in the south wall having a simple cusped arch. The lower panels of the Rood Screen still remain and are of good character with cusping &c worked in deal.

S.W. VIEW.

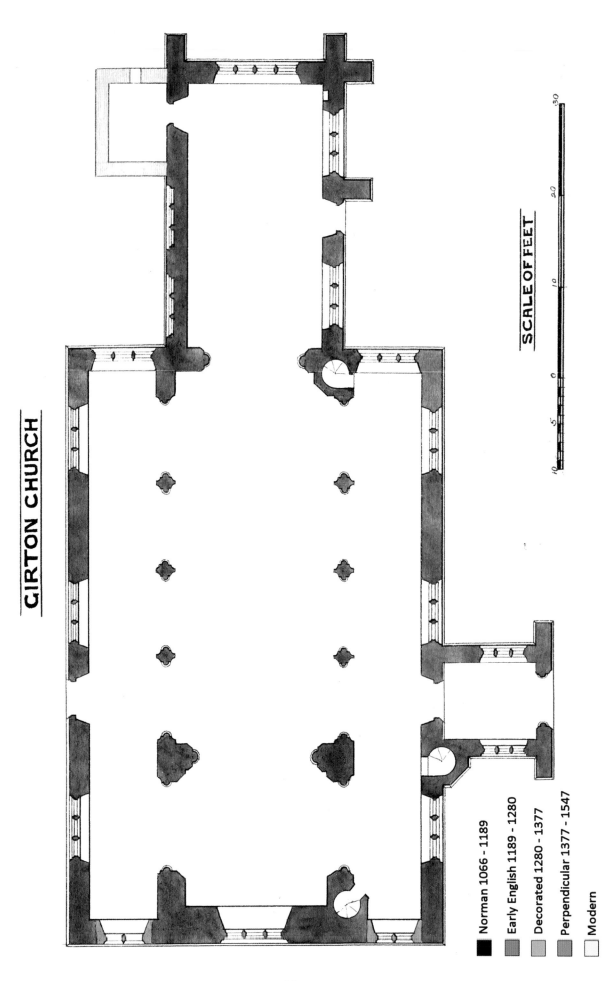

GIRTON CHURCH

Norman 1066 - 1189
Early English 1189 - 1280
Decorated 1280 - 1377
Perpendicular 1377 - 1547
Modern

SCALE OF FEET

DOORWAY TO ROOD LOFT

PANEL OF ROOD SCREEN

No traces remain of the paintings mentioned by Cole. In the east wall on the outside is a small arched opening about three feet from the ground now blocked. A range of old coffin lids much worn from the coping of the east churchyard wall.

The Nave arcade consists of four arches rising from columns of this plan. The roof is plain of flat pitch. The Font is octagonal on an octagonal base having neither moulding or carving surmounted by a plain cover of probably 18th century date. The Pulpit and Lectern are both modern Gothic, the gifts of Mr and Mrs Richard Houblon.

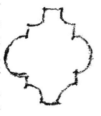

The Aisles are prolonged beyond the Nave to the west wall of the Tower. In the north and south walls of the latter are archways opening into the aisles. In the north-west corner of the South Aisle is the entrance to the Belfry staircase. Both aisles have three debased three-light windows and east windows of similar design. The two western windows of the aisles appear to be of earlier date than the rest of the fabric, they are of two lights with simple pierced heads worked with a single

chamfer flush with the outside wall. At the east end of the south wall in the South Aisle there is a Piscina and just opposite in the respond of the Nave Arcade is the doorway leading to the Rood Loft. This is the best piece of architectural detail in the Church the head being well moulded and cusped. The upper doorway formerly opening on to the Rood Loft is seen on the other side of the respond by the Chancel Arch. There are slight fragments of old stained glass in a window in the North Aisle.

Image of St. Andrew above the South Porch

The <u>South Porch</u> is bold and of good outline, it contains a chamber above, which is lighted by two three-light windows with good traceried heads formerly blocked but reopened in 1911. The doorway and staircase leading to the chamber are in the south-west angle of the Porch, the former has simple tracery in the spandrils and opens into the South Aisle.

The <u>Tower</u> is unbuttressed, in two stages with three-light Belfry windows of debased character, finished with an embattled parapet. The staircase turret on the south side stops at the Belfry floor. In the Belfry are four bells beside the clock bell with the following inscriptions.

1. Christopher Graye made me 167..
2. Charles Newman made me 1699.
3. +Non clamor sed amor cantat in ore Dei 1619
4. +Jesus::speede::us::omniafiant::ad:: gloriam::Dei::1617.

The clock bell has no inscription, one of the bells is cracked (Raven 1881).

In the Belfry are also the works of an old clock probably of late 17th century of early 18th century date, still in working order.

Visiting the Church in May 1883 the clerk told me that he remembered a good deal of stained glass in the windows of the North Aisle (now reduced to a small square of mixed fragments) and that as the windows were damaged by weather and reglazed, the glass was thrown into the churchyard and thus it gradually disappeared. He also gave me information concerning the modern glass. That in the tracery of the West Window was put in about 1840 by the Revd Alexander Cotton. The East Window in the Chancel is of foreign workmanship. About thirty years ago there were several large paintings over the Chancel Arch and also on the wall of the North Aisle. These were very distinct and plain, according to him, and were washed over with whitewash not very long back.

The following notes on the Church were taken by Cole. Feb. 24th 1743 (Cole M.S.S. Vol.IV p22.)

"On the Tower is a large wooden cross leaded on which is fastened the clock bell. The Nave and Chancel are separated one from the other by a neat screen on which are the Royal Arms painted. At bottom on the four panels of oak on each side of the door were curiously painted 8 figures at full length whereof one was a Bishop in pontificalibus with his mitre on his head and his cross in his hand but the face of this as well as of all the rest is purposely scratched out. They were exceedingly well done and the paint and gilding about them is as fresh now as ever. Over the screen and Kings Arms are the names of the Ch. wardens for this year when the Nave and Aisles were beautified."

Inscriptions.

In the Chancel are two brasses both of priests in full vestments. The first westward.

Orate aiã Magiſtri Willmĩ Malſter in decritis licentiati Canonici eccliẽ Cathedralis Ebor et Prebendarii Prebende de Fenton ac Rectoris hujus eccliẽ pochialis de Girton qui obiit xiii die menſis Januarii Anno dm̃ millio ccccºlxxxxii Cujus Anime ppicietur deus. Amen.

The second brass is smaller and has this inscription in old English letters.

Hic jacet Magiſter Willius Stedyn in Decretis Licentiatus quondam

canonic⁵ ecclīe̅ Cath Lincoln ac Rector hujus
ecclīe̅ qui obiit secu̅ do die marcii
A° dn̅ i millio cccclxxxxbii cujus anime Propicietur
deus Ame̅

On the north wall is a marble tablet with this inscription.

IN MEMORY OF
THE REVᴰ AMBROSE ALEXANDER COTTON,
OF LANDWADE IN THIS COUNTY,
YOUNGER SON OF
SIR JOHN HYNDE COTTON, BARᵀ
OF MADINGLEY,
FORTY YEARS RECTOR OF THIS PARISH,
WHO WAS BORN 10ᵀᴴ JULY 1764,
AND DIED MARCH 9ᵀᴴ 1846.
AND OF
MARIA, HIS WIFE,
DAUGHTER OF JACOB HOUBLON, ESQUIRE
OF HALLINGBURY PLACE, ESSEX.
BORN JULY 5ᵀᴴ 1771,
DIED MARCH 3ᴿᴰ 1860.

In the Nave beneath the matrix of a brass is this inscription.

Orate pro aia Johis Yaxley
quiobiit secundo die Julii
Anno Dmni mccccxli.

There are two other slabs in the Nave with the matrices of brasses, this is the only monumental inscription in the body of the Church. On a board fixed at the west end of the North Aisle is the following.

DONATIONS & BENEFACTIONS to GIRTON CHURCH
FOR THE REPAIRS & RESTORATION of the SAME
1853
REVᴰ G.B.F. POTTICARY . . . RECTOR.

		L.	S.
BERRY WAYMAN.} C. SAUNDERSON.} – *Churchwardens.*			
G. POTTICARY . . . . *Rector*	180		
CHURCH BUILDING SOCIETY	100		
MASTER and FELLOWS OF Sᵀ. JOHN'S COLLEGE	25		
THE HONᴮᴸᴱ F.D.RYDER	25		
LADY COTTON . . . *Madingley*	20		
Mᴵˢˢ COTTON, . . Dᵒ	10		
Mᴵˢˢ A.M.COTTON *Girton*	12.	10	
THE BISHOP OF THE DIOCESE	10		
Mᴿˢ COTTON *Bartlow*	10		
Mᴿ ELLIOTT SMITH *Cambridge*	10		
ARCHDEACON BROWN	5		
MASTER & FELLOWS OF CLARE HALL	5		
REVᴰ F. COOMBE *Ramsgate*	5		
REVᴰ G.BAINBRIDGE *St. John's.*	5		
Mᴿˢ GIBBONS *Ashford.*	5		
Mᴿ EKIN *Cambridge*	5		
Mᴿˢ WESTMORLAND *Girton*	5		
Mᴿ C.H.HAWKINS *Colchester*	5		
Collected by CHURCHWARDENS *of Girton* . . .	17		
Dᵒ by Mᴿ CRANFIELD	10		
Dᵒ in Small SUMS	5.	15	

THE PULPIT, READING DESK & LECTERN,
WERE GIVEN BY Mᴿ & Mᴿˢ RICHᴰ HOUBLON.

Beneath the East Window of the Chancel is a brass plate in the sill with this inscription.

DONO·GEORGII·B·F·POTTICARY·A·M·OXON
HVIVS·ECCLESIÆ·RECTORIS·A·D·MDCCCLXXXII.

Cole gives these additional inscriptions with notes on them.
"Since the year 1726 when Mr. Blomefield collected the monuments in this Church one of the six in the County that he visited out of eight (brasses) then entire and perfect as to inscriptions no less than two are stolen away. On a freestone in the middle aisle and as you enter the Nave is a small brass plate a little broke at one of the ends but the figure of a person above it is gone, but enquiring of the clerk found the very brass to fit it in the chest which was designed for a woman but headless." Mʳ. Blomefield writes out at full length Edmundus when on the brass plate is only Em. and signifies Emma I suppose, beside he had made a mistake in the date saying she died 1508 instead of 1544 as I guess it to be, however there are but three C's the two others being broke off but here follows inscript̃.

Hic Iacet Em . . Yaxley que ob... xxvi die
Decembr̃ A° Dn̅i m.c.c.c. . . xliiii cujus ai̅e
ppitietur Deu.

On a small blue marble slab close by this on the right is a small brass plate. (John Yaxley, see above.)

On a small thin grey marble lying in the middle and between the north and south doors of the Nave is the figure of a man in brass but the inscription at his feet is lost within these 3 or 4 years as the Church Clerk informed me. Preserved by Blomefield as follows.

Orate pro Anima Johannis Thielgar qui obiit ul̃t
die Marcii A° Dn̅i m.c.c.c.c.c.viii.

More to the left of this in the passage as you go into the North Aisle lie two stones close together with brasses on them the nearest the north has a figure in brass but small of a man with following inscription.

Hic jacet Wills̃ Colyn Geno̅sus. Qu̅dm un'
justic' Dn̅i Reg. ad pace in. Com̅t Cant. . . . q'
obiit iii die A
prilⁱˢ Ao Dn̅i m.ccccxxi Cuju' ai̅e ppicietur Deus.

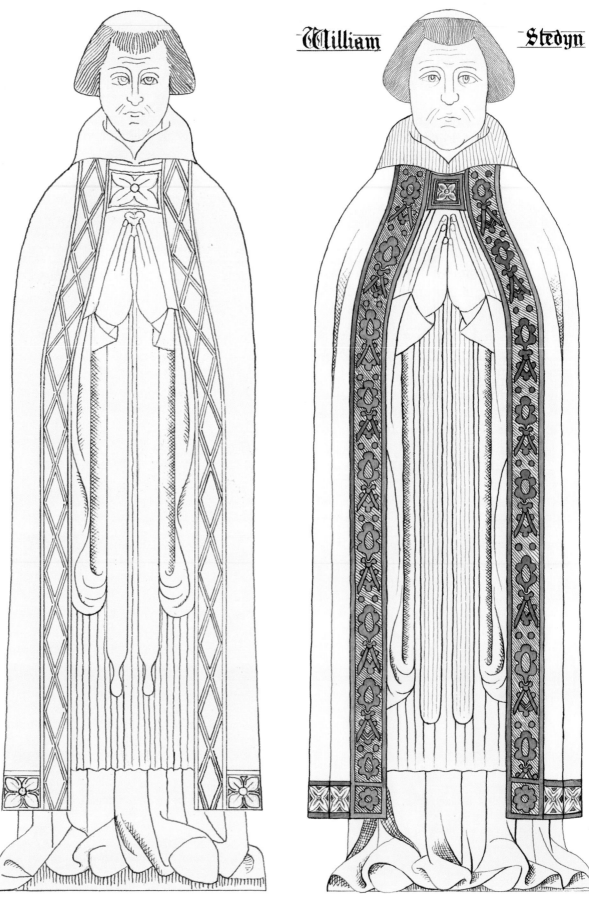

𝔚illiam   𝔖tedyn

𝔚illiam 𝔐alster

That on the other side had the figure of a man in brass now rent away together with one half of ye brass plate at his feet but fortunately I found the other half in an old chest in the Chancel which compleats the inscription.

Hic jacet Williũs Collyns qui obiit exº die Decb̃s Aº Dnĩ M.CCCCCVII cuĩ aĩe ppiciet Deus.

On a small square grey marble with round holes at each corner for brasses now lost is the figure of a man in brass but the plate at his feet is gone but happily preserved by Mr Blomefield.

Orate pro animabus Johannis Kent Katherine et Agnetis uxorum ejus qui prefatus Johannis obiit xviii die mens Nov Aº. Dnĩ M.CCCCCV quorum animabus propicietur Deus."

THE OLD RECTORY GIRTON

STAIRCASE HALL AND LANDING

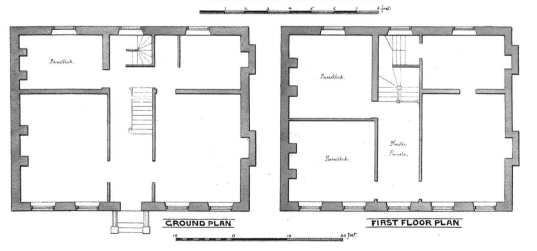

GROUND PLAN

FIRST FLOOR PLAN

GIRTON. THE OLD RECTORY

PANELLING IN FRONT BEDROOM

These figures from drawings by Cole represent the above mentioned brasses, the names in order. Kent, Collyn, Thielgar, Yaxley.

The Rectory★ was built during the Rectorship of Mr Halfhyde. It is a plain but good example of a small Georgian house but considerably enlarged at a later period and an upper storey added. It is built of yellowish brick of various shades probably from some local kiln the added portions are of white brick the whole now coloured red. The original character of the elevation is completely lost but the plan remains and is here shewn. A small room at the back and two bedrooms retain the original panelling from floor to ceiling, all the other rooms are finished with dados. The staircase is of good design with gracefully turned balusters: the walls of the staircase and upper landing are ornamented with plaster panels with the echinus moulding, the ceiling of the landing had formerly circular or oval panels of the same pattern but these have been obliterated. Two of the original ornamental pieces remain in the two front bedrooms : all the woodwork is of deal and one moulding used throughout viz. an ovolo with square raised panel. There are some points in the character of the work which are difficult to reconcile with the early date viz. the slender window bars and the front windows are set back in a reveal, at the back the window frames are flush with the wall; with regard to the former the sashes may have been renewed, but there is no evidence to shew that the frames have been moved, the unaltered state of the internal panelling to soffits and linings seem to shew that the position of the frames is the original one. A number of the old brass rim locks and finger plates remain. The house was very possibly designed by James Essex the elder who was considerably employed at Cambridge at this period.

★ Charles Bell bought the Old Rectory at Girton some time after his father's death.

104

GRANCHESTER

February 1883.

The Church.

The Church is dedicated to St. Mary and St. Andrew and consists of Chancel, Nave, West Tower, North Porch and modern South Aisle.

The Chancel is of Decorated date, c.1340, and is in a fairly original state, being but slightly repaired. The East Window is of five lights, those to the north and south of three. The tracery is flowing, two designs only are employed in the side windows.

The Nave is Perpendicular having four windows on the north. The Porch poor covered with ivy.

The Tower is plain and poor Perpendicular now used as a Vestry, the west door being turned into a window, in the spandrils are the arms of Bishop Fordham. A chevron between three crosses fleury and three ducal crowns for the See of Ely. Bishop Fordham died 1425, which gives us an

approximate date for the Perpendicular portions of the church. There is a staircase turret with door opening on the outside.

Notes.

In 1876 the Church was restored, the south wall removed and an aisle added. In 1874 there was an old South Door with good mouldings, this was demolished, also the windows and a low side opening. The new aisle is Perpendicular of good design and detail. During the restorations a few Norman remains were discovered giving evidence of an older Church, these consist of one small window, gargoyle heads and fragments of string courses, these with pieces of glazed tiles are built up in the wall of the westernmost bay of the new Aisle. A. W. Bloomfield was the architect under whom the works were carried out in 1878.

Grantchester Church from the South East

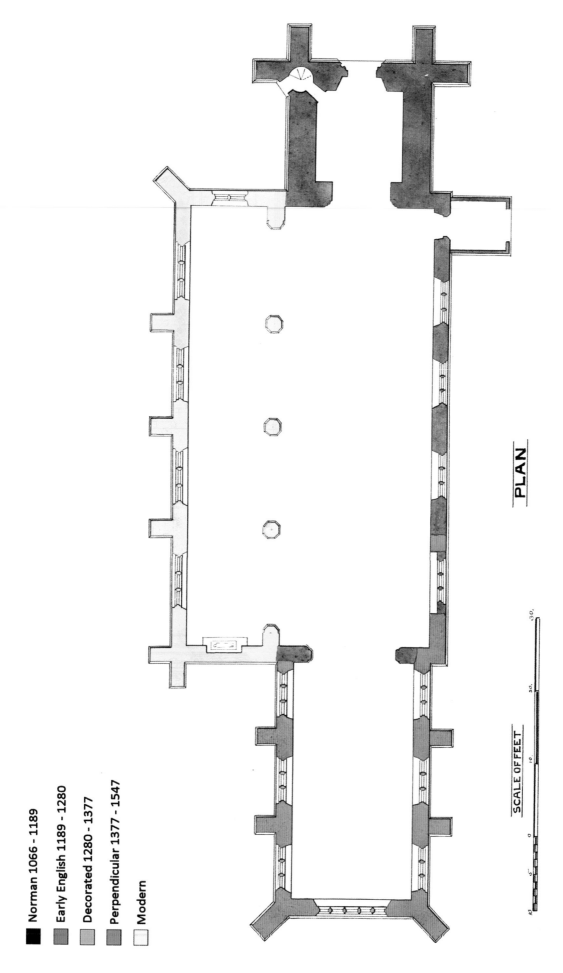

PLAN

Norman 1066 - 1189

Early English 1189 - 1280

Decorated 1280 - 1377

Perpendicular 1377 - 1547

Modern

SCALE OF FEET

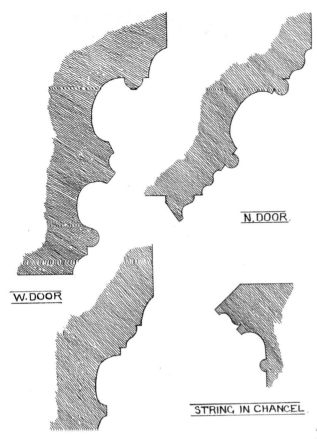

N.DOOR.

W.DOOR

STRING. IN CHANCEL.

The interior is well preserved. Between the Chancel windows are cusped arcades with ogee shaped arches and finished with finials. There are also similar Nitches on each side of the East Window. In the north wall is a recess formed with an ogee arch. On the south is a Piscina, ogee headed and triple cusped. The Sedilia is formed by the window sill which is lowered to within eighteen inches of the floor. The choir stalls are modern of oak of good plain design. The Chancel Arch has a double chamfer finishing on octagonal caps. The ceiling is boarded in panels. In the Nitches on each side of the East Window are boards on which the Ten Commandments are painted.

The Nave roof was renewed in 1876, it was formerly flat, now a hammer beam springing from moulded stone corbels. The doorway leading on to the former Rood Loft remains and there is a square opening like a low side window below it in the north wall. The easternmost window stands in a recess with an arch above of earlier character than the Nave windows. This may denote the presence of a former transept or what is more probable it may simply have been a recess for an altar.

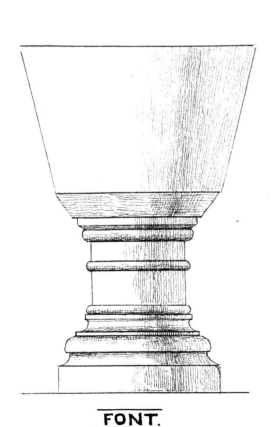

FONT.

PISCINA IN CHANCEL.

EAST END.

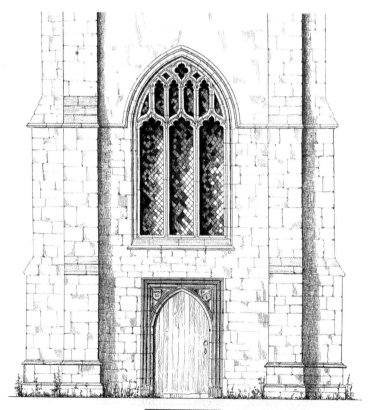

W. FRONT.

There is a fair Pulpit of Jacobean work, well moulded, and in the centre of the panel, a coat surmounted by a foliated helmet, two chevrons and a canton.

The new Aisle is of Perpendicular character with four windows to the south and one to the west. The arcade has octagonal piers with well moulded caps and plain double chamfered arches with labels. The Font is massive, circular, without ornament, the base mouldings of early character. There are a few fragments of old stained glass in the traceries of the easternmost windows on the north and south sides of the Chancel, also in the westernmost window on the north, also in the three western windows of the Nave, these are fragmentary patterns only but of rich colour. Blomefield (Col. Cant.) in 1750 mentions a coat in one of the windows, gules, a bend azure, false blazonry probably incorrect. The new windows of the Aisle are filled with modern stained glass of very good design and colouring. The subjects are as follow beginning from the east, all are of three lights.

1. Elijah, Isaiah, Jeremiah and beneath:

> To the glory
> Thomas Howard died 1843 aged 62
>
> of God and in
> Ellen Howard died 1871 aged 65
>
> loving memory of
> William Page Howard died 1862 aged 19

2. St. Peter, St. Andrew, St. Paul and beneath:

> In memory of Edw Lilley died 1847
> aged 75 William died 1871 aged 35 Caroline
>
> aged 71 & of Sarah his wife died 1854 aged 61
> died 1851 aged 47 & Sarah died 1861 aged 61
>
> & also of their children Mary Ann died 1827
> who lie buried in a vault near this window

3. St. Stephen, St. James, St. Alban and beneath:

> To the glory
> Mary Fawkes died 1854 aged 84
>
> of God and in
> Charles Fawkes died 1832 aged 27
>
> loving memory of
> Jane Fawkes died 1863 aged 58

4. Venerable Bede, Wyckliffe, Tyndale, no inscription.

The West Window is of two lights and has for subject Christ blessing little children.

Inscriptions.

The monumental remains are few and being mostly modern of little interest.

In the Chancel are four black marble slabs in front of the Altar with inscriptions as follow beginning from the north.

1.
> Here lieth the Body
> of
> *FRANCIS WILLIAM EDWARDS*
> one of the Scholars of
> Trinity College
> Cambridge
> Eldeſt Son of JOHN EDWARDS
> of Blackheath Kent
> who died 22ᵈ of July 1805
> in the 21ſt Year of his Age.

2. With coat. A fess charged with three billets between two chevronels.

Crest. A demi lion rampant issuing from a mural crown chequy with collar charged with three billets.

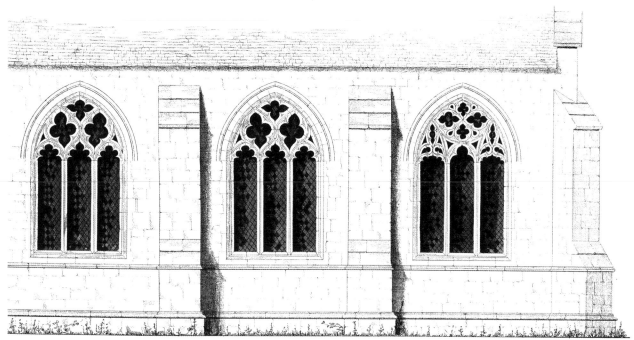

S. SIDE OF CHANCEL

ALTAR TOMB S. AISLE.

Here lieth
The Body of Mrs ANNE ROBSON
Second Daughter of Mr JAMES ROBSON
Formerly Alderman & MAYOR of CAMBRIDGE
who dyed July 15th 1731
Aged 62 Years.

(Left £50 to Grantchester schools)

3. With coat as above (Robson).

Here Lies ye Body of
Mrs MARY ROBSON
Daughter of Mr JAMES ROBSON
(Late ALDERMAN of Cambridg^e)
Who lived, and died,
like a good Chriſtian
on the 23^d day of Decem^r
1721
Aged 53 Years.

There is a fourth slab to Ekins but covered by the Reading Desk, the inscription taken by Cole as follows with coat. A bend of six lozenges inter two cross crosslets fitchy. Crest. A lion's paw holding a cross crosslet fitchy.

Here lyeth
The Body of IOHN EKINS
Master of Arts and
Senior Fellow of Trinity
College in Cambridge
who dyed Dec. 19
Anno Dom: 1706.
Ætat Suæ 71.

There are in the Chancel beside these, three stones with matrices of brasses.
At the east end of the new Aisle is a good altar tomb but it formerly stood under an arch in the south wall of the Nave but was removed at the restoration. The slab has matrices of brasses, arms, figures &c but no inscription remains. It is mentioned by Blomefield in connection with the coat above noted which may be the coat of the person here buried. The front is panelled with quatrefoils and it is finished above with a four centred well moulded arch beneath a square label. On the south wall of the aisle is a marble tablet finished with pediment, it bears the following inscription.

Near this place lyeth ye Body
of GEO: SHEPPARD, M.A. one
of ye Foundation Fellows of
CLARE HALL in Cambridge; &
5th Son to M^r EDW^d: SHEPPARD,
of Doncaſter in ye County of
York, ALDERMAN: who dyed
ye 5th of Octo:^br 1690, Aged 32
years.

At the west end of the same wall is a brass with this inscription.

+ In loving memory of
the Revd Robert Nimmo
M.A. R.N. Trin. Coll. Camb.
born 14 January 1840 Chaplain
of H.M.S. Atalanta, believed
to have been lost in that ship
on her homeward voyage from
Bermuda in February 1880.

In · the · uttermost · parts · of
the · sea · even · there · also
shall · Thy · hand · lead · me.
Psalm · cxxxix · viii · ix

On the floor of the South Aisle are two stone slabs with these inscriptions.

1. DOROTHY SPILSBURY
DIED JAN. 31ST 1837
AGED 82 YEARS.

MARY ANNE ELIZABETH
WIFE OF
JOHN LETCH MARTIN
OF CROFT LODGE
IN THIS PARISH.
SHE DEPARTED THIS LIFE
JULY 18, 1842,
AGED 59 YEARS.

2. REBECCA,
THE WIFE OF
JAMES BRADE ESQ :
OF QUEENS COLLEGE CAMBRIDGE
OBIIT DEC. 11, A.D. 1831
ÆTAT 22

ALSO
MARY FRANCES,
DAUGHTER OF
WILLIAM BRADE ESQ
OF LIVERPOOL, MERCHANT
WHO DIED AT QUEENS COLLEGE LODGE
ON THE 9TH APRIL 1834
AGED 8 YEARS.

On a marble tablet on the north wall of the Nave is the following surmounted by this coat on a lozenge. A fess between three unicorns heads couped (Spilsbury).

SACRED TO THE MEMORY OF
DOROTHY SPILSBURY,
DAUGHTER OF LUCAS SPILSBURY ESQUIRE
OF COUGHTON IN THE COUNTY OF WARWICK,
WHO DIED JANRY 31ST 1837 AGED 82 YEARS,
AT CROFT LODGE IN THIS PARISH
AND IS BURIED IN THIS CHURCH.
ALSO OF
ELIZABETH HOLLINGWORTH
SISTER TO THE ABOVE DOROTHY SPILSBURY
WHO DIED JANRY 23RD 1820, AGED 71 YEARS,
AND IS BURIED IN THE CHANCEL
OF ST. BOTOLPH WITHOUT ALDGATE LONDON.

Blefsed are the dead which die in the Lord.
REVALATION XIV.13.

There are several tablets fixed to the outside walls on the south side of the church. On the east end of the Aisle is:

SACRED TO THE MEMORY OF
THOMAS NICKISSON
SCHOLAR OF CORPUS CHRISTI COLLEGE
CAMBRIDGE. HE DIED MAY 4 1851, AGED 21
ERECTED BY MEMBERS OF HIS COLLEGE.

On one of the buttresses on the south side of the Chancel is a tablet with a Latin inscription to Farrington ob. 1837.

On the south wall of the Chancel this.

IN AN ADJOINING TOMB
BELONGING TO THE **MATTHEWS** FAMILY
ARE INTERRED THE REMAINS
OF SARAH, RELICT OF
MR JOHN BRAYSHER
OF CAMBRIDGE
WHO DIED ON THE 27TH JULY 1833
AGED 75 YEARS.

On the east wall of the Chancel are tablets. One with a Latin inscription to Basil Anthony Beck ob. 1820. One to Mandell ob. 1822 and Widnall 1865.

In the Tower are three bells with inscriptions as follow.
1. God save the church 1610.
2. John Darbie made me 1677.
3. no inscription.

Additional notes from the Cole M.S.S. Vol. IV. folio 130.

Under the north wall lies a new freestone with this inscription.

Here lieth the Body of
HENRY HEADLY
Gent:
who died Decbr ỹe 2d 1741
Aged 68 Years.

Also a stone with "John Headley 1740"

Against the south wall between the second and third window is a very neat mural monument of carved and gilt stone but much shattered and the left pillar quite gone and broken, the cherubims also at the top defaced with a hatchet, I suppose in the year 1743 (sic. 1643?) though Dowsing has omitted this Church in his journal. Under the middlemost top pyramid are blazoned these arms. Quarterly 1 and 4. Sable three lions heads erased argent. 2 & 3. Sable a chevron or inter 3 lions heads erased argent. On the first or dexter pyramid is fixed a shield with these arms. viz. Per pale 1st quarterly sable and argent in the first quarter a lion rampant for Byng impaling 2 coats. 1st sable 3 lions heads erased argent. 2nd Sable a chevron or inter 3 lions heads erased argent. On the second pyramid is a shield with these arms. Sable three lions heads erased argent. This monument fills up the Nitch in the wall. Under the cherubims is this wrote.

Usquequo Domine usquequo. Rev. 6.50.
Etiam venio cito amen, etiam veni Domine Jesu.

Under this in a table of black marble is the following inscription in gold letters hardly legible.

KATHERINA BYNG, RELICTA ET ANIMO ET PIETATE PRECELLEN TISSIMI VIRI THOMÆ BYNG, JURIS RETRIUSQUE DOCTORIS EMINENTISSIMI, ET IN CELEBERRIMA ACADEMIA CANTABRIGIEN :
(line illegible   )
IBIDEM CUSTODIS VIGILANTISSIMI ALMEO, CVRIÆ CANTAUR
RIENSIS DE ARCUBUS LONDINI DECANI LONGE DIGNISSIMI,
CUI FILIOS DECEM ET DUAS PERPERIT FILIAS, PLACIDE HIC IN DO
MINO REQUIESCIT, SECUNDEM EIUS ADUENTUM QUEM AS
SIDUIS PRECIBUS, ET VOTIS SEMPER ARDENTISSIMIS EXPETEBAT
AD SUI RESUSCITATIONEM IN DIES, VEL IN HORAS POTIUS
SINGULAS FIDEI CHRISTIANÆ ET BONÆ SPEI PLENA AVIDISSME EXPECTANS.
ADHUC ENIM MODIEUM ALIQUANTULUM ET QUI VENTURUS EST VENIET ET NON TARDABIT HEB. 10. 37.
QUONIAM IPSE DOMINUM EUM HORTÆTIONEM CLAMORE ET VOCE ARCHANGELI AC DEI TUBA DESCENDET A CŒLO ET QUI MORTUI ERUNT IN CHRISTO RESURGENT PRIMUM. THES. 4. 16.
OBIIT JULY AN. DOM̃ 1627 ÆTATIS VERO SUÆ 74.

Under this on a soft kind of stone was wrote 36 long and short Latin verses which are quite illegible. I took this extract from the Parish Register which begins very soon here 31st of Hen. 8th 1539.

Venerabilis Katherina Byng mater Henrici ad legem servientis sepulta fuit vigesimo primo die Julii 1627.

Dr Byng Dean of Arches was first fellow of St. Peters College, Proctor of the University 1565 and the year after when the Queen was at Oxford he was incorporated Master of Arts at that University. He was Public Orator, Master of Clare Hall and the King's Professor of Law and afterwards official of the arches and Dean of the Peculiars. (Thomas 2nd son of John Byng of Wrotham Kent seated at Grantchester, temp Eliz. Collin 6.364).

In the middle south window at top in a large shield are the arms of Vere Earl of Oxford. viz. quarterly Gules and or, a mullet in the first quarter (guard Ar'.) In the opposite window are two coats. First Vert a fess Dancetti Ermine (Somers) impaling gules a chevron inter 3 owls argent. In the same window Somers impales gules, on a bar sable a mullet inter 2 annulets argent. These two impaled coats are both false heraldry as well as another which is in the Nave but I take them as I find them. There is no mistake by any alteration for it is the old original glass remaining in them flowered, beside one in the Manor House is blazoned in the same colours.

About a foot from Mr Shepherd's gravestone lies another freestone with two swords in saltire in an oval at top, under them is this inscription.

Here lyeth the body of John
Athan Rowledge the son of
Jonathan Rowledge who de
parted this life Aug. 10th 1740
aged 48 years.

At the head of this are the shapes of two coffins in the bricks, on the breast of that to the south on a square brick is

M. B. 1733

for one Mary Bell. On that close to it on the north.

M. M. 1734

for Mary Morris her daughter.

The Nave and Chancel are separated from one another by a screen over which are the King's Arms and the Ten Commandments.

All the windows of this Church at top are full of very curious and neat figures of Saints; among the rest of St. Anthony, St. Lawrence, St. Thomas of Canterbury &c. In the lowest south window are these arms. Gules a bend B. Over the arch of the Belfry is painted Death and Time in the shape of a saltire. The arms with bend B is false heraldry. I have seen an old seal in Kings College pendant from a deed with only a bend on it in this manner, which belonged and was executed by John, the son of Sir Walter de Huntingfield of Grantchester 15th Edward III.

BYNG MONUMENT. 1627.

EKINS 1706.

ROBSON 1731.

HARDWICK

May 22 1883.

The Church.

The Church is dedicated to St. Mary the Virgin and consists of Chancel, Nave, South Porch, West Tower and Spire.

The Chancel appears to be of Perpendicular date. There are two windows on the north and two on the south, the westernmost of which seems to be of slightly earlier character. The East Window is of three lights, the cusping destroyed. The floor is tiled with red and black tiles, the Altar Rails are of wrought iron, the choir seats of deal. On the south side is a Piscina with a four centred chamfered arch. The roof is good with moulded tie beams, embattled wall plates, octagonal queen posts with caps and bases, these are connected again by lateral braces curved. The East Window is filled with stained glass in three subjects, The Nativity, the Crucifixion and the Resurrection, the work is below criticism.

The windows in the Sanctuary are filled with pattern glass. The Chancel Arch is Perpendicular, there is one step here and another to the Altar, none of the windows have labels.

The Nave is of the same period as the Chancel with three windows and a door on each side. The windows on the south have traceried heads, those on the north merely cusped arches, all without labels. The roof is similar to that in the Chancel, the tie beams supported by curved braces that spring from moulded stone corbels. The Font is octagonal with a plain bowl, the shaft is ornamented with cusped panels. The doorways to the Rood Loft, although blocked, are plainly discernable on the north side of the Chancel Arch, one exactly above the other. The seating and Pulpit are of poor character worked in deal. The Porch is Perpendicular and has the original oak open roof. The proportions of the Tower and Spire are good but the detail meagre. The former is unbuttressed with an embattled parapet from which rises an octagonal spire, the Belfry windows are single lights.

S.E. VIEW

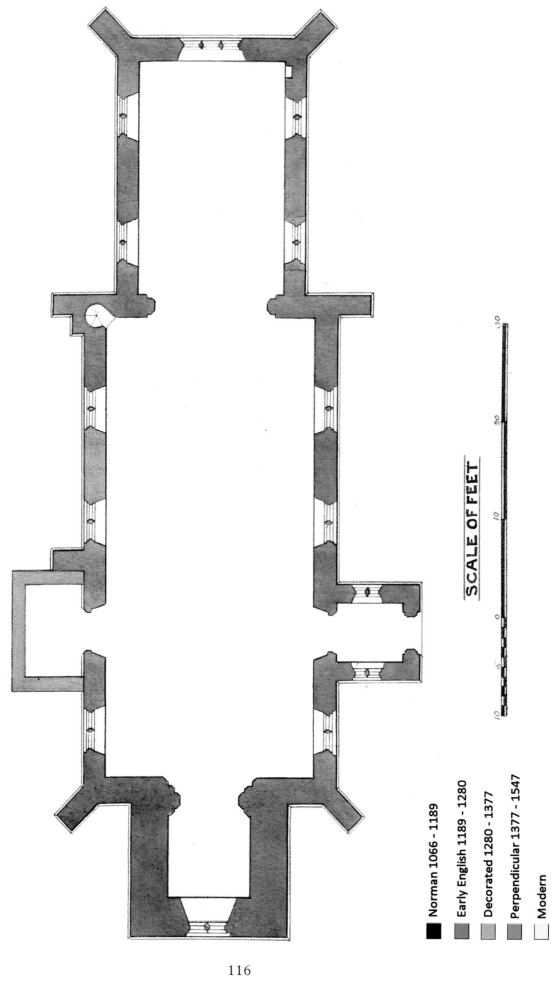

SCALE OF FEET

Norman 1066 - 1189

Early English 1189 - 1280

Decorated 1280 - 1377

Perpendicular 1377 - 1547

Modern

INTERIOR LOOKING EAST

The Tower Arch is lofty finished with double chamfers. The West Window is of two lights with stained glass in the tracery. Within the Tower are two old chests, in one of which are fragments of armour.

<u>Bells.</u> There are three bells with these inscriptions.
1. Peter Whittel Churchwarden.
   Robert Taylor founder 1797.

2 and 3. Peter Whittel Churchwarden.
   Robt. Taylor St. Neots founder 1797.

Notes.
Whatever features of interest this Church possessed were destroyed at its restoration. In "Parkers Architectural Topography" 1842, the following items were noted. "There are a few old open seats and a heavy Jacobean Rood Screen across the Chancel

Arch, also some quarries and fragments of good painted glass." There were also painted on the south wall of the Nave, the legend of St. Cyriac, the six acts of mercy and over the North Door, St. Christopher.

Inscriptions.

The Church possesses only two monumental inscriptions and an obliterated slab.

A tablet on the north wall of the Chancel.

SACRED TO THE MEMORY OF
MARY, WIFE OF THE REV^D WILLIAM BIRCH,
RECTOR OF THIS PARISH,
WHO DIED NOVEMBER 4TH 1858, IN HER 58TH
YEAR.
HER REMAINS ARE LAID IN A VAULT
AT THE SOUTH EAST CORNER OF THE
CHURCHYARD.

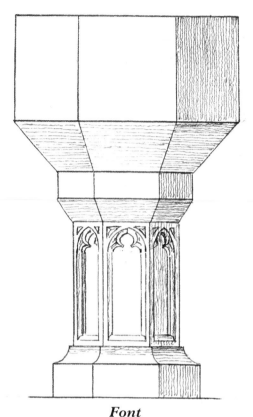

Font

On a slab removed to the Tower.

In memory of
Thomas Barron
who died Feb^{ry} 1st 1762
aged 46
and of Sarah his Wife
who died Nov. 18th 1784
Aged 67.

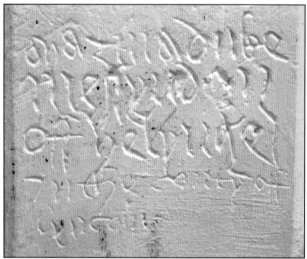

Early Graffiti on an interior wall

16th Century Oak Chest in the Chancel

118

HARLTON

The Church, c.1370, is dedicated to St. Mary and has Chancel, Nave, North and South Porches and a low Embattled tower with three bells.

Font.

Church Interior.

Harlton Church as it is today.

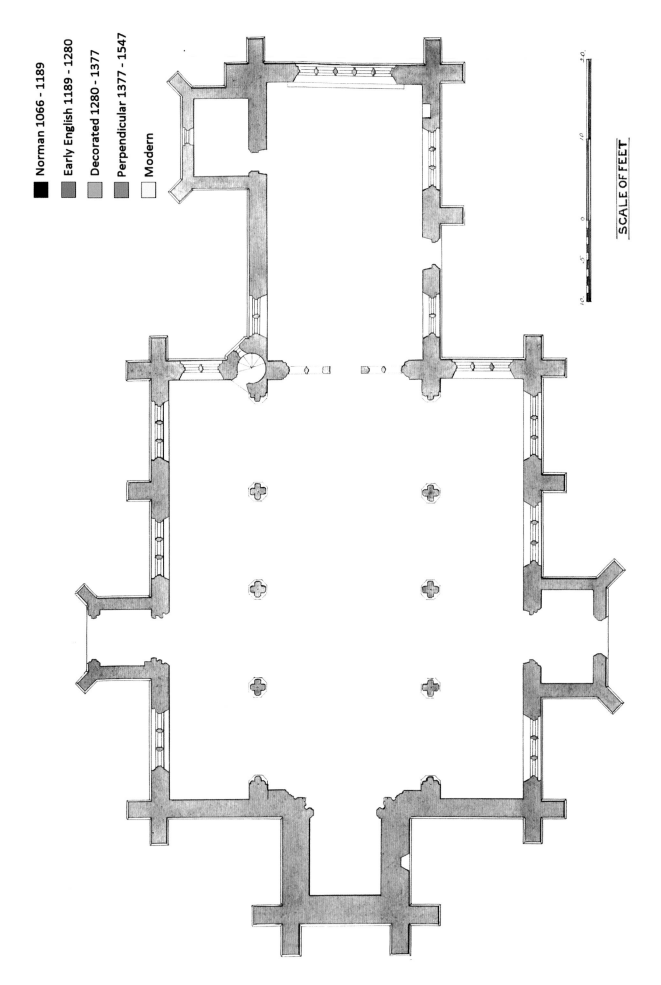

SCALE OF FEET

The Fryer Monument, 1631.

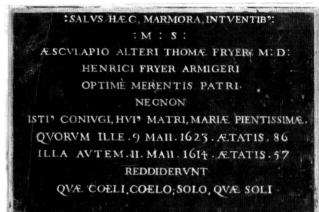

:SALVS HÆC, MARMORA, INTVENTIB":
:M : S :
ÆSCVLAPIO ALTERI THOMÆ FRYER, M: D:
HENRICI FRYER ARMIGERI
OPTIMÈ MERENTIS PATRI.
NECNON
ISTI' CONIVGI, HVI' MATRI, MARIÆ PIENTISSIMÆ.
QVORVM ILLE .9 MAII. 1623. ÆTATIS. 86
ILLA AVTEM.II. MAII. 1614. ÆTATIS. 57
REDDIDERVNT
QVÆ COELI, COELO; SOLO, QVÆ SOLI

THIS MONVMENT OF MEMORY IS RAYSED BY Ẏ EXECVTORS
OF HENRY FRYER ESQ. SECOND SONNE OF THE
SAYD THOMAS FRYER DOCTOR IN PHYSIQVE.
WHO DYED Ẏ 5 OF IVNE 1631 &
IS HERE INTERRED LEAVING
HIS DEARE WIFE BRIDGET TO LAMENT HIS LOSSE.&
HIS LARGE ALMES TO Ẏ POORE TO COMMEND HIS FAITH.

INCLOISTER'D IN THESE PILES OF STONE
THE RELIQVES OF THIS FRYER REST,
WHOSE BETTER PART TO HEAVEN'S GONE:
THE POORE MANS BOWELS WERE HIS CHEST:
AND MONGST THESE THREE, GRAVE, HEAVEN, POORE,.
HE SHAR'D HIS CORPS, HIS SOVL, HIS STORE.

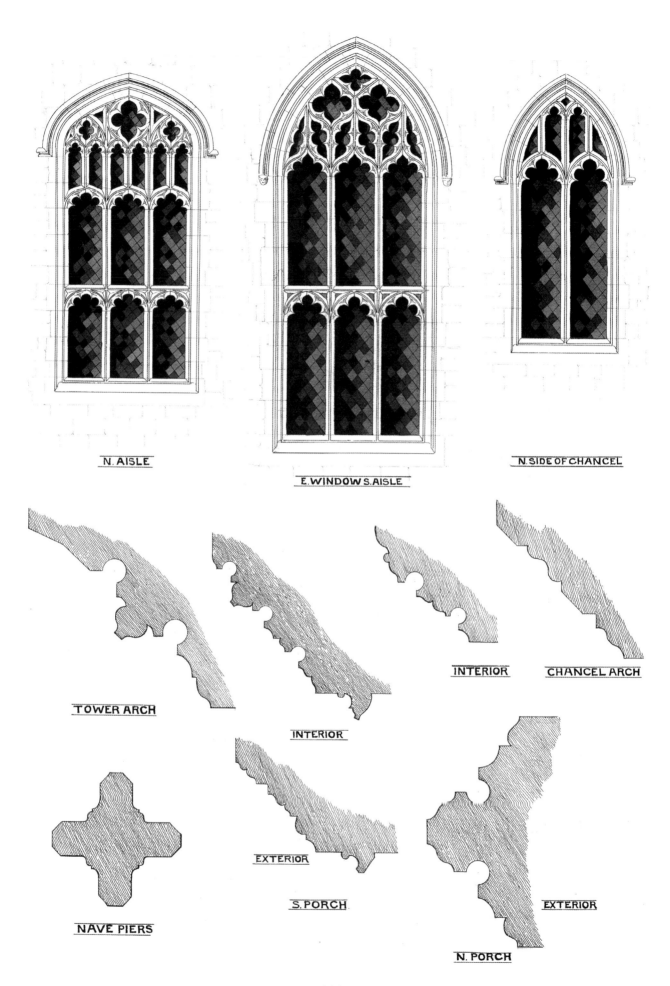

N. AISLE

E. WINDOW S. AISLE

N. SIDE OF CHANCEL

TOWER ARCH

INTERIOR

INTERIOR

CHANCEL ARCH

NAVE PIERS

EXTERIOR

S. PORCH

EXTERIOR

N. PORCH

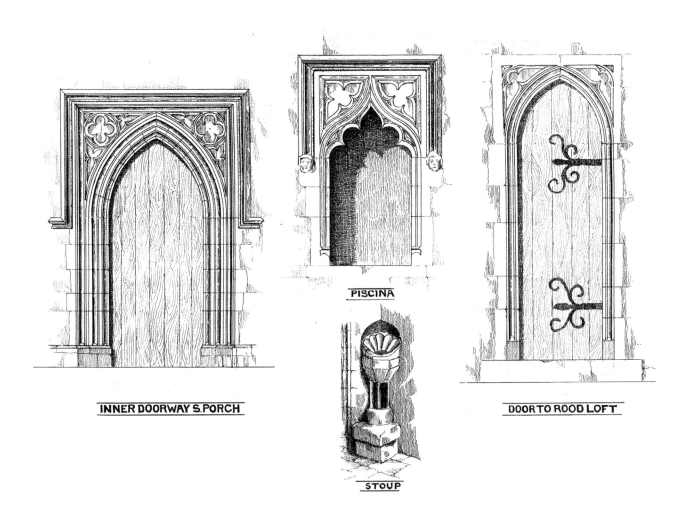

INNER DOORWAY S. PORCH

PISCINA

STOUP

DOOR TO ROOD LOFT

SKETCH ELEVATION OF REREDOS

FRYER

FRYER

FRYER

ON THE FRYER MONUMENT

ARMS NOTED BY COLE

HINXTON

The Church is dedicated to St. Mary & St. John. It consists of Chancel, Nave, South Aisle, South Chapel, South Porch and Embattled Tower with Spire, a Clock and two bells, plus a Priest's Bell on the Spire.

Hinxton Church Interior. The present building dates from about 1150.

Hinxton Church as it is today from the South.

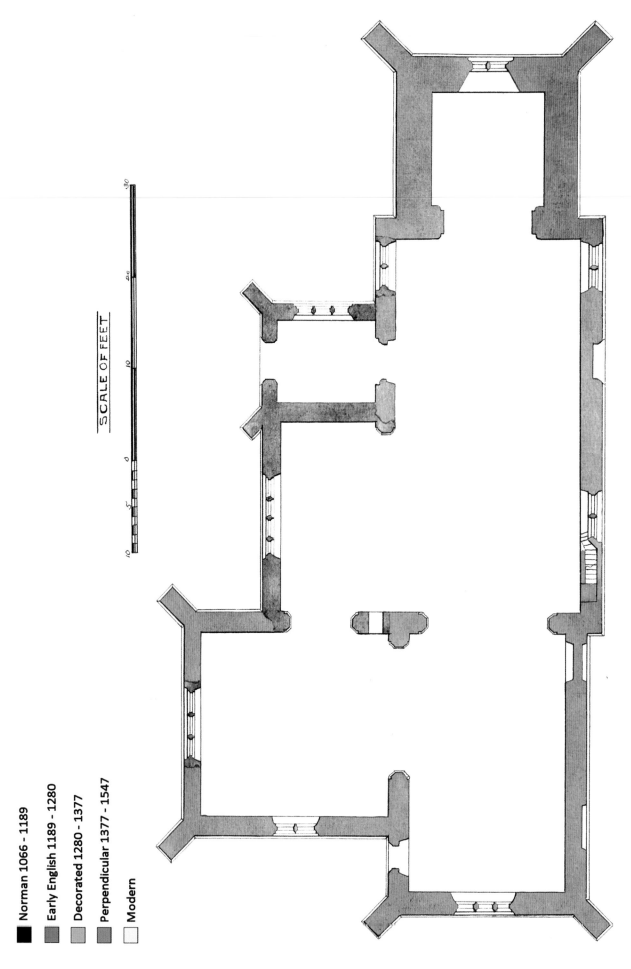

SCALE OF FEET

Norman 1066 - 1189
Early English 1189 - 1280
Decorated 1280 - 1377
Perpendicular 1377 - 1547
Modern

Inside the South Porch

17th Century Jacobean Pulpit with some 20th Century restoration

Font believed to be Norman but with later base

One of the delicately carved panels on the Pulpit

Hatchments hanging on the wall above the font. The Church has five more requiring some restoration. These are currently in storage.

Edward Green
1770 - 1804

Charles Raikes
1828

HISTON

April 1883.

The Church.

The Church is dedicated to St. Andrew and consists of Chancel, Nave, North and South Transepts, North and South Aisles, North Porch and Central Tower.

The Chancel is Early English, much restored, the easternmost portion being rebuilt from the designs of Sir G. G. Scott. The East Window has five lancets with clustered shafts and mouldings enriched with the tooth ornament. On the south side are two windows of coupled lancets and one single one. On the north side is the same arrangement, with the addition of a door. On the south side is a good Sedilia with shafts and cusped arches terminated by gablets above, all modern. There are four steps to the Altar and one at the Chancel Arch. The roof is of oak divided into panels by moulded ribs. The choir stalls are the old ones very much restored of good Perpendicular design. The floor is paved with Mintons tiles. The Communion Table is of Jacobean date. The side

windows as well as the east have shafts in the jambs and the labels are finished with knots of very good design. The Chancel Arch is plain with a double chamfer.

The Transepts are Early English with Perpendicular insertions. That to the south forms the Manor Chapel and is divided from the Nave by an oak screen of Early English design, the work of Sir G. G. Scott, by whom the transepts were restored in 1872. On the top of the screen are carved these arms. Vert, a fess wavy between three trotting nags bridled and saddled or. Crest. A Wyvern for Sumpter.★ On the east side are two triplets of Early

★ This screen has been demolished but the arms illustrated are preserved inside the church.

S.E. VIEW.

129

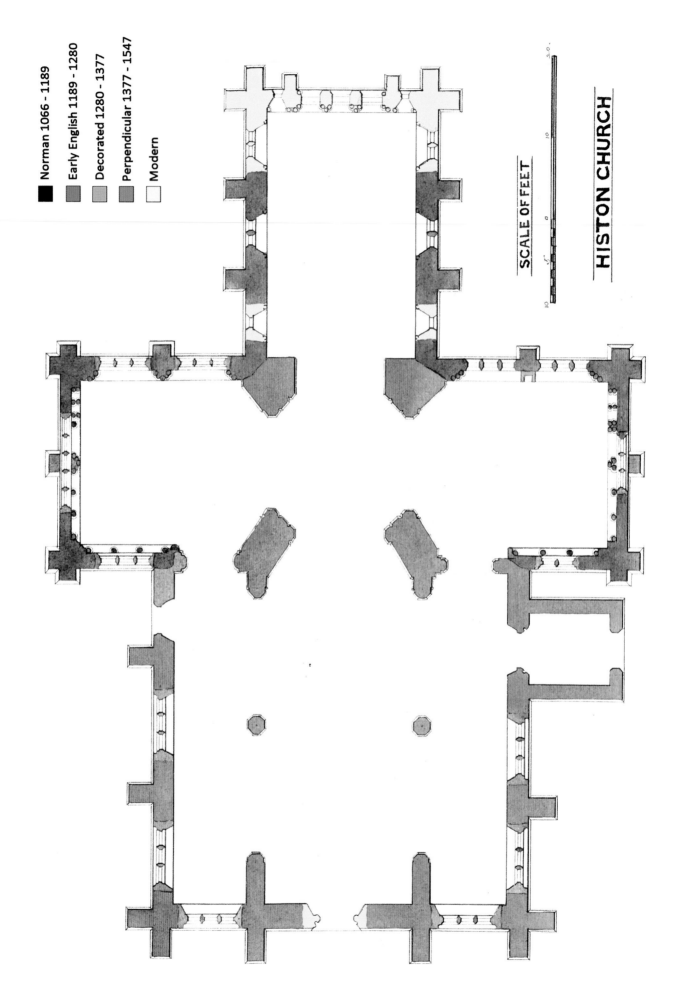

Norman 1066 - 1189
Early English 1189 - 1280
Decorated 1280 - 1377
Perpendicular 1377 - 1547
Modern

SCALE OF FEET

HISTON CHURCH

ARCADE S. TRANSEPT.

Hujus transepti partem
meridionalem mortuarium Familiæ
sacellum Catherina, Gulielmi
Ricardi Sumpter vidua pretioso et
pulcherrimo opere reficiendam penitus
et ornandam curavit; in honorem
Dei et in piam memoriam conjugis
desideratissimi ultimi stirpis antiquæ
viri fidei et honorum operum pleni
A.D. MDCCCLXXIII.

The South Window is Perpendicular of three lights.
On each side are bases of Early English shafts in the
wall shewing that there formerly existed an Early
English triplet. Below this is a good Early English
arcade with double Piscina beneath interlacing
arches on Purbeck shafts. This arcade continues
along the west wall. The seats are modern oak, the
two nearest the Nave being panelled with rich tracery
carved and finished with good poppy heads. The
roof is flat of oak, plain but good. The caps of
archway leading to South Aisle are roughly carved.
The original Cross displaying the Crucifixion now
much weather worn remains on the gable.

English work enclosed by richly
moulded arches and clustered
shafts, the central cluster is
broken and a Decorated Nitch
inserted supported by a modern
sculptured corbel representing
the burial of St. Catherine.
Below is a brass plate surrounded
by the arms of Sumpter as
above with this inscription.

131

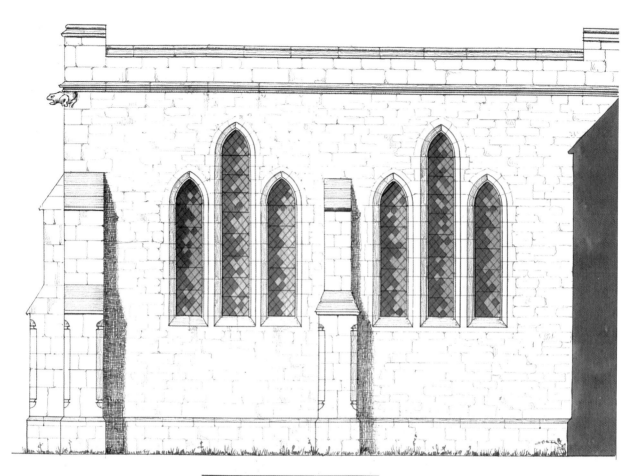

E.SIDE S. TRANSEPT

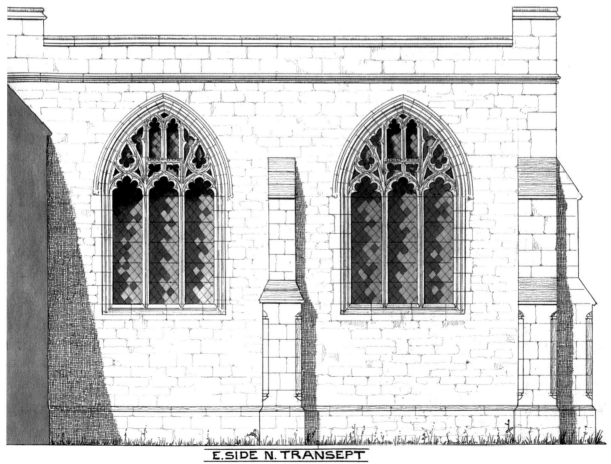

E.SIDE N. TRANSEPT

The North Transept is in design similar to the south but all the windows are later Perpendicular insertions. On the east are two three-light Perpendicular windows in place of the triplets originally there but the richly moulded Early English enclosing arches with shafts still remain on the inside. The North Window is a three light Perpendicular. There is an arcade round the walls of this Transept similar to that on the south and with a Piscina of similar design. The seats of pitch pine, the roof of oak. This Transept was restored in 1874.

The Nave was restored some time back by Bodley, externally the old work being completely destroyed. It is Decorated and consists of two bays with octagonal piers and double chamfered arches. The Clerestory windows are modern, circular, with cusped cinquefoils and quatrefoils. These take the place of two-light Perpendicular windows which were here in 1845. (vide Churches of Cambs). The old work in the West Front was also demolished at the restoration previous to which the West Window was Perpendicular and beneath it was a four centred west doorway. There are now two modern Decorated windows above and a corresponding doorway below. The roof is pitch pine with arched principals. The Royal Arms are above the arch leading to South Transept. The seating is modern of pitch pine. The Pulpit stands on oak columns and is surrounded by a brass railing, in front is a life size figure of St. John with an eagle crouching on his shoulders which forms the desk, this is carved in oak. The Lectern is of oak, poor and small. The floor is tiled.

The Aisles are Perpendicular or rather Decorated with Perpendicular insertions. Each has two Perpendicular windows of three lights to the north and south and a similar one at the west end. The roofs are of poor character. In the South Aisle is one old bench remaining with good poppy heads and animals carved on the elbows. Above the South Door is a board commemorating some benefactions &c. dated 1729 but too high to read. Against the central pier of the Nave stands the Font with octagonal basin and stem, in the panels of the former are sunk quatrefoils of two designs, very much chipped.

Glass. There are no old remains of stained glass. All the windows of the Chancel are filled with modern glass by Mayer of Munich. Beginning at the east end. The small lancet to the north, is filled with patterns and medallions and has inscription.

·DONO·S·PEED·

The central triplet has the following subjects. The lancet to the north, The Descent from the Cross. The central lancet, The Resurrection and the Marys at the Sepulchre. The South lancet, The Advent of our Lord. These have inscriptions.

·IN·MEM:GULIELM·TAYLOR·

The lancet to south is similar to that on the north, with inscription.

DONO·J·WENTWORTH

On the south side above the Piscina is a two-light subject, The Descent of the Holy Ghost on the assembled Apostles and Christ Teaching, with this inscription.

DONO·CAR·ET   MARG·ANGIER

A two-light window of six subjects with inscription.

IN·MEM·S·N·UNDERWOOD

Lancet window with symbolical design and inscription.

IN·MEM·CATH·BAUMGARTNER

On the north side a two light window, The Betrayal, Christ leaving the Prætorium with inscription.

DONO·CLERIC·ARCHDIAC

(This is over the door.)

A two-light window with subjects, The Annunciation and the Nativity.

DONO·L·A·UNDERWOOD·

A lancet, Adam in Eden.

❋❀DONO·I·ELLIOT❀❋

South Aisle. The westernmost window has three subjects,
1. The Angel appearing to Joseph.
2. The Nativity.
3. Herod and the Wise Men.
The West Window, The Purification, The Flight into Egypt and Christ in the Temple. Inscription.

TO·THE GLORY OF·GOD·AND·IN MEMORY ·OF· HENRY ·ANGIER AND ·OF· MARY HIS WIFE

South Transept. The east lancets are filled with figures of the Evangelists. The South Window has three subjects.
1. Raising of Lazarus.
2. Giving sight to the Blind.
3. Healing the Leper.

NAVE ARCADE

CAP

BASE

NAVE ARCH

The North Transept. The North Window has numerous subjects and this inscription.

IN·MEMORY·OF·WILLIAM RICHARD·SUMPTER·AND CATHERINE·HIS·WIFE.

Monumental Inscriptions

These are remarkably few and uninteresting. On a tablet on the north side of the Chancel Arch is this.

SACRED
TO THE MEMORY OF
THE REV^D ROBERT BROUGH M.A.
OF
CORPUS CHRISTI COLLEGE CAMBRIDGE,
SOME YEARS CURATE OF THIS & THE
ADJOINING PARISH OF
IMPIMGTON.
HE DIED THE IXTH DAY OF APRIL
A. D. MDCCCXXIII,
AGED XXXII YEARS.

THIS TABLET WAS ERECTED BY HIS FRIENDS
& PARISHIONERS,
AS A TOKEN OF REGARD FOR HIS MEMORY, &
A SMALL BUT SINCERE
ACKNOWLEDGEMENT OF THE DILIGENCE
WITH WHICH HE DISCHARGED
THE DUTIES OF HIS SACRED OFFICE.

In the South Transept on the south-west pier of the Tower on a marble tablet.

To the Memory of
THOMAS SUMPTER ESQ^R
of this parifh
who died 18th April 1806
in the 71st Year of his Age.

Alfo of ELIZABETH his Wife
who died 10th Octr. 1806. Aged 67.

And also of the Revd JAMES FRENCH SUMPTER,
Son of WILLIAM & SOPHIA SUMPTER,
& Grandson of the above,
who died 27th Octr. 1836,
Aged 29 Years.

Above this on the same pier is another tablet filled with close writing too high to decipher.

Bells. The bells have been recast. There are six and a clock bell. They have the following inscriptions.
1. John Warner & Sons London 1873 (patent) (Royal Arms).
2. 3. 4. 5. 6. John Warner and Sons London 1866 (patent) (Royal Arms).

Clock bell. J. Osborn Downham. Fecit 1781.
The old peal were as follows.
1. Tho. Newman made me 1723.
2. Cantabo laudes tuas Domine per atria.
3. 4. X Ricardus Bowler me fecit 1604.
5. William Peck and Robert Read Churchwardens 1683. W. B.

The following notes from Cole.

"14 July 1745. This Church is a very regular building in ye shape of a cross with a square Tower in ye middle between ye Nave and Chancel, in it hang 5 good bells and a small bell in ye small Spire without serves for a clock. The Nave 2 side Isles 2 cross Isles and a South Porch are all leaded but the Chancel is tiled. The Parish is now repairing ye outside of ye Church it being but in ordinary condition; besides they have 10 or 12 pounds a year as the clerk told me to keep ye church in repair. The Chancel has been longer in ye east end of it has fallen down for ye present wall is modern of wood and mortar ye whole in nasty order."

Notes.

This Church was one of the most interesting near Cambridge but many of its ancient features have been destroyed through restorations. At the restoration of the Nave and Aisles by F. W. Bodley the old Perpendicular windows of the Clerestory and West Front were destroyed and modern Decorated substituted. In 1872 the South Transept was restored and in 1874 the north under Sir G. G. Scott who practically rebuilt the Chancel at the same time. The walls are partially faced with old stones from St. Etheldredas Church which were discovered at Madingley when the long gallery of the mansion was taken down about 1874. The then vicar carefully collected all that could be used. At the restoration, on removing the plaster from the walls, two Early English lancets were discovered, one in either wall north and south. Half the door leading to Sacristy was discovered in the north-east corner and a shaft supporting a head of the Virgin. From these circumstances the conclusion was arrived at that the Chancel had extended another bay eastward which was confirmed by a Tudor door being found on the south side which seems to have been put there to supply the want of the Priests Door which had been cut off. There was originally a Chancel Screen which was taken away at the restoration.

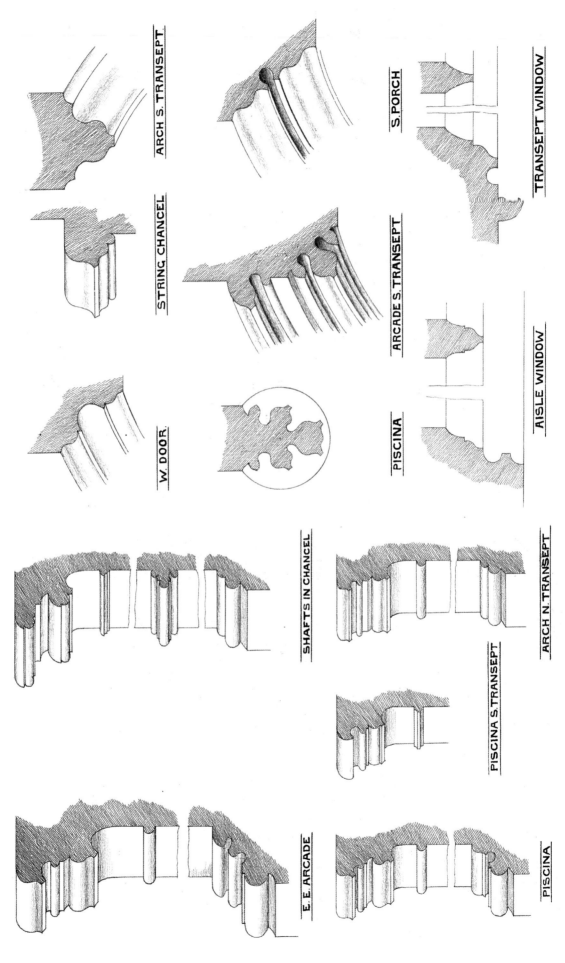

ARCH S. TRANSEPT

S. PORCH

TRANSEPT WINDOW

STRING CHANCEL

ARCADE S. TRANSEPT

AISLE WINDOW

W. DOOR.

PISCINA

SHAFTS IN CHANCEL

ARCH N. TRANSEPT

PISCINA S. TRANSEPT

E. E. ARCADE

PISCINA

FONT

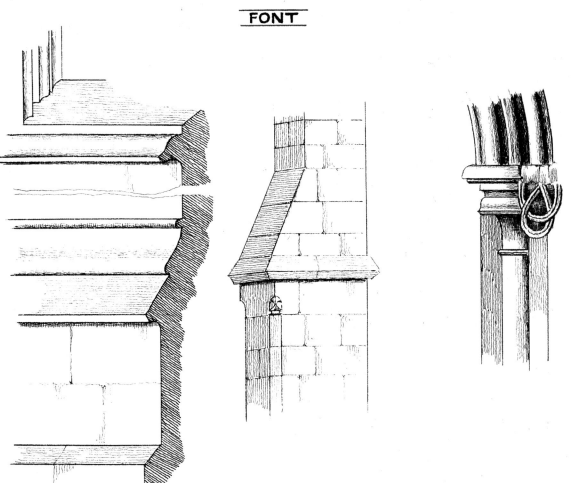

BASEMENT NAVE   **CHANCEL BUTTRESS**   **SHAFT CHANCEL WINDOW**

Pedigree of Gardner

Arms. Gardner quartering Berkeley or Calybut.

Humfrey Gardner of = ... d. of . . . . Helinghed.　Frances Callybutt = William Callybutt of
　Maxfeild in 　　　　　　　　　　　　　　　of Castell Acre. 　　of Cockforth
　Com. Chester. 　　　　　　　　　　　　　　vide Norf. 　　　(Cockthorpe) 4 son.

Margarett d. of Hen. = Hugh Gardiner of March = Margarett d. of Wm. Trussell of
　Barrett. 1. 　　　　in the Isle of Ely. 　　St. Edmunds Bury in Com. Suff. 2 wife.

1 Thomas ob. s.p.　2 Richard ob. s.p.　4 James.　5 Frances.　3 Thomas Gardiner = Anne d. and h.
　　　　　　　　　　　　　　　　　　　　　　　of Cockforth 3. 　　of Wm. Callibutt
　　　　　　　　　　　　　　　　　　　　　　　　　　　　　　　　of Cockforth.

2 Barkley.　1 Humfrey Gardiner of Histon = Elizabeth d. of Rob. Audley　Catherine ux. Thom
　　　　　in Com. Cambridge 1619. 　　of St. Ives in Com. Hunt. 　Cromwell, 2 sonn of
　　　　　　　　　　　　　　　　　　　　　　　　　　　　　　Gregory Lord Cromwell.

1 William Gardiner sonn and heire. = Elizabeth d. of Hen.　　　2. Frances.　3 Thomas.　Elizabeth.
　　　　　　　　　　　　　　　Laurence of St. Ives.

　　　　　　　　Humfrey Gardiner.

HORNINGSEA

The Church.

The Church is dedicated to St. Peter and consists of Chancel, Nave, North and South Aisles, South Porch and West Tower.

The Chancel and Nave are of equal width and of almost equal length, and there being no Chancel Arch the Church appears to be of extraordinary length.

The Chancel is of Early English date. Several of the trefoil headed original lancets remain, there are four on the north side, and one lancet and an Early English Priests Door on the south. On the south are also two windows of Perpendicular date, the East Window is of the same period. In the south wall is a double Early English Piscina but much restored. In the north wall near the centre of the Chancel is a plain Niche, and in the south wall about on a level where the upper Rood Loft door would open is another opening of similar character. The choir stalls are modern, the floor tiled. There are two steps at the entrance to the Chancel and four more to the Altar. In the East Window are remnants of old stained glass.

The Nave has been restored, the roof modern and the floor tiled. The seating for the most part is modern but two or three of the old benches remain. The Font is octagonal standing on five octagonal shafts of 13th century date. The Pulpit is Elizabethan with linen pattern in the panels and canopy above. The Lectern is modern.

The Elizabethan Pulpit

VIEW FROM S.W.

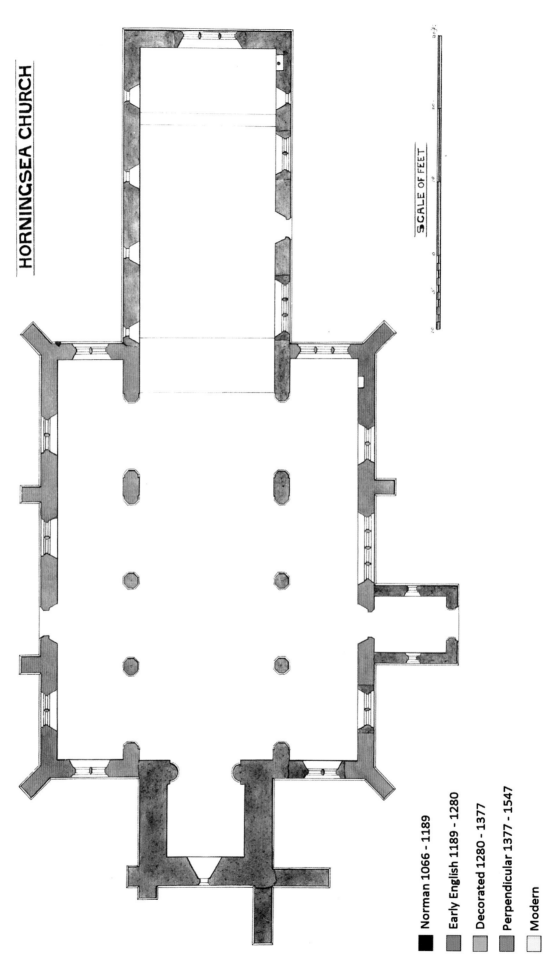

HORNINGSEA CHURCH

SCALE OF FEET

■ Norman 1066 - 1189

■ Early English 1189 - 1280

□ Decorated 1280 - 1377

■ Perpendicular 1377 - 1547

□ Modern

WINDOWS S. AISLE.

Carved Panel from the Elizabethan Pulpit

The North Aisle is of Decorated date with a Decorated arcade, the windows have been renewed, there are three in the north wall and one at the east and west, all modern, also a north door. There are some remnants of coffin slabs in the floor at the east end and also fragments of old stained glass in the East Window.

The South Aisle has an arcade of early 13th century or perhaps late 12th century date. The piers are octagonal, the easternmost appears to be of earlier date than the others, the arch springs from a slightly higher level but is of similar character. The East Window and two easternmost in the south wall are of Decorated date of good design especially the former of three lights. The western and westernmost windows are Perpendicular, the South Door Decorated. There is a Piscina in the south wall at the eastern end and a Nitch in the adjoining angle. In the East Window and easternmost are fragments of old stained glass. In the floor are three coffin slabs.

The Tower is Early English with a chamfered arch. The West Window a lancet filled with bad modern stained glass. The Belfry stage of Perpendicular date with two-light Belfry windows and finished with a stepped battlemented parapet. At the southwest angle are two later buttresses projecting nine feet from the Tower wall.

Bells. In the Belfry are four bells with inscriptions.
1. 2. 3. J Taylor & Co. Bell founders Loughborough 1871.
4. Johannes Draper me fecit 1608: with the crown and arrows in saltire for Bury.

The first three before recasting were as follow.
1. J.H. made me 1654. John Crispe C.W.
2. Thomas Draper made me 1590. With a star.
3. Christopher Graye made me 1680.

Inscriptions.
There is but one inscription in the Church. A slab in the Nave with coat.
Party per fess (gu. and arg.) three lions rampant within a bordure ermine. (Willys). See Fen Ditton.

Hic requiefcit Thomas Willys Armiger, qvi obiit Nono Die Februarij anno Domini Mileffimo Sexcentefimo. Viceffimo qvinto, ætatis fuæ. Sexcefimo Septimo.

N. SIDE.

S. SIDE

NAVE ARCADES   HORNINGSEA CHURCH

HORNINGSEA

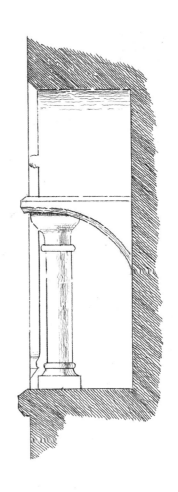

PISCINA.

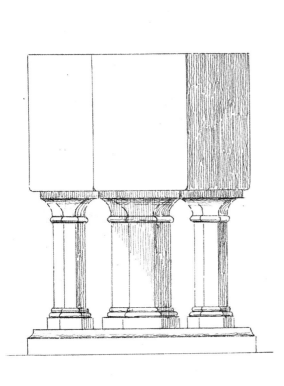

FONT

WINDOW S.AISLE

Fragments of early glass in the East Window of the South Aisle

Hall of Horningsea

Arms as above in Visitations 1575 and 1619.

Randolf Hall of Horningsea Co. Cantabr. = Catherine dau. of John Burrell Serjeant at Arms.

| Martha mar. Lancelot Calpot. | Robert Hall of Stretham in the Isle of Ely. = Margerett dau. of John Welsh of Norfolk. | Thomas 2 son. | Richard 3 son. | Michael 4 son. |

Catherin.   Margerett.

ICKLETON

The Church.

The Church is dedicated to St. Mary Magdalene and consists of Chancel, Nave, North and South Aisles, South Transept, South Porch, Central Tower and Spire. Originally cruciform but the North Transept is destroyed.

The Chancel, practically rebuilt 1882 - 83 is of Perpendicular character. On the north is an archway enclosing a window and also a blocked up door. On the south are three windows and a Priests Door, the sill of the easternmost window is continued to within a few inches of the floor and forms a Sedilia, the back of which has cusped panelling, adjoining is a Piscina. The East Window is of three lights. The piers of the Chancel Arch are of good early Norman date, the Arch itself later, of 14th century work. There is no step at the Arch but three to the Altar. The floor is tiled, the ceiling octagonal. The seating is modern of good design. The Reredos consists of oak panels on which the Ten Commandments are painted. The Chancel Screen is original, c.1400, and in good preservation.

The South Transept is of Decorated date and divided from the Aisle by a broad Arch now filled in with a plastered partition. The South Window is of four lights with excellent tracery beneath a segmental pointed arch. In the east wall is a good cinquefoiled Nitch. This Transept is used as a lumber deposit.

The Nave is Norman with four plain unmoulded arches resting on circular columns with square caps and bases, the latter with angle foot ornaments. These columns are monoliths and shew an entasis, it is probable that they are of Roman workmanship. The Clerestory windows on the north are circular, on the south they have been altered. These are not immediately above the arches. Below these and over the centre of the arches are small round headed openings with a deep splay inward, these now form a sort of triforium opening into the Aisles and may be of earlier date than the Norman Arcade. The two easternmost on the north side have considerable remains of painting in the jambs fairly perfect. The West Window is of Churchwarden type with wooden mullions and a round arch. The West Door is Norman with jamb shafts to the exterior.

Ickleton Church as it is today.

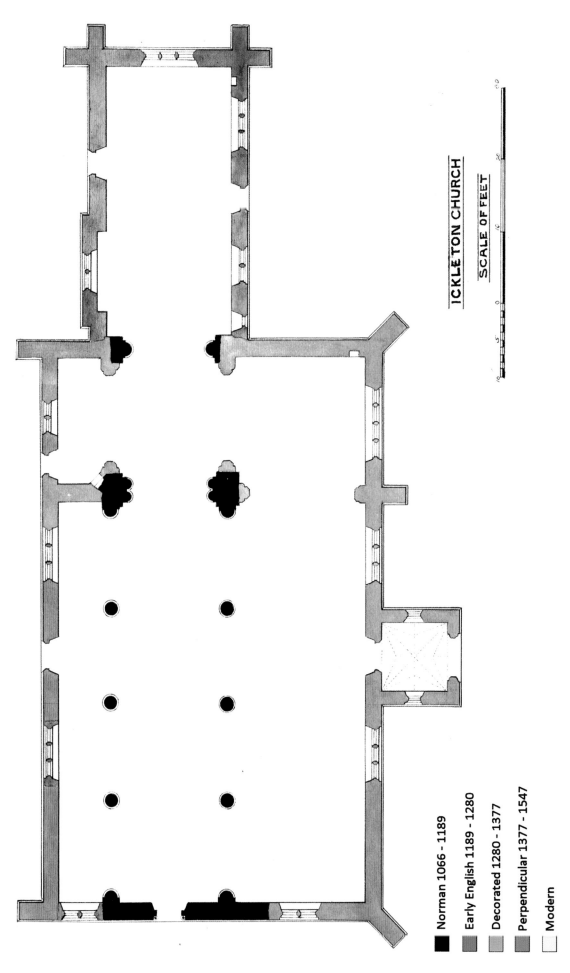

ICKLETON CHURCH

SCALE OF FEET

Norman 1066 - 1189

Early English 1189 - 1280

Decorated 1280 - 1377

Perpendicular 1377 - 1547

Modern

The roof is flat with a plaster ceiling. The piers of the Tower are Norman with double shafts, the arches are of Decorated date.

The North Aisle, c.1350, is very narrow, the eastermost portion (the remnant of the former Transept) is walled off from the rest and opens into the crossing beneath the Tower by a Decorated arch and is used as a Vestry. The Aisle has one Decorated window, a door, and one Perpendicular window at the west end. The easternmost window is filled with very bad stained glass and bears this inscription.

✝ To the beloved and honoured memory of the Honbⁱᵉ ALGERON HERBERT who died at Ickleton June 11ᵗʰ 1855.

There are slight remains of old stained glass in the Perpendicular window. Over the door are the Royal Arms.

The South Aisle is of extraordinary breadth, three feet broader than the Nave. It is of the same period as the North Aisle and has two fairly good windows, under the eastermost is a sepulchral recess. The roof is good with well moulded principals and wall posts resting on carved corbels.

The Font is octagonal on an octagonal base altogether devoid of mouldings, probably of Decorated date.

There are remains of good seating both in the Nave and Aisles with well carved poppy heads. One is exceptionally fine representing St. Michael weighing souls, others have been mutilated.

The Porch is Decorated with an excellent groined ceiling with bold ribs and bosses at the intersections, the door has the original ironwork.

The Tower is built on four Decorated arches, the piers to those at the east and west being of Norman work, those to north and south, c.1350. The Tower itself is of the same period, the ceiling above the crossing is divided into panels with moulded ribs and coloured. The Belfry windows are of two lights with traceried heads differing in design. The Tower is surmounted by a broach Spire covered with shingle with a sacring bell outside. Over the south and east Belfry windows is a cross patonce worked in flint. In the Belfry are six bells with these inscriptions.

1. James Keath and Henry Hanchett, Churchwardens. Lester and Pack of London fecit 1761.
2. Thomas Newman of Norwich made me 1729.
3. William Chapman London fecit 1781.
4. John Haleyard and Matthias Ribster. Churchwardens. Lester and Pack fecit 1755.
5. I tell all that doth me see, that Newman of Norwich new cast me 1729.
6. Charles Shepherd and Robert Miller. Churchwardens 1751. Thomas Lester of London fecit.

Priests bell without.
Tenor 18 cwt diameter 47in. Note F.

On the coping of the churchyard wall are grotesque figures carved in relief, a crocodile devouring a nondescript animal, a fox running away with a goose. &c.

Inscriptions.
Chancel tablet on the north wall.

SACRED
TO THE MEMORY
OF
ZACHARY BROOKE D.D.
LADY MARGARET PROFESSOR OF DIVINITY
IN THE UNIVERSITY OF CAMBRIDGE
RECTOR OF FORNCETT IN NORFOLK
AND
VICAR OF THIS PARISH
HE DIED AUGUST VIITH. MDCCLXXXVIII
AGED LXXIII YEARS.
AND OF
SUSANNA HIS WIFE
WHO DIED MARCH XXTH. MDCCCXII
AGED LXXIII YEARS.

On the floor immediately beneath is a black marble slab to the said Zachary Brooke, the inscription being identical but in Latin.

On a tablet surmounted by this coat. Sable 3 dexter hands couped argent impaling. Argent a chevron surmounted by a cross pattée between 3 boars heads gules.

Near this place lieth
Mary the wife
of John Hanchett Esqre
who died 7th of March
1778 aged 23.

On the floor are nine slabs with inscriptions to this family as follow.

1. HERE LIETH ENTERD
SARAH HANCHETT THE
WIFE OF THO. HANCHETT
WHO DEPARTED
THIS LIFE MARCH 1716.

2. Here Lieth interr'd ẙ
second wife of THO:
HANCHETT whose
maiden name was SARAH
ELLEOTT she departed
this life Dec^br ẙ 22nd 1729
left no Iſsue Aged 54.

Here Alſo lieth interr'd ẙ
Body of THOS. HANCHETT
Eſq^r. who departed this Life
ẙ 24th of Aug^ft 1744 in ẙ
73^d year of His Age.
Left Iſsue JOHN HANCHETT.

3. Here Lieth Interr'd
the body of Elizabeth the Wife of
JOHN HANCHETT ESQ^R
whose Maiden Name was
ELIZABETH CHELLINGWORTH
who departed this Life Oct^br ẙ 11th 1747
Aged 49 years.
Left Iſsue Rachel and Suſanna

Here also lieth interr'd the
body of IOHN HANCHETT
Esq. who departed this Life
April 28th 1758
Aged 61 Years.

4. HERE LYETH INTERR'D
THE BODY OF IOAN
HANCHETT WIFE OF
SAMUEL HANCHETT
AND DAUGHTER OF

IOHN CRUD AND ANN
HIS WIFE WHO DEPARTED
THIS LIFE OCTOB 7TH
1713 AGED 63
AND HAD ISSUE ELIZ.
HANCHETT, THO.
HANCHETT, SUSANNA
HANCHETT, SAM. HANCHETT
ANN HANCHETT
AND IOHN HANCHETT.

5.   HERE LIETH ENTER'D
THE BODY OF ANN
HANCHETT . . . .
DAUGHTER OF IOHN
AND ANN CRUD
WHO DEPARTED THIS LIFE
MARCH 11TH 1720
AGED 77.

6.   Here lieth the body of
Mary the wife of John Hanchett
who died ẙ 30th of October 1721
aged 21 years left three children
Mary, Anne and John.

7.   Here lieth Inter'd ẙ Body of
JOHN HANCHETT of Chriſhall Grange
Eſqr who departed this life ẙ 28th, of
Octobr: 1737 in ẙ 50th year of his Age.
left Iſsue MARIE, ANN, & JOHN.

8.   Here lieth the body of
John Hanchett Esqre single man
Son of John Hanchett Esqre and Mary his wife
who died May 9th 1756 in the
35 year of his age.

9.   Here lieth Mary the wife of
John Hanchett Esqre who
died the 7th of March 1773
aged 78 years.

In the Nave is a tablet surmounted by the
Hanchett coat.

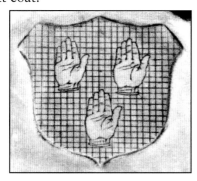

IN MEMORY OF
WILLIAM HANCHETT,
BORN JULY 14, 1814, DIED AUG. 1, 1873.
ALSO OF
CAROLINE HIS WIFE
BORN FEB. 26. 1812. DIED JULY 2. 1871.

On another tablet.

To the Memory of
MRS MARY HANCHETT,
Wife of MR JOHN HANCHETT,
who died October 6th 1796
Aged 20 years.

————

Alſo of HENRY HANCHETT,
who died Novr. 13th 1795. Aged 76.

On a slab.

Here lieth the body of
Henry Hanchett
who died November 12th 1794
aged 78 years
also Mary the wife of
Henry Hanchett
who died November the 1st 1801
aged 75 years
also Samuel Hanchett
who died December 29th 1814 aged 7 years.

In the south aisle on a tablet with a coat for
Hanchett as above.

In a vault beneath
are deposited the remains of
John Hanchett Esqre
who died Aug. 29. 1844 aged 41 years.

Besides these inscriptions to the Hanchett family
are the following.

In the Chancel two slabs.

1.   HEAR LYETH IN THE
. . . BODY OF
THO. CRUD ESQRE
SINGLE MAN OF JOHN CRUD AND
AND ANN HIS WIFE WHO
DEPARTED THIS
LIFE APRIL THE 5TH
1714 AGED 67.

2.   Here lieth interrd
the body of Sarah Cass
. . . . Hanchett who
departed this life . . . 1757
aged 42 left one daughter.

On a slab in the Nave.

Here lieth the body
of
Mary the wife of Joseph Pyke
who departed this life Sept. 6. 1750
aged 45

Here also lieth the body of
Joseph Pyke
who departed this life Feb. 18. 1779
aged 68.

South Aisle on a tablet.

NEAR THIS PLACE
ARE INTERRED THE REMAINS OF
JANE ELIZABETH JONES,
WHO DIED ON THE 6TH OF DECEMBER, 1831,
AGED 74 YEARS,
WHOSE MIND WAS ADORNED WITH
CHARITY, BENEVOLENCE,
AND THE
TRUE FEELINGS OF
A CHRISTIAN.

On a brass plate by the South Door with this coat. Sable a lion rampant within a bordure embattled or, impaling. Per pale azure and gules 3 lions rampant argent a crescent in chief or (Herbert).

In · Pace · obiit · Anno · ætatis · XLIII · Rev^dus ·
Gulielmus
Lempriere · Lewis · A · M · Coll · S · S ·
Trinitatis · apud
Oxoniam · Quondam · Scholaris · ac · Sorius ·
Cujus
quod · mortale · erat · In · Ajaccio · Cerni ·
Insulæ · Mense
Januarii · MDCCCLXXII · Uxor · mærens ·
Terræ · credidit.

Extracts from the Register.

The Register begins in 1558, the early part is a transcript made during the incumbency of Michael Cowle who was instituted 1588.

1559.   Robert son of John Crud at the Rose and Alice his wife, bap. April 10.

1562.   Sara Crud da. of John Crud at the Churchgate and Joane his wife. bap. Nov. 10.

1565 - 6. Martha Crud da. of John Crud jun^r bur^d Jany 24.
There are a large number of entries of this family to the middle of the eighteenth century, indifferently spelt Curd and Crud.

1572.   John Brignel, John Chambers & Richard Barker slayne at the clay pitt & overwhelmed with clay, bur^d Nov. 21.

1575.   Richard Lorkin & Agnes Titmouse married April 21.

1575.   Agnes Proctor wife of Robert Proctor, Vicarii Ickeltonii, buried Aug. 17.

1576.   Robert Procter Vicar of this Towne & Joane White, mar^d Aug. 20.

1576.   Grace da. of Richard Lorkin, bap. June 24.

1578.   Alice Spicer drowned in the river bur^d June 24.

1582.   Margaret Lorkin widow buried Aug. 6.

1586.   Mother Wakefield buried Nov. 20.

1587.   Joane Procter wife of Robert Procter (Vicar) bur^d. March 2.

1588.   Michael Cowle Vicar entered (not interred) 20 April. The Register signed by this Vicar from the commencement 1558 to 1611.

1589.   John Addam a great drunkard excommunicat, bur^d. Nov. 25.

1589.   John Backstur & Margery Byllingay when they had lived as man and wife 18 years confessed their folly and did penance and were married Nov. 24.

1590.   Old Mother Thriplow dyed June 22.

1590 - 1. William the bastard sonne of Elizabeth Stirling was begotten in adultery bap. Feb. 2.

1591.   George son of Michael Cowle (Vicar) bap. April 18. (Many more children of this vicar appear among the baptisms.)

1591 - 2. Old Father South buried March. 4.

1592.   Goodwife Curd wife of John Curd at the Churchgate buried June 16.

IMPINGTON

The Church.

The Church is dedicated to St. Andrew and consists of Chancel, Nave, West Tower, South Porch and modern Vestry.

The Chancel is of 14th century date : it has two two-light windows on the south enclosed within two broad arcades extending the height and length of the Chancel. There is a similar arcade on the north side, this refers to the interior. The East Window is Perpendicular of poor character but the label is of Decorated date. The Sedilia is formed by a low seat extending the whole width of the easternmost arcade on the south side. The floor is tiled. The Chancel seats are new, of oak with traceried backs. The roof is oak with open rafters framed octagonally. The Chancel Arch has a double chamfer.

The Nave is Perpendicular with two windows and a porch on the south side and the same number of windows with a blocked up doorway on the north. Inside in the south angle are two doorways with depressed arches, one leading to the stairs of the former Rood Loft and the other above it opening to the loft itself. The Font is octagonal on an octagonal base probably coeval with the Chancel, c.1350. There are four good old bench ends finished with poppy heads, the remainder are new of oak worked in character with them. On the north side between the windows is a large fresco of St. Christopher bearing the infant Christ, it is fairly perfect though much faded. In the jamb of the easternmost window on the north side is a small Nitch with traces of green and red painting. The old moulded tie beams and king posts of the roof remain. The ceiling above is modern boarding.

Small niche, now with a modern sculpture by L Pendred, c.1975

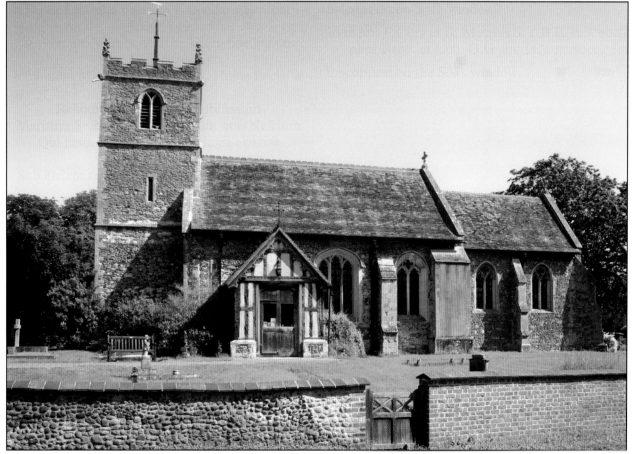

Impington Church as it is today.

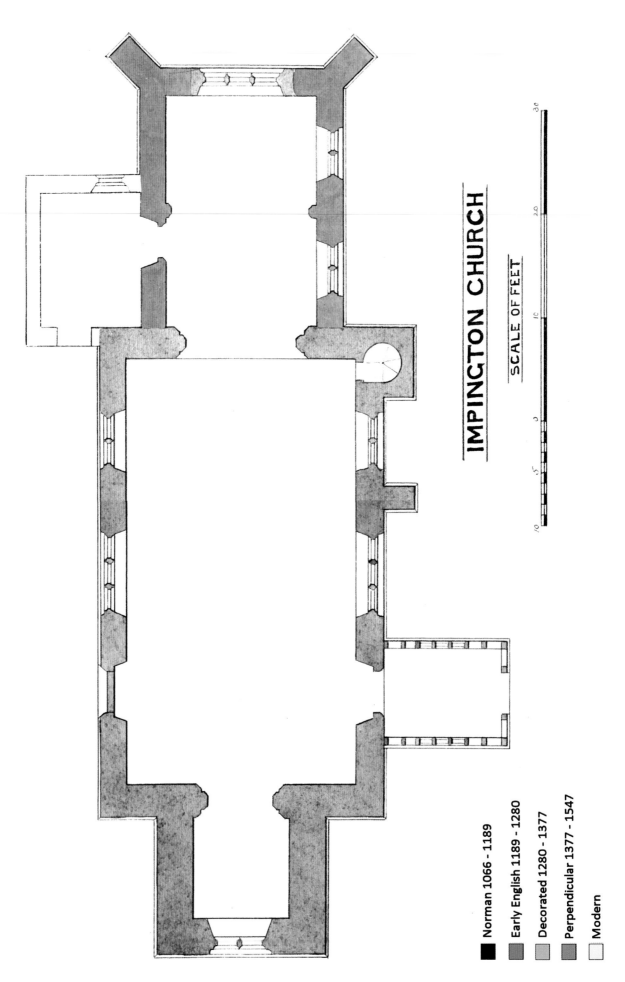

IMPINGTON CHURCH

SCALE OF FEET

Norman 1066 - 1189

Early English 1189 - 1280

Decorated 1280 - 1377

Perpendicular 1377 - 1547

Modern

WEST ELEVATION   IMPINGTON CHURCH   S. E. ANGLE OF NAVE.

South Porch

Decorative Spandrel on South Porch

The Porch is wood and plaster with cusped and traceried windows, moulded doorway, large board &c, after the original design, some of the old timbers of which are worked in.

The Tower is small and unbuttressed, finished with an embattled parapet and four crocketted pinnacles. There are two-light Belfry window openings and a West Window. A peculiarity is that the putlog holes are left unfilled.

At the extreme west of the south wall of the Nave is what appears to be the remains of a lancet window but the head is wanting. It is so close to

N. SIDE OF NAVE

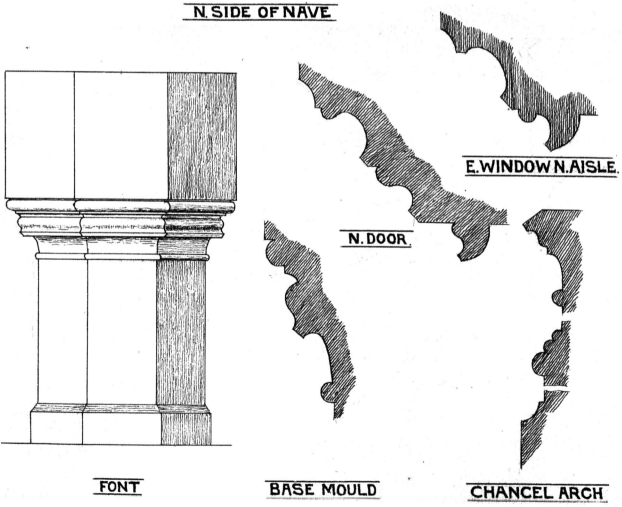

E. WINDOW N. AISLE.

N. DOOR.

FONT

BASE MOULD

CHANCEL ARCH

the angle that this can hardly have been the original position, for had the Church extended further westward it would have been with difficulty preserved in situ. There is no evidence anywhere of earlier work than the middle of the 14th century. The fragment in question is simply two upright lines of stones about a foot apart.

Bells. The Tower contains three bells with inscriptions as follow and these devices.
1. A fleur de lis and a shield (a bend between a cross and an annulet within a bordure).
   + Sancte Petre ora pro nobis, in old English lettering.
2. Has the four symbols of the Evangelists also a shield (a chevron, on a chief three mullets, in base a crescent reversed) a crowned fleur de lis. Sancta Katerina ora pro nobis.
3. R. G. made me 1652.
The tenor has a three legged pot at the beginning of the inscription.

Notes.

There is no stained glass in the Church, ancient or modern.

This Church was restored in 1878. It was formerly in a ruinous condition. The work was carried out under the direction of Mr R. R. Rowe, Architect of Cambridge. At this time the remains of a Rood Screen and an hour glass were lost or destroyed, the Burgoine brass removed to its present position in the Tower, the Porch rebuilt and the exterior scraped and pointed, but altogether the work was carried out in a fairly conservative spirit. The expenditure was about £1400. About twenty years ago (1865), before the Church was restored, I remember seeing a book chained to a desk in the Chancel. In May 1883 the clerk of Girton Church told me there used to be two books chained, one being Foxe's Book of Martyrs, these, he said, were there just before the restoration of the Church.

Inscriptions.
On the Chancel floor a black marble slab.

Thomas Wilborow vir pius et doctus
hujus ecclesiæ vicarius et privatæ
scholæ moderator postquam per
multos annos utramque spartam
egregie adornasset tandem diu
turnis confectus curis et laboribus moi
temque anlielantis Jesu amoris io annimam
huic sacrario ossa patientissime commen
davit. Anno {Dni 1669} Sept. 7th
{ Æts 62 }

On a marble tablet south wall of Nave.

SACRED
TO THE BELOVED MEMORY OF
CATHERINE HOVENDEN,
(RELICT OF WALTER HOVENDEN,
MAJOR IN HIS LATE MAJESTY'S SERVICE.)
SHE DIED AT AN ADVANCED AGE
ON THE 24TH OF MAY 1826.
IN REMEMBRANCE
OF THE KINDEST AND DEAREST OF MOTHERS
THIS TABLET IS PLACED
BY FILIAL AFFECTION.

In the Tower is a good brass of John Burgoyne and wife beneath whom are the figures of seven sons and two daughters. There are also matrices of coats of arms. The man is in armour his feet resting on a dog and his tabard charged with his arms a talbot passant. The woman wears a mantle emblazoned with her coat, a chevron a fess in chief three leopards faces, portions of the brass on both figures has been torn away. The figures are surrounded by a rim of brass containing the inscription, the corners ornamented with medallions containing symbols of the evangelists. The inscription is perfect with the exception of about two feet on the south side being the last words. It is in old English characters as follows.

✠ Hic jacet Johannes Burgoyne Armiger et
Margareta uxor ejus, quidẽ Johannes obiit deciõ
bidie menſe Octobr̃ A°. Dñi
Millim̃ o Quingenteſimo quinto et prædicta
Margareta obiit die menſe Anno Domini Millim̃ o
Quingenteſimo quorum . . . .

The date of the womans decease was never inserted, she died in June 1528 (Cole). Cole gives the four coats of arms now defaced.
1. Above his head. A talbot passant. (Burgoyne)
2. Above her head. A chevron and fess in chief three leopards faces.
3. Under him. These two coats impaled.
4. Under her. Burgoyne.
Cole also gives the following notes taken by him. (M.S. Vol 4. p88)

Against the north wall an achievement with these arms.
Sable on a bend or inter 2 horses heads erased 3 fleurs de lis sable (Pepys) impaling. Sable a chevron ermine inter 3 fer de molines or, on a chief argent a lion passant gardant gules (Turner). Crest. A horse's (camel's?) head erased gu. (or?) gorged and strung with a ducal coronet sable.
In the south window in modern glass painting are the arms of Pepys.

IMPINGTON CHURCH

SYMBOLS & LETTERING
ON THE BURGOYNE BRASS

On a handsome freestone much worn.

Here lieth the body of
Mr John Horborne who
departed this life
1707
aged 67 years.

Blomefield gives the fleurs de lis on the coat of Pepys as azure which is incorrect. He also notes that on a Chalice are the arms of Pepys quartering Turner as above. Roger Pepys of Impington born 1667 mar. Anne dau. of Charles Turner of Weasenham Co. Norf. The Chalice probably given by his son Charles the last Pepys of Impington died 1778 (See pedigree.)

Miscellaneous.
Eustacius Bishop of Ely (1197 - 1215) gave the patronage of this Church to the Prior and Convent of Ely for the use of transcribing books for their library (Hist. Eliensis) but in another place Nigellus, Bishop of the same See, is said to be the donor for the same purpose. Since the Reformation it has been vested together with the advowson of the vicarage in the Dean and Chapter. This Parish was enclosed pursuant to an Act of Parliament 1801 by which allotments of land were made to the Dean and Chapter as impropriators, to the Vicar and to the Pepys family for a considerable portion of great tithes annexed to their estate. The living of the value of £128 was in 1871 in the gift of Charles Bamford Esq.

In 1871 the area of the Parish was returned at 1200 acres with a rateable value of £3137. By the Divided Parishes Act 1882, the Local Government Board order No. 18936 (March 24. 1886) detached parts of Histon were added to Impington so that in 1901 the area of the Parish is returned at 1668 acres with a rateable value of £3823.
The Population in 1801 was returned at 92. In 1871 at 387. In 1901 at 418.

A market on Thursdays and a fair for 8 days to begin on the Saturday in Easter week were granted to Peter de Chauvent in the year 1300. Both long discontinued.

An obelisk in the fields south of the village marks the spot where Elizabeth Woodcock, a native of the village, on her return from Cambridge Market 2 February 1799 was lost in a snow drift under which she remained nearly eight days and nights. She was taken out alive and under the care of Mr Okes a surgeon of Cambridge, was so far recovered on the 17th of April, after the loss of all her toes

and most of the fleshy parts of her face, as to be deemed in a state of convalescence. A pamphlet drawn up by Mr Okes and the Reverend Mr Holme, then curate at Impington, was published for her benefit. Through imprudence in not abstaining from the immoderate use of strong liquors her health never became completely re-established and she died in the month of July the same year. ?Query. But for the liquor would she have survived at all?

Norwich Taxation 1256, "Impetone XVIII marc. vicesima. XII sol. Prior de Ely in eadem XX sol. vicesima XII sol.
Value of Temporalities of the Priory of Barnwell."
In Ympetone. lxvııs.

Customary Dues. Impiton. "Philippus de Insula tenet feodum 1 militis de episcopo Elyensi. Ibidem Alexander de Impiton tenet feodum 1 militis de episcopo Elyensi et debet j sectam, et de auxilio vicecomitis iijs." (Mem. Esq. Barnwell. Clark. 241.)

Manors.
The Manor was given to the Abbot and Convent of Ely in 991 by Brithnoth and held under the See passed to the families of de Lisle, and Chauvent. Peter de Chauvent bought the Manor of Simon de Lisle (see Fine 1268). It was held 1324 by John de Chauvent who appears to sold it to Jeffery de Cantebrugge or Jeffery Seeman of Cantebrigge (see Fines 1324). His name occurs in the list of assessments from lay subsidies 1326. It was acquired by the Burgoyne family probably about the end of the 15th century for in 1505 John Burgoyne died possessed of it, but the name does not occur in connection with the village among the Fines relating to the County up to 1485. A portion of it called Ferme part was sold by the coheirs of the Burgoynes to the Pepys family 1632, another part called the Manor of Burgoyne became the property of the Master and Fellows of Christi College. Fermepart on the Death of Mrs Pepys 1805 (widow of Charles Pepys who died 1778) descended to the Revd John Pine Coffin of Portledge, Devon nephew to the above named Charles Pepys.

The Hall was begun by John Pepys in the middle of the 16th century and finished by his Executors in accordance with his will dated 2nd July 1589. The house was rebuilt about 1725 by Roger Pepys or rather remodelled for the central portion still retains the original hall, a wing was added 1862 and the exterior practically renewed.

Domesday.

"In Epintone tenet Walterus de Picot iij hidas et dimidiam. Terra est iij carrucis et ibi sunt cum iiij bordariis et iiij Cotariis. Pratum j carrucæ. Inter totum valet lx solidos : quando recepit l solidos : tempore Regis Edward iiij libras. Hanc terram tenuerunt iij sochemanni Abbatis de Ely. Horum ij habuerunt j hidam et virgatam : vendere potuerunt sed soca Abbati remancit. Tercius vero ij hidas et j virgatam habuit, sed vendere non potuit."

Suit of the Prior of Barnwell against Peter de Chauvent for customary services.

"De placito contra dominum Petrum de Chavent pro servicio de Impetone".

Temporibus domini Symonis de Insula et domini Philippi de Insula patris ejus, et ante cessorum suorum a tempore quo non extat memoria, solebant villani sui de Impetone facere servicium ad manerium Regis de Cestertone: vide licet corruras, falcationes prati, messiones in autumpno, gallinas ad Natale, ova ad Pascha, panes ad opus mesores ad Natale, et garbas in autumpni pro habenda communa cum averiis suis in pastura de Sestertone. Processu vero temporis vendidit dominus Symon de Insula manerium suum de Impetone cum pertinenciis domino Petro de Chavent et heredibus suis in perpetuum. Predictus vero Petrus prohibuit villanis suis ne ampluis facerent predicta servicia manerio Regis de Cestertone et sic subtracta erant servicia antedicta per multos annos: Prior tamen de Bernewelle fecit distringere dictos villanos de Impetone pro dictis serviciis, et dictus Petrus fecit averia replegiare usque ad Comitatum Cantebrigie, et per breve quod dicitur pone ponebatur loquela ad Bancum apud Westmonasterium. Ibique fuit placitum inter dictum priorem et dictum Petrum de Chavent per decem annos et ampluis et tandem posuerunt se super patriam.

Postea in octabis Sancti Michaelis anno regni regis Eadwardi. xiiº venerunt juratores qui dicunt super sacramentum suum quod quilibet villanus terram tenens in Impetone debet dare de jure, et a tempore quo non extat memoria, dedit quilibet eorum per annum unam galinam ad Natale domini, et decem ova ad Pascha et duos panes et unam garbam in autumno pro habenda pastura in campo de Cestertone: et quod predictus Prior et predecessores sui a tempore quo non extat memoria fuerunt in seysyna de predicto servicio: et quod nullus villanus de Impetone tenet ultra dimidiam virgatam terre. Et quia predictus Prior et predecessores sui a tempore quo non extat memoria fuerunt in seysina de predicto servicio de villanis predicti Petri pro predicta communa habenda in predicto campo de Cestertone, et illi villani illud semper facere solibant de jure et non de gracia, consideratum est quod predictus Prior habeat returnum averiorum, et Petrus in misericordia pro falso clamore. Et similita predictus Prior in misericordia pro injusta districtione facta super predictum Petrum, eo quod distrinxit eum pro pluribus serviciis quam ei recognoscuntur. Et misericordia predicti Prioris perdonatur per justiciarios &c.

Brive Regis. E(dwardus) Dei gracia &c. vicecomiti Cantebrigie salutem. Scias quod Prior de Bernewelle in curia nostra coram justiciariis nostris apud Westmonasterium per consideracionem ejusdem curie nostre recuperavit versus Petrum de Chavent returnum quatuor equorum. Et ides tibi precipimus quod eidem Priori predicta averia sine dilacione returnari facias. Teste Th(oma) de Weyland &c.

Concerning the above. Apparently the Prior avowed the taking good and lawful on the ground that Peter's villains at Impington were prescriptively bound to make certain payments in kind to the Prior in return for rights of pasture in the field of Chesterton. A return of the horses that had been relevied is awarded to the Prior; but he is amerced, as the verdict has not in all respects borne out his avowry. (Lib. Mem. Eccl. Bern. 138. lv.)

List of names and assessments from Lay Subsidies Cambridgeshire 1. Edwd III. 1326.

De Galfrõ Seman	viijs	viijd	q"
" Henr̃ Vicar	ijs	ijd	q"
" Galfrõ ate Grene		xiijd	
" Willo p'põito		xxd	
" Rogo' le March	ijs	ijd	
" Joħe de Meppale		vijd	
" Joħe de Ove'		xviij	ob.
" Joħe fil˜ Simoñ		vijd	
" Agnẽt Ryngewale	ijs		
" Ric le Taylour		xvid	
" Nicħo Bungeys		xiiid	
" Henr̃ Toly		xvid	ob' q"
" Joħe Bigge		xd	
" Simoñ Messor		vi	q"
" Nicħo de Tame	ijs		
" Joħe Estrild		vijd	q"
" Joħe Power		xiijd	
" Joħe de Westwich		xxd	
" Alex̃. Toly		viijd	
" Joħe le Marcħ	ijs		

" Henr̃ Bele	vijd		
" Henr̃ Warde	xiiijd		
" Rogo' Toly	vijd		
" Joħe Carpent'	vijd		
" Agnet' Steyk'	xijd	q"	
" Galfrõ Chapman	vjd	q"	
" Thom̃ Chapman	iiijs	ob' q"	
" Robt̃o Mold	vjd	q"	
" Joħe de Cretig'	vjd	q"	
" Martino Toly	vjd		
" Petro Amaunde	viij		
" Henr̃ de Wyte	viij		

Sm̃   xl   vs   jd

Calender of Fines relating to Impington.

1201. 3rd John

Walter fil' Walter v. William fil' Thomas in Impinton.

1205. 7th John

Simon de Ka.. v. Walter . . . in . . . Empitone.

1246. 31st Henry 3rd.

Eadmund fil' Thomas v. Robert fil' Roger in Impiton.

1247. 32nd Henry 3rd.

Gilbert Pollard and Cecil his wife v. William Vicar of Impiton in Impiton.

1250. 35th Henry 3rd.

Hugh de Impyton v. John de Harleton and Matilda his wife in Impyton.

1252. 37th Henry 3rd.

Alex fil' Torald v. Michael Bassett and Fria his wife in Impinton.

1268. 53rd Henry 3rd.

Peter de Chavent and Agnes his wife v. Simon de Insula and Ela his wife of Impynton manor.

1271. 56th Henry 3rd.

Nicholas fil' Petronill' de la Grene and Matilda and Julian his sisters v. Godfrey de Empyton in Empynton Hyston and Howes.

1271. 56th Henry 3rd.

Gilbert Knyght and Johanna his wife v. Auger fil' Lodewyc de Chestreton and Agatha his wife in Impington.

1271. 56th Henry 3rd.

Peter Alyot and Ysobel his wife v. Gilbert Knyght and Johanna his wife, Thomas de Ufford and Alice his wife, Benedict de Gretton and Muriel his wife, Nichs. de Impeton and Juliana his wife & Auger fil' Lodowyci & Agatha his wife in Impeton.

1272. 1st Edward 1st.

Peter de Chavent and Agnes his wife v. Simon de Insula and Elena his wife of Manors of Impington.

1273. 2nd Edward 1st.

Peter de Chaumpuent (Chavent?) by Wm. de Bonevill v. Amandus de Impiton in Impiton Histon Midelton and Cestreton.

1286. 15th Edward 1st.

Philip de Colevile v. Martin de Brinkele and Amicia his wife in Empyton.

1296. 25th Edward 1st.

William de Honylane and Laurence his brother v. Richard Crocheman of Cantebrigg and Muriella his wife in Impiton and Hyston.

1312. 6th Edward 2nd.

William de Stanton of Dryedrayton and Sibilla his wife v. Nicholas le Clerk of Impinton in Drydrayton.

1317. 11th Edward 2nd.

John de Chavent and Eva his wife v. John de Cretynge of the Manor of Impiton.

1324. 18th Edward 2nd.

Geoffrey de Cantebrigge v. John de Chavent and Eva his wife of the Manor of Impington.

1324. 18th Edward 2nd.

Geoffrey Seman of Cauntebrigge v. the same.

1324. 18th Edward 2nd.

The same.

1361 - 2. 36th Edward 3rd.

Master Thomas de Eltesle senior and others v. Dedericus de Somerton and Amia his wife of Manors of Tadlowe & Impyngton.

1366 - 7. 41st Edward 3rd.

William West of Histon v. Hugh le Eyr of Wilberton & Agnes his wife in Impyton.

1373. 48th Edward 3rd.

Edmund Laurence and others v. John Goldsmyth and Margaret his wife in Impynton.

1373. 48th Edward 3rd.

Roger de Herlaston and others v. John Morys of Cantebrigge and others of $\frac{1}{3}$ of the Manor of Impynton.

1405. 7th Henry 4th.

Thomas Skelton Knight and others v. John Ashwell Clerk in Impyton.

1411. 13th Henry 4th.

John Heche and others v. Roger Scot of Impyngton and Flora his wife in Impynton.

1420 - 1. 9th Henry 5th.

Robert Hervy v. Thomas Everard and Agnes his wife in Impyngton and Histon.

Pepys of Impington

John Pepys of Cottenham ╤ Edith Talbot dau. and sole heir of
will dat. 2 July 1589.   Edmund Talbot of Cottenham.

Talbot Pepys of Impington Co. ╤ Beatrice dau. of John Castle   John   Thomas ╤ Kezia . . . .
Cantabr. elected Recorder of   of Ravenham Co. Norf. Esq.
Cambridge 27. Oct. 1624. ob.   John of Brampton Hunts
March 1666, æt. 84.   ob. 1680. ╤

                                                    Samuel the diarist.
                                                    1632 - 1703.

John born 1 Dec. 1618 = Catherine widow   3. Thomas born   Paulina born 30 Jan. 1622   Henry
Bapt. 8. Dec. L.L.D.   of Thos. Hobson   5 June 1621.   mar. Hammond Caxton   ob. infant.
living 1684. 2 son.   of Cottenham.   M.D. ob. s.p.   of Broughton Norf.

1. Roger born 3 May 1617, bap. 8th. He was Recorder of Cambridge 1660 ╤ Barbara.
and M.P. for the Borough 1661. Of Impington Esqre.

Francis born 1648   Talbot 1 son and heir born 20 March 1646 of Impington. ╤

Roger Pepys of Impington Esqre born 1667 ╤ Anne dau. of Charles Turner of
rebuilt the Manor house c.1725.   Weasenham Co. Norf.

Charles Pepys of Impington = . . . dau. of . . . Spellman   Talbot born 25 June 1703, ob. 23 July
ob. 1778 æt. 68. He was the   of Norf. ob. 1805 æt. 83.   1717 bur. St. Nicholas Chapel, Lynn.
last Pepys of Impington.

LANDBEACH

2 April 1884.

The Church.

The Church is dedicated to All Saints and consists of a Chancel with North Chapel now used as a Vestry, Nave, North and South Aisles, South Porch and West Tower with Spire. The Church dates from about the middle of the 14th century but underwent considerable alterations in the 15th.

The Chancel has an East Window of three lights. On the south is a two-light window and Priests Door of 14th century date and a three-light Perpendicular window. In the south wall is a square double Piscina and the Sedilia is formed of the sill of the adjoining window which is lowered to within about two feet of the ground. The floor is covered with modern tiles, there are two steps at the Chancel Arch and two more to the altar. The seating is new with the exception of two old stalls with elbows and misericords, the latter carved with these coats. Or a fess between two chevrons sable, a mullet in the dexter quarter all within a bordure of the second (de L'Isle). Quarterly 1 and 4 Gules a lion rampant or, 2 and 3 Checky or and azure (Arundel). The Screen is of good but rather coarse workmanship, it was removed from the west end some years ago.

On the north side is a broad double chamfered archway and eastward a door both opening into a North Chapel, now used as a Vestry. The Chancel has been much restored and a great deal of the stonework of the windows is new.

Landbeach Church as it is today.

161

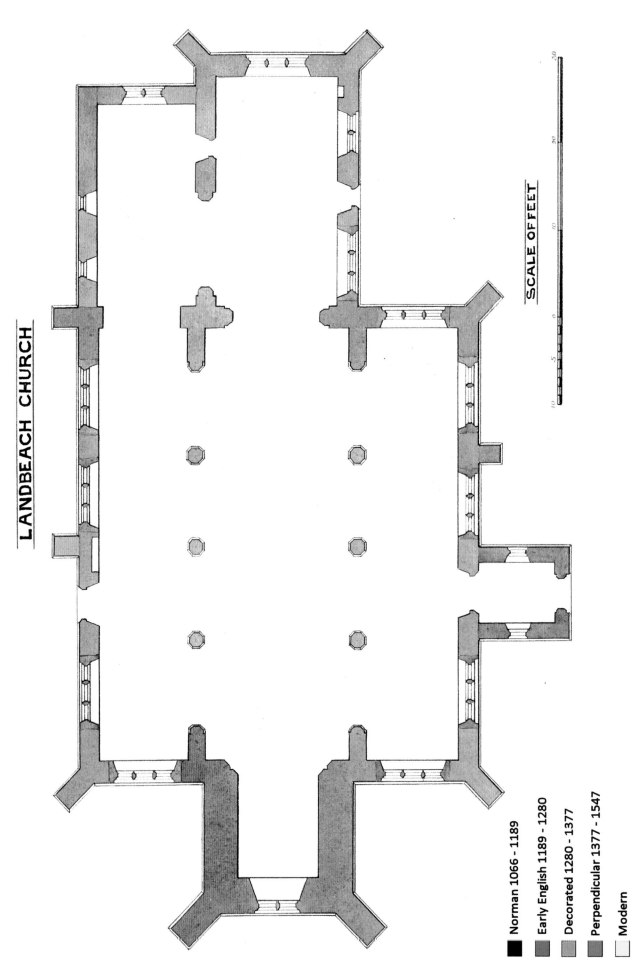

LANDBEACH CHURCH

SCALE OF FEET

Norman 1066 - 1189

Early English 1189 - 1280

Decorated 1280 - 1377

Perpendicular 1377 - 1547

Modern

162

supported by angels with carved bases at the intersections of purlins and rafters.

The South Aisle has Perpendicular windows and a 14th century doorway exactly corresponding to the North Aisle. There is a Decorated Piscina and credence in a double arch by the door a Stoup. In all the windows are remains of old stained glass. The roof is similar to that of the North Aisle but less enriched.

The Tower is of 14th century date and has a West Window of two lights. The Tower Arch is double chamfered, above which are the Royal Arms, placed there in 1826. The Belfry windows are of two lights. The Tower has angle buttresses, is embattled and finished with a low octagonal Spire; beneath the battlements on the west side a shield semée of fleurs de lis three barrulets (Chamberlayne).

Bells. In the belfry are four bells with these inscriptions.
1 and 2. John Draper made me 1619.
3. De Buri Santi Edmondi Stephanus Tonni me fecit 1577. W.L. Favet Jova populo suo. with a device between each word.
4. Xrs + Perpetue Dei nobis Gaudia vite, with a coin between each of the last five words and a device at the end.

Heraldry.
The following coats of arms are in the Church windows.
In the Vestry some old quarries formerly in the East Window of the Chancel; they were placed there by the Revd Robert Masters soon after his induction to the living about 1750. They were taken from the parlour windows of the Rectory house. A considerable number have been lost; the remaining coats are:

De Beche. Or three dragons heads erased sable, impaling. Argent on a bend ingrailed sable three dolphins naient of the field.
Quarterly 1 and 4. Or three bars gules. 2 and 3. Or four palets gules impaling. England and France per fess. Attributed to De Beche. Or a bend wavy coticed gules, impaling. Argent on a bend sable between three saltires of the last 3 crosses botony of the field.
The East Window of the Chancel has some good remains of old stained glass. In the tracery are three coats of modern work.
1. As the first mentioned in the Vestry above but the dragons heads vert and marshalling reversed.
2. As the second mentioned in the Vestry but instead of four palets it shews paly of eight.
3. As the third in the Vestry but the marshalling reversed.

The Nave and Aisles are mainly of the Decorated period but the windows are insertions of Perpendicular date. The arches of the Nave Arcade are plainly moulded with a chamfer and a hollow. They rest on octagonal pillars with moulded caps, although contemporary those on the north side are of rather earlier character. There are some remains of old seating of interest. The roof is good framed with moulded tie beams with curved braces resting on stone corbels, the intermediates are supported by angels. The Clerestory windows are two-light Perpendicular of poor character. The Font is modern a plain octagon. The Pulpit has traceried panels of very good work originally brought from Jesus College. The Lectern represents an angel carved in oak, rather awkwardly perched on a pedestal of Flemish workmanship. There are slight remains of colour on the south respond by the Chancel Arch. Over the Chancel Arch is a small window and above the Tower the Royal Arms are painted.

North Aisle. The windows in the North Aisle are of similar design, of three lights of Perpendicular date. The door is of 14th century work and adjoining it eastward is a recess with a crocketted canopy and double foliated cusps supposed to be the tomb of Sir Thomas Chamberlayne, c.1350, whose arms are in the adjacent window. There are remains of stained glass in the tracery of all these windows. The roof is good framed with principals

CANOPIED TOMB N.AISLE

CAP S. SIDE

CAP N.SIDE

NAVE ARCADE AND AISLE WINDOW

Arms of De Beche in the Church windows

Coats of Arms in the East Window

<u>Masters.</u> In the South window eastward three coats.
1. Gules a lion rampant gardant or double tailed holding in its sinister paw a rose argent seeded gules slipped and leaved vert (Masters).
2. Masters impaling. Sable on a chevron between three eagles heads erased or three etoiles gules.
3. This last coat repeated with a crest. A demi eagle rising from a ducal coronet or. "Spero meliora".

<u>Bryan Walker.</u> In the South Window westward. Argent a chevron sable between three Cornish choughs ppr, (Bryan Walker) impaling. Gules a lion rampant regardant between three wells argent.

<u>Chamberlayne.</u> In a window of the North Aisle. Argent two bendlets dancetty gules (Chamberlayne).

Inscriptions.
In the Chancel. On the north wall a small brass plate.

<u>Clifford 1616.</u>

> Henrye Clifford Master of Artes Preacher
> and Parson of this Church: after residence
> of full 47 yeres, endinge his lyfe, departed
> in the faith of Christ, and was buried Aᵒ. 1616.
> Unto me yester day: to the day. ECCL. 38.
> ætatis suæ 77.   Guil Bro: posuit.

<u>Mickleborough 1756.</u> On a tablet with this coat. Argent on a pile sable 3 lozenges of the field in base 2 crosses botony fitchy gules. (Mickleborough)

165

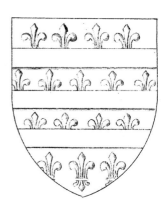

HERALDRY

Pro ſuo ipſius juſsu deponitur infra
Quod reliquum est JOHANNIS
MICKLEBOURGH,
Apud Cantabrigienſes Chemæ Profeſsoris, Caput
mortuum
Et (ut loqui amant Chemici) Die Secundo Maii,
MDCCLVI,
Exhauſto ſpiritu, terra itidem damnata
Ad vitam beatam, quod faxit Deus,
Reſurrectura.

De me res acta eſt, Sed non ſine Crimine vixi,
O Jeſu Judex! Tu miſerere mei.
Ad me quæ ſpectant, Lector, vis inoſcere plurã.
Ultima monſtrabit, cum venit illa, dies.
Hæc ſuprema Dies, et ineluctabile Fatum
Te manet, Una Salus Vita fideſque pia.
Vale, in Æternum Vale.

Mickleborough 1749. On an adjoining tablet.

Quos per viginti annorum Spatium
Felices ter et ampluis,
Amor, Fides, et irrupta Connubii Copula
Conjunctos ſimul tenuit
Hos Uxoris dilectiſſimæ Heſter Mors non
immatura
Subita tamen et inopinata dictum factum divulſit
Egit annos Ætatis Sexaginta & unum, Ætatem
in vitâ futurâ Sempiternam et beatiſſimam Actura
Quâ Spe ſuffulta primum Kalendaru Februarii
A.D. 1749
Supremum Vitæ bene actæ Diem ſine gemitu
Sine Suſpirio exegit
Johannem Micklebourgh S.T.B. Hujus Eccleſiæ
Rectorem
Reliquit Superſtitem mæſtiſſimum
Maritum Suæ ipſius Vitæ tantum non Neſcium
Qui juxta hoc marmor Conjugis exuvias
curavit deponendas;
Sub eâdem terrâ Suas ipſius tandem aliquando
Depoſiturus.

Addison 1843. On another tablet

SACRED
TO THE MEMORY OF THE
REV^D EDWARD ADDISON,
22 YEARS RECTOR OF THIS PARISH,
WHO DIED MAY 28, 1843,
AGED 67 YEARS.

ALSO MARIA SARAH ADDISON
HIS SISTER,
WHO DIED APRIL 8, 1843.

Burroughes 1821. In the pavement

THOMAS
COOK BURROUGHES,
M. A. T. P.

RECTOR OF LANDBEACH
FOR 23 YEARS
DIED APRIL 23, 1821,
AGED 64 YEARS.

Burroughes 1816.

ROBERT
MASTERS
BURROUGHES,
SECOND SON OF
T. C. BURROUGHS,
RECTOR
DIED JULY 30, 1816,
AGED 14.

Sproule 1813.

Beneath are
deposited the remains of
two beloved Daughters of
The late J. R. Sproule
Vicar of Great Bradfield Essex
and Annie his wife Daughter of
The Rev. Robert Masters
a former Rector of this Parish
Catherine Sproule
Died Jan. 19 1813 Aged 19
Marianne Sproule
Died Sept 14 1813 Aged 21

Inscription on S. E. window.

In mem. J. Cory et R. Masters S.T.B.B. huj. eccl. olim Rect^t. et Coll. G.G apud Cant. Socc.

Inscription on the S.W. window.

: Haec : Sua : Mano : Sollerti : Picta :
: Dicabat : Deo : Erpani : Rectoris :
: Francisca : Coniox : Coniunctissima :

In the Nave.
Rawley 1667. At the west end on a slab with this coat. Chequy a chief vairée impaling. Argent on a bend sable between three cornish choughs ppr. two garbs saltireways or between 2 buckles Arg.

Hic jacet *Gulielmus Rawley* S.T. Docter
Vir *Gratÿs* et *Mufis* æquo charus
Serenifs Regibus Car. 1º et 2ᵈᵒ a Sacris
Dº Franc Verulamio Sacellanus primus atqe ultimo
Cujus Opera Summa cum fide edita et debent Literæ
Uxorem Habuit Barbaram ad latus Mariti pofitam
Jo. Wixted, Aldermanni nuper *Cantabr* filiam
Exea filium Sufcepit unicum, *Gulielmum*
In Cujus cineribus Salus haud parum latet
Ecclefiam hanc per annos 50 prudens adminiftravit
Tandem placide, ut vixit, in Domino obdormavit

Anno {Domini MDCLXVII Jun. 18
{ Ætat 79

Cory 1727. On a slab opposite to the last.

Hic requiefcit
IOHANNES CORY S. T. B.
Vir Pietate Infignis & Omni literarum genere
præclarus afsidºus Concionator et hujus ecclefiæ
Per Annos 39 Rector Indefefsus
Adhæret lateri Uxor amantifsima præ dolore
Obruta eheu! quam Sabito Sequuta est
Semel, Simul & Semper
Hic animan placide Deo reddidit Sept. 17
Anno Ætat: 76
Salut: 1727
Illa Nov. 23. Ætat 57.

Hall 1867. On a tablet

In memory of Thomas son of William Wilson
Hall and Mary Ann his wife. Midshipman of the
ship Louisa who died at Calcutta Aug. 31ˢᵗ 1867
aged 17 years.

Tinkler 1871. In the Chancel on a brass plate

Prope hunc locum sita sunt ossa
viri Reverendi Johannis Tinkler S.T.B.
collegii Corporis Christi in universitate Cantabrigiensi
per multos annos socii tutorisque,
et per annos prope xxviii
huius ecclesiæ rectoris.
natus est A.S. mdcccv mortuus A.S. mdccclxxi.

Masters 1798, 1759, 1764.

Sacred to the memory of Robert Masters B.D.
F.S.A. the faithful and diligent Rector of this
church 41 years; whose charity to the poor
rendered his life truly exemplary. He died July 5ᵗʰ
1798 aged 84 years.
William Masters Gent. ob. Oct. 15.1759 æt. 79.
Lucretia Richardson sister of Robert Masters.
William Masters Vicar of Waterbeach ob. 1791.
Constance wife of Robert Masters ob. Aug. 29.
1764 aged 33.

East Window, late 13ᵗʰ century, with man in the central light holding an Armilliary Sphere

LANDWADE

The Church, now actually in Suffolk, was built by Walter Cotton in 1445. It is dedicated to St. Nicholas and consists of Chancel, Nave, North and South Transepts, South Porch and a low embattled West Tower.

North Transept.

Inside South Porch.

Landwade Church as it is today.

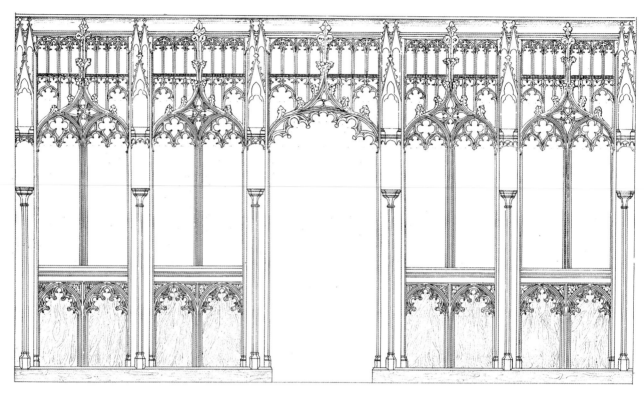

CHANCEL SCREEN

INNER DOOR S. PORCH.

TOMB S. TRANSEPT

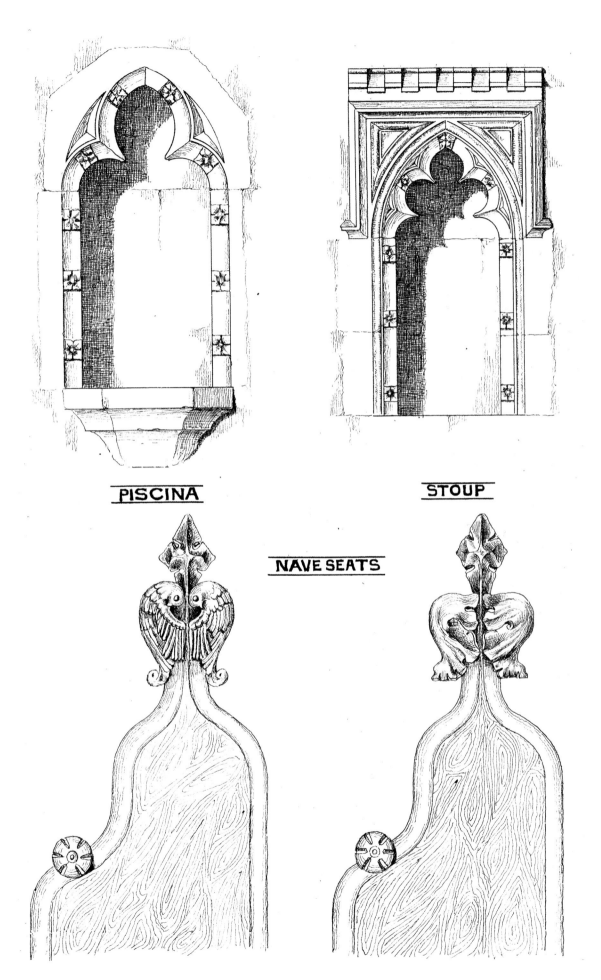

PISCINA

STOUP

NAVE SEATS

Coats of Arms in the Nave Windows

Coats of Arms in a Chancel Window

Here lieth
the Body of Sʳ Iohn Cotton
Knight, son and heire of Sʳ
Iohn Cotton, he married three wives, the
firſt Elizabeth daughter to Tʜomas Carrell
Esq. oꜰ Warneham in Suſsex, yͤ second Elizabeth
daughter to Sʳ Humphrʏ Bradbume Knight oꜰ
Bradbume in yͤ County of Darby, by whome he had
noe iſsue, yͤ third was Anne dauɢhter to Sʳ Richard
Houɢhton Baronett of Houɢhton towre in yͤ Countʏ
of Lancaſter, by whome he had iſsue, Iames, Iohn and
Katherine, which Iames & Katherine died in the life time
of there Father, he departed this life in yͤ 77 year
of his age Anno Donĩ 1620 & lieth in a Vault
on yͤ ſouth Ile of this Church made by himſelf.

Here Lieth the Body of Sʳ *IOHN COTTON*
Baronett Son of Sʳ *IOHN COTTON* he Married
Iane Hind daughter & Heire of Edward Hind
of Maᴅɪɴɢʟᴇʏ in this County Esqʳ he had
Iſsue by her 2 Sons & 2 daughters Iohn~
Thomas Iane & Anne of Which Iohn and
Iane Surviu'd them he died March · 25ᵗʰ : 1689
Ætatis Suæ 74·

Landwade Church.

Mon. Walter Cotton 1445.

Mon. Walter Cotton 1459.

Mon. Johanna Cotton (Sharpe) 1496.

Mon. Sir John Cotton 1593.

Mon. Sir John Cotton 1593. (Spencer.)

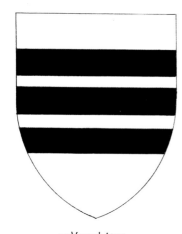

Houghton

Mon. Sir John Cotton 1620.

Cotton — Houghton

LONGSTANTON

The Church.

The Church of All Saints consists of Chancel, Nave, North and South Aisles, South Transept or Chapel, South Porch, West Tower and Spire.

<u>The Chancel</u> is wholly unrestored within, the walls whitewashed and the floor laid with bricks or slabs. The Sacrarium is tiled, there are two steps to the Altar, the rails of which are modern of poor Gothic design. The ceiling is plastered. On the south side is a Piscina with two basins, a triple Sedilia with cusped ogee arches, a Priests Door and two two-light Decorated windows, the westernmost enclosed by a broad recessed arch. On the north is one Decorated two-light window and a door. There are low side windows to north and south, that on the north of 14th century date with cusped arch, the bars remain. These are blocked and are only visible from the outside. The East Window is of five lights of curvilinear tracery much restored or rather renewed. Above the arch outside is a small Nitch. Inside there is a square locker or Aumbrey in the east wall. There are no remains of old stained glass in the Chancel.

<u>The Nave</u> consists of four bays with octagonal pillars and well moulded caps and bases. The arches display the double wave moulding. The roof is ceiled and framed with tie beams and braces. The seats are high old fashioned deal pews. At the west end is a gallery blocking up the Tower Arch, the Pulpit is deal. The pew on the south side nearest the Chancel has some good carved panels of Jacobean date. The Chancel Arch has octagonal caps and jambs: there are no Clerestory windows.

<u>The North Aisle</u> has three windows and a blocked up door on the north, a three-light window in the east wall (this has been renewed) and a two-light window in the west wall. The parapet is of red brick. In the east respond of the Nave Arcade is a Piscina and in the opposite angle on the north is a rough bracket. The seating is similar to that in the Nave. The roof is good, framed with moulded ties and braces. In the west, and westernmost windows on the north are fragments of stained glass.

Longstanton All Saints Church as it is today.

175

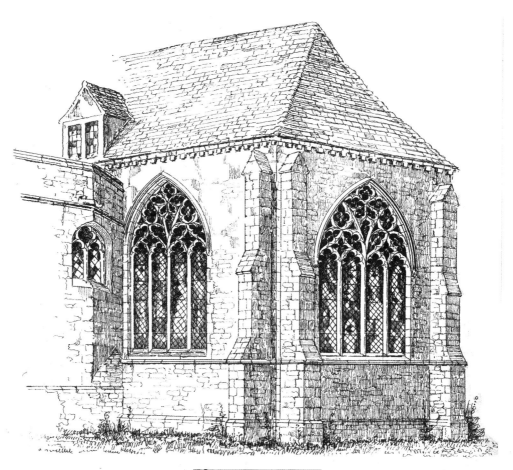

S. TRANSEPT

FONT

LONGSTANTON ALL SAINTS

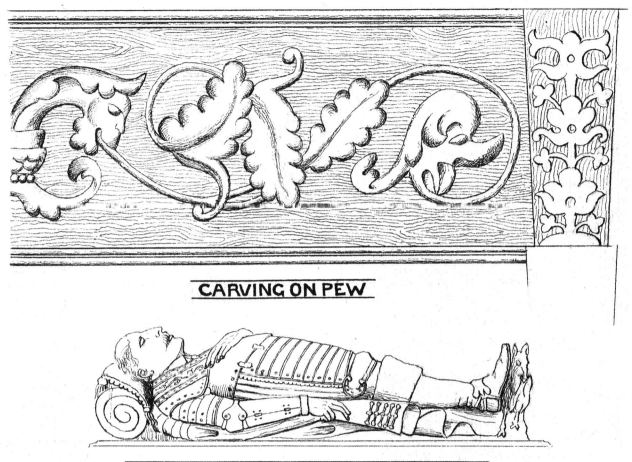

CARVING ON PEW

EFFIGY OF SIR THOMAS HATTON 1658

<u>The South Aisle</u> has seating and roof similar to the north. There are two three-light windows, beneath the sills of which runs a moulded string. The west end is raised a step on which stands the Font which is octagonal, with elaborately panelled sides and octagonal base coeval with the Church. At the east end of this Aisle is a Chapel arched off from the rest. Being narrower than the Aisle the wall is canted inwards instead of forming an angle, the cant contains a small two-light window some distance from the ground, an unusual arrangement. The arch opening into the Chapel finishes on the south wall with a carved head forming a corbel. There is one step down to the chapel in which there are monuments to the Hatton family. It is divided from the Nave by a portion of an old oak screen. On the south is a door leading to the blocked up Transept now used as a mortuary, above it is painted "Sepulchrum 1770" (since opened out, see below). This Transept has good buttresses with gabled heads and richly traceried Decorated windows of four lights, these are all blocked. The roof is hipped and finished with a modern cornice of red brick. This form of roof although unusual in a Transept is probably original for the south window and buttresses finish well below the cornice. In the roof just above the Aisle is a modern dormer window.

<u>The Tower</u> and Spire are Perpendicular of poor character, the West Window of two lights. On each side of the arch are remains of painting in red and black.

<u>Belfry.</u> There are three bells each with this inscription. "Miles Graye me fecit 1637."

Notes.

The Church underwent restoration in 1886 - 88 and 1891 when the partition separating the South Transept from the Aisle was removed and the windows opened out and glazed. This exposed a canopied Nitch in the south-east angle. During the restoration also the mean fittings of Nave and Chancel were replaced by the present seating and floors relaid.

Monument to Sir Thos. Hatton 1658

Tablet to Sir Thos Hatton 1787

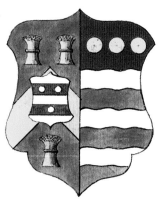

Tablet to Sir Thos Hatton 1735

Tablet to Sir Thos. Dingley Hatton 1812.

There is a chest of somewhat late date. On the south side of the Church remains the base of the Churchyard Cross.

Inscriptons.

The monuments excepting those of the Hatton family are of little interest.

In the Chancel on the north a small black slab with inscription "Ann Hatton". On the south a similar slab.

MRS ANNA BAILLIE
RELICT OF
HUGH BAILLIE ESQRE
OF MONKTON
IN AIRSHIRE, N. B.
DIED 2d OF AUGUST 1818.

On the south wall is a large marble tablet surmounted by this coat. Azure a chevron between 3 garbs or. Crest. An antelope trippant or. (Hatton)

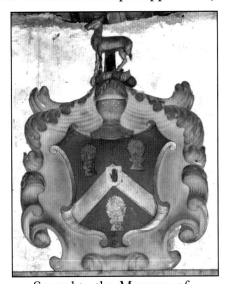

Sacred to the Memory of
ANN HATTON
Daughter of GEORGE STEAD Citizen of London,
Twenty fix Years the affectionate Wife
of the Reverd CHRIS: HATTON
She died July 6th 1770
in the 50th Year of her Age,
after a long and Painful Illnefs
which She bore with an
Exemplary Patience and Refignation
and died as much lamented
as fhe was beloved when living.

On another large tablet of marble are these arms and inscription. Hatton as above with an escutcheon of pretence. Argent 2 bars gules charged with 3 plates 2 and 1 (Orlebar) impaling. Barry wavy of 6 argent and azure on a chief gules 3 bezants. (Astrey).

Underneath ly the Bodies
of
Sr THOMAS HATTON of this Place Bartt.
Who departed this Life *Iune* 22d 1733,
In the *59*th Year of his Age
And of
His first Wife ELIZABETH only Daughter & Heir
of COOPER ORLEBAR of *Henwick*
In the *County* of *Bedford* Esqr.
To whofe Memory
HENRIETTA HATTON his Relict and Executrix
Daughter of Sr IAMES ASTRY of *Harlington*
Woodend in the *County of Bedford* Knit.
Erected this Monument
As a small Teftimony of her great Regard
And Affection for them both;
Defiring to be Buried
In the fame Grave with them.

In the Chapel at the east end of the South Aisle is a fine monument with two life size recumbent figures carved in alabaster of Sir Thomas Hatton and Lady Mary Hatton. On the side of the Baronet are small figures of his sons, on that of the Lady of her daughters. These are all detached and simply placed on the marble base of the monument. The Baronet is in armour, his legs encased in high boots, bare headed his left hand on his breast, his feet resting against an antelope, the feet of his Lady rest against a dog. Above them against the east wall of the Aisle rises an elaborate Corinthian canopy surmounted by the Hatton arms and crest. Immediately above the effigies is this coat. Hatton as above empaling. Sable a bend (engrailed) between 6 billets argent (Allington).

Monument to Sir Thomas Hatton and Lady Mary Hatton

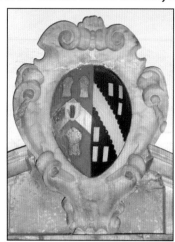

In the Vault under this Monument lieth buried
the Body of
Sir THOMAS HATTON Kn^t and Baronet, Lord of
this Mannor:
who Married Mary the Daughter of Sir Giles
Allington of Horſeheath in the County of Cambridge
Kn^t. by whom he had Iſſue, ſeven Sons, and four
Daughters: but left Surviving at
his Death only three Sons Viz: Thomas, John,
and Chriſtopher; and three Daughters, Viz:

Elizabeth, Mary, and Jane. He put on
Immortality the 23^d of September 1658,
Aged 75 Years. For whoſe pious Memory, Mary
his loving Wife Erected
this Monument, and Intendeth to be here alſo Buried.

Reddidit illuſtrem Natura, Academia doctum,
Curia facundum, Lex juſtum, Templa beatum
Jacobi Miles, Caroli Baronnettus utriq̃
Et Comus et Famulus: gratus Famuluſq̃ Mariæ
Anglia Dynaſten; Legatum Gallia novit
Hauſit Stantoniæ Lucem primam atq̃ ſupremam.
Siste, Viator, et tace; loquuntur Marmora
Illuſtris Virginis, Conjugis, et viduæ Decus
Allingtoniam Virgo decoravit Proſapiam,
Hattoniam Conjux utramq̃ vidua.
Urbana ſine Fuco; benefica, nec glorioſa
Non Fanatica, non religioſa, aſt ſincere pia.
Prænobilem hane Dominam
Invida rapuit Climactera.

*This Monument was Cleaned and Repaired by
Sir THOMAS HATTON Baronet 1770.*

Sacred to the Name & Memory
of Sir Thomas Hatton Baronet
who, defpifing the Follies of his Age,
cultivated amidft a multitude of Virtues,
every Sentiment of Humanity.
His charities were rather felt than known;
Whofe opennefs of Temper & Benevolence of
Difpofition procured him general Veneration.
He died on the 7th Day of Novr. 1787
Aged 60.

In grateful teftimony of the Virtues
he pofsefsed, this Monument was erected
to his Memory, by his Surviving & fincerely
afflicted Lady.

2. With the arms of Hatton and escutcheon of
pretence as above on a lozenge.

Sacred to the Memory of
Dame HARRIOT HATTON,
Relict of the late Sir THOMAS HATTON Bart.
of whom it may be said without Flattery that
she was a bright Example of every Virtue for
future Ages to follow, she was eminent for Piety
& Charity. Her Humility & Sweetnefs of Manners
endeared her to all her Acquaintance, particularly
to he disconsolate Family, who must ever feel the
Lofs of her kind Affections; but tho' they mourn,
it is not without Hope, for that patient Resignation,
& heavenly Calmnefs of Mind, which ever attended,
& never to the last forsook her, must have procur'd
a Place for her in that blefsed Kingdom, where
every Virtue meets its just Reward.
She died March 20th 1795,
Aged 60 Years.

This Monument is erected by her afflicted Family
in Gratitude for her Affection & Kindnefs.

On the south wall of the same Chapel are three
tablets.

1. Surmounted by the arms of Hatton with an
escutcheon of pretence. Quarterly 1 and 4 gules a
fess between 3 dolphins embowed or. 2 and 3
Azure an eagle displayed argent.

3. With the arms of Hatton impaling quarterly 1
and 4 Hatton. 2 and 3 quarterly 1 and 4 gules a
fess between three dolphins or. 2 and 3 Azure an
eagle displayed argent.

In this Vault are deposited
in the Hope of a joyful Resurrection,
the Remains of
Sir THOMAS DINGLEY HATTON, Baronet
who died unmarried Septr. 19th 1812,
Aged 41 Years.

The many excellent Qualities of his Heart
were eminently displayed
by his
Universal Benevolence,
which was
more particularly exercised in his
Acts of Charity to those around him;
He being always the kind
& constant Benefactor to the Poor.
He lived
Beloved and respected
and died
Regretted & lamented
by
all who knew him.

There are two hatchments on the south wall of this Chapel.
1. Hatton impaling quarterly 1 and 4 Hatton, 2 and 3 quarterly 1 and 4 gules a fess between three dolphins or. 2 & 3 Azure an eagle displayed argent.
2. Quarterly 1 and 4 Hatton, 2 quarterly 1 Azure an eagle displayed argent . . . 2 and 3 Or three piles gules . . . 4 Argent a lion rampant azure.
3. Quarterly 1 or a lion rampant within a double tressure flory counter flory gules. 2 & 3. Gules a fess between three dolphins embowed or.
4. Azure a cross flory between 4 martlets or.

On the wall of the South Aisle this tablet.

Oppofite this Place lies the Body of
WILLIAM the Son of
CUPISS & MARY MARKHAM
who died Jany 23^d 1782 Aged 26 Years.

Affliction fore long Time he bore,
Phyficians were in Vain ;
'Till God Above in tender Love,
Reliev'd him of his Pain.

In the North Aisle a tablet.

Oppofite this Place
Lieth the Body of
RICHARD the Son of
THOMAS & MARY WALLIS,
who departed this life Decr y^e 4th. 1767
Aged 23 Years.

Young Men prepare yourfelves to die,
For life is fhort and Death is Nigh:

Coats in the South Aisle Windows

Prepare yourfelves make no Delay,
For I in my prime was fnatch'd away.

On a stone slab by the North Door.

Oppofite this Place
Lieth the Body of
THOMAS WALLIS
who died June y^e 2^d 1773
Aged 71 Years
Also MARY WALLIS
Wife of the Above THOMAS WALLIS
she died Feby. the 13th 1776,
Aged 64 Years.

Above the North Door.

Opposite this Place lyeth the Body
of MARY the Wife of JOHN DAINTREE
(and Daughter of THOMAS & MARY WALLIS)
who died Sept. 30, 1769.
Aged 29 Years
Alfo her Daughter aged 2 Months.

There are no inscriptions in the Nave, but by the Chancel Arch is a large black marble slab, with the matrix of a brass.

Names and assessments in Lay Subsidies
132.6. Longa Stanton

Name	s	d
De Joha de Chene	iijs	vid
” Johe Stevene		xvjd
” Rico Sigar		xiijd
” Margia Lamas		xviijd
” Johe Lamas	ijs	vjd
” Johe Gilberd		xvd
” Rado Syre		xiijd
” Alic ad Crucem		xijd
” Matild de Lolleworth	ijs	vjd
” Willo Besson		xiijd
” Deyetaup		xijd
” Willo Plante		xviijd
” Johe de Torhm		xijd
” Robto Double		xiijd
” Willo Cole	iiijs	vjd
” Robto Abbot		xiijd
” Willo Tom		xijd
” Johe Reyd		xiijd
” Johe Reyd	ijs	
” Willo Bec		viijd
” Willo Gilberd	iijs	
” Johe Kyng		xiijd
” Henr Baroun	iiijs	ijd
” Ad Yester		xvjd
” Galfro Geffrey		xiijd
” Stepho Squier		xxd
” Johe Beche	ijs	vjd
” Alicia Gilberd	ijs	vjd
” Johe Michelhowe	iiijs	
” Alic Vrlic	ijs	vjd
” Rico Vrne		xviijd
” Willo ad Eccam		viijd
” Hugon Capllo		xixd
” Johe Laur	iijs	
” Nicho Cundy		xijd
” Willo fil Hugon		xijd
” Johe Wysch		xd
” Robto Sodecomp	ijs	xjd
” Robto Gilberd	iiijs	
” Alicia Lentelowe		xijd
” Johe Gibbe		viijd
” Simon de Hesyghm	iiijs	
” Simon Berford		xviijd
” Johe de Chene	ijs	ixd
” Johe Adam		xiijd
” Lin Wyting		xvjd
” Johe Wente	ijs	
” Robto Wys		xiijd
” Robto Pigate	iijs	vjd
” Simon Salman		xiiijd
” Johe Fox		xjd
” Willo Geffrey		xviijd
” Johe Page	iiijs	
” Galfro Baroun		xviijd
” Joha de Cam	iijs	vjd
” Willo Wente		viijd
” Johe Sodecomp		xijd
” Simon Kyng		xviijd
” Willo Harlewen	ijs	
” Johe Stel		xvd
” Henr Longe		xijd
” Rico Capoun	ijs	vjd
” Johe Walweyn	vs	jd
” Willo Spend		vijd
” Rico Herford		xd
” Henr Sodecomp		vjd
” Nicho Vndyrbyl		vjd
” Willo Shate		vjd
” Rogo Lord		viijd
” Johe Lord		viijd
” Johe Lucas		viijd
Sum vjli	iijs	vijd

The number of names and the large amount assessed shews this to have been a village of some importances but it includes both parishes.

Fines Relating to Longstanton.

1287 16th Edward I.
William fil' Andre de Longestaunton and Agnes his wife v. Albreda widow of William de Chenney in Longestaunton.

1287 16th Edward I.
Robert fil' Richard de Flyxthorp v. John fil' Robert de Grenlay whom Hugh de Grenlay calls to warrant in Longastaunton & Hokerton.

1292 21st Edward I.
John le Graunt of Bokesworth and Emma his wife v. Henry de Cheyny of Longa Staunton in Bronne.

1297 26th Edward I.
Robert fil' Constance de Swavesey and Margaret his wife and John son of the said John v. John Freysel of Longstanton and Matilda his wife.

1297 26th Edward I.
Reginald le Bobier and Katherine his wife v. John Freysel of Longa Stanton and Matilda his wife in Swavseye.

1297 26th Edward I.
Robert fil' Constance of Swaveseye v. John Freysel in Swaveseye.

1298   27th Edward I.
Nicholas le Fevere v. Robert de Westwyk of Longa Stanton and Mageria his wife in Longstanton.

1314   8th Edward II.
Margaret de Rothyngge v. John de Cheny of Longa Stanton in Long Stanton.

1315   9th Edward II.
John de Kaam and Joan his wife v. William le Longe of the Manor of Long Staunton.

1330 - 1 5th Edward III.
Simon fil' John de Brunne v. William de Haukedon vicar of Waterbeche in Long Staunton and Wyvelingham.

1336 - 7 11th Edward III.
William fil' Nicholas de Cheyney and Joan v. John de Sobbury and Walter Waleys in Lange Staunton.

1342 - 3 17th Edward III.
Thomas de Heslarton Knight and Alice his wife and John parson of the church of Shelford Parva v. Thomas fil' Robert de Heslarton of the manors of Longstanton &c (many others mentioned).

1344 - 5 9th Edward III.
John Sygar of Longa Stanton v. John Chauntour of Maddyngle & wife in long Stanton.

1347 - 8 22nd Edward III.
John de Granteceste and Thomas parson of the church on Esthattle v. John Walewayn chivaler of the manor of Longstanton.

1361 - 2 36th Edward III.
Robert de Thorp v. Dedricus de Somerton and Amia his wife of the manors of Histon Lolleworth and Longa Stanton.

1364 - 5 39th Edward III.
William de Blonnham v. Robert Harsent of Longa Stanton and wife in L. Stanton.

1364-5 39th Edward III.
John Cheynee of Longa Stanton v. John Pariz of Melreth and Agnes his wife in Longstanton.

1377   7th Richard II.
Stephen Gamon capell' and others v. John Dengayn Knight of the manor of Walewyns in Longestanton.

1377   7th Richard II.
John la Warre and others v. William de Thorpe chivaler of the manors of Histon Lolleworth and Long Stanton.

1403   5th Henry IV.
John de Stynecle and others v. John Cheyne of Longstanton and Margery his wife in Longstanton.

1440   19th Henry VI.
John Pulter v. Thomas Grenley and Sibilla his wife of the manor called Longstanton Greneleys manor.

The following under the name of Stanton only probably relate to these parishes.

1202   4th John.
Alan de Feugieres v. John fil' William in Stanton and Lollesworth.

1227   12th Henry III.
William fil' Robert v. Stephen le Bloy and Avicia his wife in Stanton.

1227   12th Henry III.
William Alard v. Stephen le Bloy and Avicia his wife in Stanton.

1231   16th Henry III.
Spephen le Bloy and Avicia his wife v. Roger de Balham and Felicia his wife in Stanton.

1231   16th Henry III.
Harris le Gous and Quenina (?) his wife v. William Pigate and Agnes his wife in Stanton.

1239   24th Henry III.
Henry de Colevill and Matilda his wife.

1246   31st Henry III.
Thomas de Wyvill v. William de Chedney in Stanton.

1250   35th Henry III.
William de Chenne (Cheney) v. Henry de Colville and Matilda his wife in Staunton.

1252   37th Henry III.
Adam fil' Adam le Butiller v. Margaret widow of John de Oure in Staunton.

1252   37th Henry III.
Henry de Colevill v. Henry de Swavesey in Swavesey Stanton &c.

1262   47th Henry III.
Roger de Touny v. John Maunsel by Thomas de London of advowson of the church of All Saints of Staunton.

1282   11th Edward I.
Thomas fil' Ralph de Balesham v. William Giffard and Katerina his wife in Stanton and elsewhere.

1369 - 70 44th Edward III.
John Knyvet and Alianora his wife v. William le Man of Stanton & Elena his wife in Fendrayton.

1373 - 4 48th Edward III.
William Blown of Stanton and others v. Geoffrey Porter of Milton and Alice his wife in Milton.

Holford of Longstanton

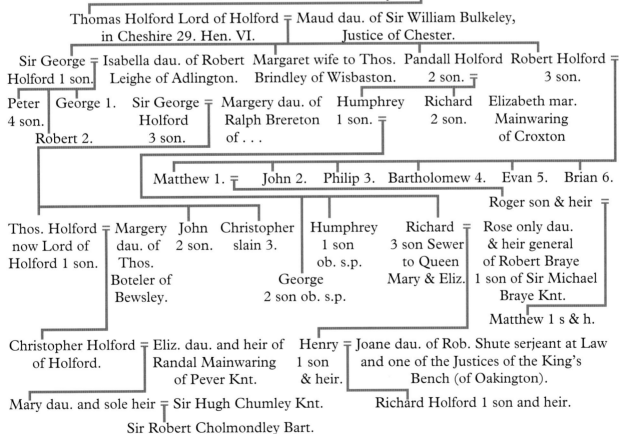

William de Holford 1. Henry VI

Thomas Holford Lord of Holford = Maud dau. of Sir William Bulkeley,
in Cheshire 29. Hen. VI.   Justice of Chester.

Sir George = Isabella dau. of Robert   Margaret wife to Thos.   Pandall Holford   Robert Holford =
Holford 1 son.   Leighe of Adlington.   Brindley of Wisbaston.   2 son. =   3 son.

Peter   George 1.   Sir George = Margery dau. of   Humphrey   Richard   Elizabeth mar.
4 son.   Holford   Ralph Brereton   1 son. =   2 son.   Mainwaring
    Robert 2.   3 son.   of . . .   of Croxton

Matthew 1. =   John 2.   Philip 3.   Bartholomew 4.   Evan 5.   Brian 6.

Roger son & heir =

Thos. Holford = Margery   John   Christopher   Humphrey   Richard =   Rose only dau.
now Lord of   dau. of   2 son.   slain 3.   1 son   3 son Sewer   & heir general
Holford 1 son.   Thos.   ob. s.p.   to Queen   of Robert Braye
              Boteler of   George   Mary & Eliz.   1 son of Sir Michael
              Bewsley.   2 son ob. s.p.   Braye Knt.

Matthew 1 s & h.

Christopher Holford = Eliz. dau. and heir of   Henry = Joane dau. of Rob. Shute serjeant at Law
of Holford.   Randal Mainwaring   1 son   and one of the Justices of the King's
                of Pever Knt.   & heir.   Bench (of Oakington).

Mary dau. and sole heir = Sir Hugh Chumley Knt.   Richard Holford 1 son and heir.

Sir Robert Cholmondley Bart.

LONGSTANTON
St. Michael

St. Michael's Church.

The Church of St. Michael is now redundant. Bell does not give any notes about this.

CHURCH FROM S.W.

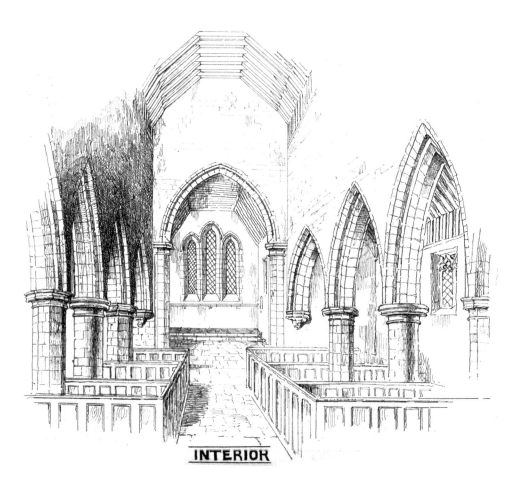

INTERIOR

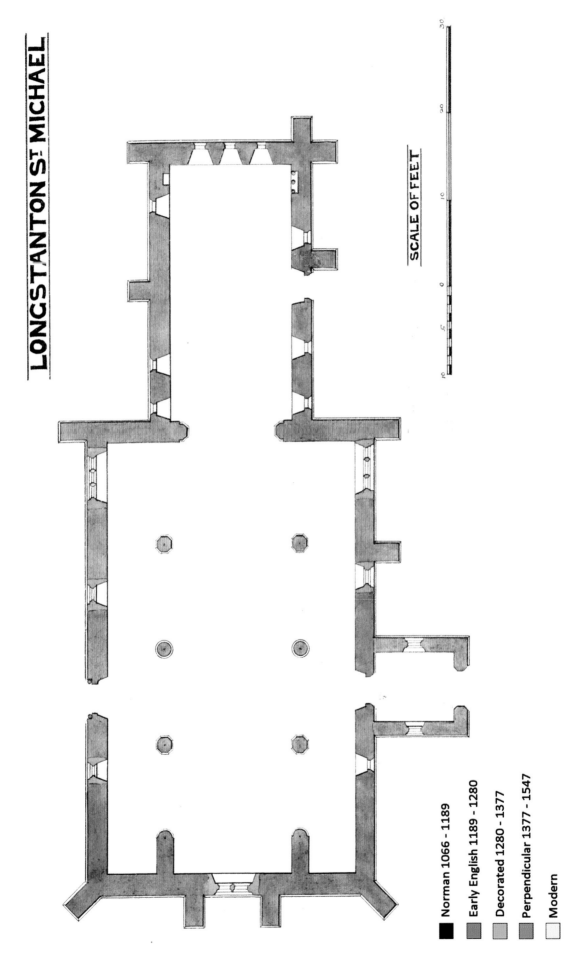

LONGSTANTON ST MICHAEL

SCALE OF FEET

Norman 1066 - 1189

Early English 1189 - 1280

Decorated 1280 - 1377

Perpendicular 1377 - 1547

Modern

LONGSTANTON S⸆ MICHAEL.

NAVE ARCADE

PISCINA

Burgogne of Longstanton

Arms Quarterly.   1. Burgogne.   2. Perient.   3.   4.   5.   6. Freysell.
As above in Visitations 1575. 1619 (Cole)

Bartholomew de Burgoine of Bokesworth temp. Edwd. III ⊤

Bartholomew Burgoine of Bokesworth ⊤ Anne dau. and heir of John Fresille

John Burgoine 22. Richard II ⊤ . . . dau. of Roger Harleston of Essex.

John Burgoine ⊤ . . dau. of Thomas Peyton   Richard 1 ob. s.p.   John 3 ob. s.p.   William 4 ob. s.p.
of Cambridgeshire

Alice dau. of . . Tay 2 wife ⊤ Thomas Burgogne 2 son & heir = Isabelle dau. of . . . . 1 wife.
of Longstanton.

Thomas Burgogne 1 son & heir ⊤ Elizabeth dau. of . . Stafferton (of Strode Hall Co. Berks.)

Thomas Burgogne ⊤   John 2   Christopher Burgogne 4 son ⊤ Thomasine dau. of Robert Freville
1 son & heir   William 3   of Longstanton Co. Cantabr.   of Shelford Co. Cantab.

Thomas 1 son   Thomazine mar.   Godfrey   George Burgoyne ⊤ Dorothy dau.   Mary mar. Anstey
& heir ob. s.p.   Robert Shute   2 son.   of Quickwood in   & coheir of
Clothall Herts.   Thos. Perient.   Alice mar. John
Cotton.

Elizabeth mar. 1 Willm Rudston

John 6   Edward 4   Thos. Burgoyne ⊤ Catherine dau. of Lord   Ralph 7   Charles 9
Oliver 5   William 3   of Longstanton   Chilcock Pawlett   Francis 8

Mary   George Burgoyne of ⊤ Elizabeth dau.   Arthur living at   Elizabeth ux. Henry
Spawfford in Co.   of . . . Cheyney   Spawfford   Blacksham of London
Yorks 1638.   unmar. an. 1638

Frances ux. Thos. Walton
of Shapwick Co. Som.

Peter Burgoyne about   Will'm Burgoyne apprentice in London
19 years old in   with Mr German Honeychurch,
Aug. 1638.   Marchaunt Aug. 1638.

Transcribed from the Cole M.S.S. This pedigree differs in some respects from that in the Visitations
1575.1619 printed by the Harleian Society in which another generation is given and included here.

LONGSTANTON St MARY

NAVE ARCADE

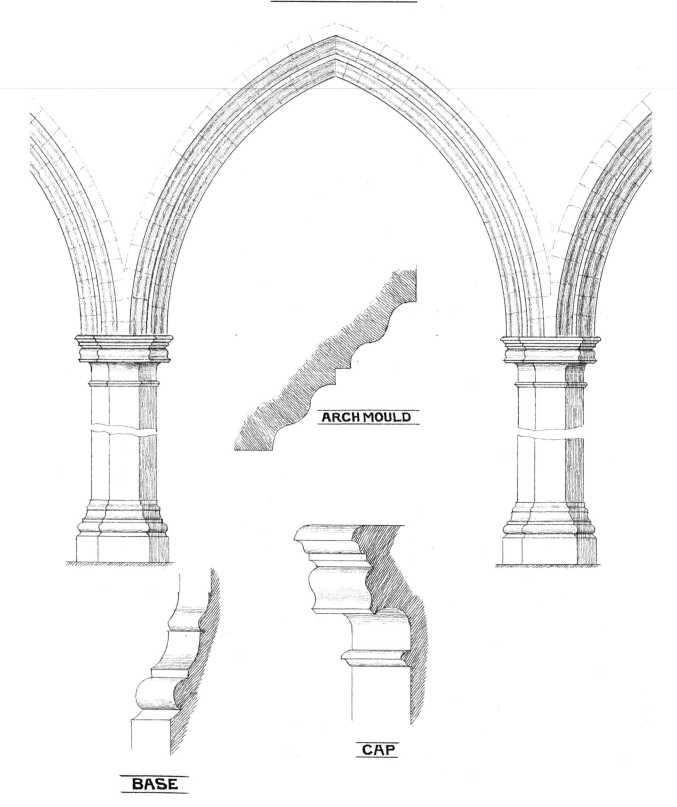

ARCH MOULD

CAP

BASE

This drawing is incorrectly labelled but is believed to be from St. Mary and All Saints Church, Willingham

MADINGLEY

11 May 1883.

The Church.

The Church is dedicated to St. Mary Magdalene and consists of Chancel, Nave, North Aisle, North and South Porches and West Tower with Spire.

The Chancel was rebuilt a year or two ago (1876) the old materials being reused. The East Window is an Early English triplet with plain splayed jambs on the inside of modern date. On the north side are two lancets, on the south one lancet and a two-light Decorated window. The roof is new, the floor tiled. The altar rails are of good Jacobean character: the choir stalls are new, plain but good. There are some interesting remains of old stained glass: the lancet on the south has three figures, the two-light window contains a figure of St. John and beneath "Deo honor et gloria in secula." Also the Crucifixion and some medallion patterns.

The Nave is of 14th century date. There are five arches on the north side resting on clustered columns of four large and four small shafts. The Clerestory windows are two-light Perpendicular. In the south wall are two original Decorated windows with segmental pointed arches one of three lights with flowing tracery. There are two other two-light windows of Perpendicular date. The door is 14th century and has floriated hinges, the Porch of nondescript character. At the south-west angle of the Nave roof the coping has masks cut in the hollow of the springer. In one of the windows in the south wall are two very good medallions of 18th century date in bistre and yellow.

The Font is Norman, square with angle shafts, the bowl ornamented with shallow sculpture. It was brought from the now destroyed Church of St. Etheldreda, Histon, but for many years stood in the grounds of Madingley Hall and was reinstated in the Church about the year 1906 when the Hall was restored.

The North Aisle is of 14th century date. It has two windows in the north wall, the west window is of three lights, poor Perpendicular, the door is Decorated and well moulded, the Porch Perpendicular, the Aisle parapet is embattled.

The Tower is unbuttressed rising in three stages finished with a small octagonal spire. The Belfry windows and West Window are of two lights and

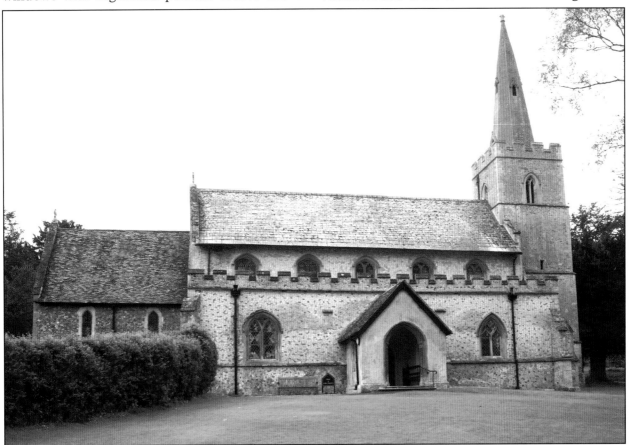

Madingley Church as it is today.

The Norman Font

of similar character, the whole of 14ᵗʰ century date.

Bells. In the Belfry are three bells with the following inscriptions.
1. Preceeded by an initial cross and with a stamp of three roundells in pale between each word "Dicor ⁞ Ego ⁞ Thomas ⁞ Laus ⁞ est ⁞ Xri ⁞ sonus ⁞ omas." A peculiar inscription translated "My name is Thomas and I can Sound forth the praise of Christ O man."
2 and 3. "T. Tymbs and R. Stephens, C. W. Tho. Newman made me 1723."

In 1881, there were preserved in the Tower a series of six paintings measuring 3 feet by 2 feet each within a moulded frame. They represented St. Andrew, St. John, St. Jude, St. Paul, St. Peter and St. James. They were probably of 18ᵗʰ century date and coarsely painted, and may formerly have been part of a Chancel Screen.

In the churchyard are some fine old yew trees.

Inscriptions.
These are fairly numerous. In the Chancel on the north wall are two tablets.
1. In white marble surmounted by a sculptured column and beak of a ship.

SACRED TO THE MEMORY OF
COMMANDER CHARLES COTTON R.N.
WHO DIED ON BOARD H.M.S. ZEBRA IN THE
MEDITERRANEAN ON THE ELEVENTH OF FEBRUARY
1828,
IN THE TWENTY-FIFTH YEAR OF HIS AGE,
AND WAS INTERRED NEAR THE PRACTIQUE CHURCH
AT MALTA, WHERE A MONUMENT WAS ERECTED BY
HIS OFFICERS AND MEN ATTESTS, WITH THEIR OWN
GRIEF THEIR DEEP SENSE OF HIS LOSS TO THE SERVICE.
HE WAS THE YOUNGEST SON OF ADMIRAL SIR
CHARLES COTTON BARᵀ
AND HAVING EMBRACED HIS FATHERS PROFESSION
HE DISPLAYED THAT ZEAL AND TALENT
WHICH SECURED TO HIM THE HIGH APPROBATION
OF HIS COMMANDER IN CHIEF AND
THE CONFIDENCE OF THOSE WHO SERVED WITH HIM.

HIS DEATH WAS OCCASIONED BY A FEVER
RESULTING FROM THE FATIGUES OF AN ARDUOUS
SERVICE,
IN THE COURSE OF WHICH HE WAS EMINENTLY
CONSPICUOUS IN RESCUING THE CREW OF H.M.S.
CAMBRIAN
OFF CARABUSA IN THE ISLAND OF CANDIA.

TO HIS AMIABLE QUALITIES IN PRIVATE LIFE, TO THE
GENUINE GOODNESS OF HIS HEART, AND THE
FRANKNESS OF HIS DISPOSITION, THE
AFFECTIONATE REGRET OF MANY FRIENDS, AND
DEEP AND LASTING
SORROW OF HIS NEARER CONNECTIONS, BEAR
AMPLE TESTIMONY : NOR DOES RELIGION
CONDEMN THEIR GRIEF,
WHILE SHE TEACHES THEM NOT TO "SORROW AS
MEN WITHOUT HOPE," AND POINTS TO A REUNION
IN A WORLD WHERE DEATH AND TEARS AND
SEPARATION SHALL BE NO MORE.

THIS MONUMENT IS ERECTED BY HIS AFFLICTED
MOTHER.

2. A tablet in white marble surmounted by sculpture signed "Flaxman R. A. Sculptor."

SACRED TO THE MEMORY OF SIR CHARLES
COTTON BART
ADMIRAL OF THE WHITE, AND COMMANDER IN
CHIEF OF THE CHANNEL FLEET.
AT AN EARLY PERIOD OF LIFE HE ENTERED INTO
THE SERVICE OF HIS COUNTRY.
FROM THE ACTIVE AND ALMOST INCESSANT
OCCUPATIONS OF WHICH
NEITHER THE SUBSEQUENT POSESSION OF AN
AMPLE FORTUNE NOR THE STILL
MORE POWERFUL TIES OF DOMESTIC AND LOCAL
ATTACHMENT
WERE SUFFICIENT TO WITHDRAW HIM.
TO THE QUALITIES OF A DISTINGUISHED OFFICER
HE ADDED THE VIRTUES
WHICH MOST WARMLY ENDEAR THE PRIVATE
CHARACTER.
IN THE MIDST OF HEALTH AND JUSTLY ACQUIRED
HONOURS,
IN THE STRENUOUS DISCHARGE OF THE DUTIES OF
THE HIGHEST NAVAL COMMAND
HE WAS SUDDENLY SUMMONED BY THE DECREES
OF PROVIDENCE!

THE POIGNANT DISTRESS OF THOSE TO WHOM HE
WAS MOST DEAR IT WOULD BE
A VAIN ATTEMPT TO RECORD :
THE MORE TEMPERED, YET LIVELY REGRET OF AN
EXTENSIVE CIRCLE OF FRIENDS
WILL LONG ATTEST THE UNAFFECTED
BENEVOLENCE, THE PROBITY, THE
CANDOUR AND THE DISINTERESTED SPIRIT, WHICH
HAD SO JUSTLY SECURED
THEIR ESTEEM AND ADMIRATION.
HE DIED ON THE 23D FEBRUARY 1812, AGED 58 YEARS.
HIS REMAINS ARE DEPOSITED WITH THOSE OF HIS
ANCESTORS IN THE FAMILY VAULT
AT LANDWADE, WHILE THIS MEMORIAL IS PLACED
AMIDST THE SCENES
WHICH HE MOST LOVED AND CHERISHED WHEN
LIVING.
HE MARRIED FEBRUARY THE 24TH 1788,
PHILADELPHIA, DAUGHTER OF
SIR JOSHUA ROWLEY BARᵀ, VICE ADMIRAL OF THE
WHITE
BY WHOM HE HAS LEFT TWO SONS SAINT VINCENT
AND CHARLES
AND TWO DAUGHTERS PHILADELPHIA LETITIA AND
MARIA SUSANNA.

Below is this coat of ten quarterings.

1. Sable a chevron between three griffons heads erased argent (Cotton).
2. Argent a fess engrailed gules in chief a rose of the last.
3. Ermine on a chief azure two mullets or.
4. Gules a chevron between three pears or.
5. Argent three eagles heads erased sable beaked gules within a bordure engrailed of the second.
6. Sable a cinquefoil within an orle of eight martlets argent.
7. Azure three eagles displayed a canton ermine.
8. Ermine on a bend gules three eagles displayed or.
9. Argent on a chevron gules between three goats heads erased azure collared and horned or three lozenges of the last.
10. Argent on a chevron gules three swans of the field beaked and footed or on a canton gules a rose argent.

Crest. A griffons head argent beaked or on a torse sable and argent.

On the north side of the Chancel within the rails is a small marble tablet.

SACRED TO THE MEMORY
OF JOHN HYNDE COTTON, ELDEST SON
OF SIR CHARLES COTTON, BARᵀ & PHILADELPHIA,
HIS WIFE
WHO DIED MARCH 27TH 1807.
COULD THE MOST PLEASING GIFTS OF NATURE
HAVE ARRESTED THE HAND OF DEATH,
THIS STONE HAD NOT RECORDED AN IMMATURE
DESTINY
OF EIGHT YEARS AND NINE MONTHS.
YET LET NOT AFFECTION LAMENT TOO DEEPLY :
UPON THE FAIREST PROSPECTS OF EARTHLY
HAPPINESS
ATTEND UNCERTAINTY AND MISCHANCE ;
WHILST HE EVEN IN THE MORNING OF LIFE, HAS
SECURED
AN ENTRANCE INTO THE MANSIONS OF HEAVENLY
BLISS.

A large tomb of alabaster and black marble stands against the north wall, upon it is a reclining figure life size and this inscription surmounted by the following coat. Argent on a chevron gules between three goats heads erased azure collared and horned or three lozenges of the laste (Hinde) impaling.

Sable three griffons heads erased argent (Cotton).

Here lyes ẙ Body of Dame IANE COTTON
ſole-Daughter & *Heireſs* of EDWᴰ HINDE *Esqᵣ*
of this Pariſh & Relict
of Sʳ IOHN COTTON Barᵗ.
She departed this Life Oct. 13ᵗʰ 1692
in the 62ᴰ year of her Age.

Sʳ IOHN dyed March. 25ᵗʰ 1689,
in the 74ᵗʰ year of his Age,
& was buryed amongſt his Anceſtors
in ẙ Vault at Lanwade in this County.

They had Iſsue
IOHN, THOMAS, IANE & ANNE.
THOMAS & ANNE dyed young.
IOHN & IANE surviv'd *Them*.

This has been the burying place of the Hindes for many ages.

On a small alabaster monument on the north wall with the figure of an infant between two angels surmounted by a crown.

AFFERTE ROSAS VIRGINEI CHORI SPARGITE
VIOLAS SIC SIC
ORNATE TVMVLVM, CELEBRATE FUNUS
TRIVMPHALI POMPA,
NEC IN CASTIS PROFANENTVR LACHRIMIS
FAVILLÆ SACRÆ
VIRGINIS, QVAM LVX VNA VIDIT NATAM,
EXTINCTAM,
ET MOX LVCE LVCIDIOREM, ET IN EADEM FERE, HORA
SPIRANTE ANIMAM DEO RESPIRAVIT,
EXVLTANS VIRGO ET GRATE RETRIBVIT
CREATORI QVAM DEDIT.

Within the Altar rails are five slabs.

1.   Here lieth the Body of
        ANN ẙ Wife of TIMOTHY
        TIMBS who was Born at
        Coats in Stafford-Shire &
        died Dec. yᵉ 26th 1734
        Aged 82.

2.   Here lieth the Body of
        Timothy Tymbs
        who was Born at
        Great Yarmouth
        in Norfolk and he died . . . .
        (inscription defaced.)

He was Churchwarden in 1723. See inscription on bell.

3.   VXORIS AMANTISSIMÆ, MATRIS INDVL=
        GENTISSIMÆ, FÆMINÆ PIJSSIMÆ AGNETIS
        STEWKELEY ADVMBRATVR HIC CINIS :
        QVÆ POST ANNOS TRIGINTA NON INFÆ=
        LICITER PERACTOS BEATIORI SPE
        PRÆGNANS PVERPERIO DIS=
        CASSIT 15º DIE AVG :
        1641.

4.   Here Lyeth ẙ body of
        ANNE, Daughter of
        JOHN STEWKELEY Eſq
        & Relict of HUGH GOVE Eſq
        of Cheſingbury in Wiltſhire
        She died Aprill ẙ 24th 1707

        This Stone was ordered by her
        Brother WILLIAM STEWKLEY Esq
        Ætatis Sue 73.

5.   Here lyeth the Body of
        WILLIAM STEWKLEY
        of Wiltſford in the County
        of Wilts Esq:
        Eldeſt Son to IOHN
        STEWKELEY of Hampſhire
        Esq: & Agnes his Wife
        he departed this life May ẙ
        31th Anno : Doṁ . 1717
        In the 76th year of his Age.

On a stone lozengeways in the middle of the Chancel

        Here Lieth the Body of
        Ursula Stewkeley 4th Daughter
        of Iohn Stewkeley Esq of
        Hant-shire and Agnes his wife
        Daughter of Sʳ Tho: Maples
        Barᵗ. of Huntington-shire &
        Relict of Edward Hinde Eſq
        she departed this Life ẙ 24th
        day of May 1704 in ẙ 66th
        year of her Age.

At the west end of the North Aisle is a stone monument with a kneeling figure of a woman holding a book. The carving is very coarse and the base is painted black and white in imitation of marble. Above are the arms of Cotton in a lozenge.

Here lyeth the Body of
M^ris JANE COTTON, daughter
of Sr JOHN COTTON, and
dame JANE his wife, who
departed this life, the fourth
day of July 1707 in the 59th
year of her Age.

On a white marble tablet on the south wall of the
Nave with this coat. Sable a lion rampant (Ermine)
between three crosses pattée fitchée or (King).

IN MEMORY OF
JOHN HYNDE KING C.B.
COLONEL COMMANDING 2ND BATTALION
GRENEDIER GUARDS
BORN 22ND DECEMBER 1826
DIED AT ALDERSHOT 9TH JULY 1870.
HE WAS THE SON OF
VICE ADMIRAL SIR RICHARD KING BAR^T. K.C.B.
AND MARIA SUSANNA DAUGHTER OF
ADMIRAL SIR CHARLES COTTON BAR^T.

In the churchyard on the south are these
inscriptions relating to the family of Swan.

1.   In memory of
WILLIAM SWAN GENT.
Born at Moulton in Norfolk
who died Dec. 14 1752
Aged 52 Years
Also of MARY Daughter of
WILLIAM and MARTHA SWAN
who died . . . 1747
Aged 16 days.

2.   In Memory of
MARTHA the Wife of
WILLIAM SWAN
who died May 15th 1783
Aged 60 Years.

3.   Here lieth the Body
of Elizabeth the Wife
of William Swan, born
at Pulham S^t. Maries
in y^e County of Norfolk
died 20th Septem
1743 Aged 43.

4.   John Swan died 1857 aged 66.

Some of the fine painted glass in the Church

1. *Cotton,* 2. *Fleming,* 3. *Hastings,* 4. *Abbot,* 5. *Sharpe,* 6. *Staunton,* 7. *Fitz Simon,*
8. *Bagot or Bagholt, The visitation of Cambs 1619 the eagles emblazoned or,*
(also in the Fitz Simon coat), 9. *Hinde,* 10 *Sheldon*

Hinde impaling Cotton

King

MILTON

Notes taken February 1883.

The Church.

The Church is dedicated to All Saints and consists of Chancel, Nave, North and South Aisles, South Porch and West Tower.

The Chancel is Decorated and has Perpendicular insertions. The East Window is of four lights with flowing tracery, the walls are plastered and much restored, the east end is entirely new. Within there is some good Jacobean woodwork which the Clerk told me came from Kings College. The backs of the choir stalls, the Altar rails and Vestry door are very good. In the south wall is a triple Sedilia with double cusped arches, also a Piscina, the mouldings of which have been cut away and a modern foliated cap has been added to the shaft. Farther eastward is a square Aumbrey. The elbows and misereries of the choir stalls are of old and original work. The Chancel Arch is Norman with a large roll moulding, the only portion remaining of the original Norman Church. On the south side of it is an arched opening with good Decorated mouldings. It now forms simply a recess but was probably a hagioscope.

The Nave and Aisles are Decorated, there is no Clerestory. The Nave roof is original with tie beams and cornice cut and moulded but it is finished above with a modern plastered ceiling. The Font is plain octagonal on an octagonal stem. The Pulpit, reading desk, and Lectern are of oak moulded with traceried panels, these and the seating are all modern. The Nave Arcade is good with clustered columns and hollow moulded arches. The North Aisle was rebuilt in 1864 and the columns which are original work laid open, the old Aisle was demolished in 1779. It is Decorated and has three two-light windows of the same design. The aisles extend from the Chancel westward three bays only, the Nave is longer. Whether the space between the westernmost respond of the Arcade and the Tower which is nearly of the same date as the Aisles, is as originally planned is doubtful. This part of the Nave contains two square headed Perpendicular windows of poor character. In the South Aisle there are two windows to the south and one to the east all Decorated. In the eastern respond of Nave Arcade there is an Aumbry. On the north side of the East Window there is a bracket and on the

CHURCH FROM S.W.

197

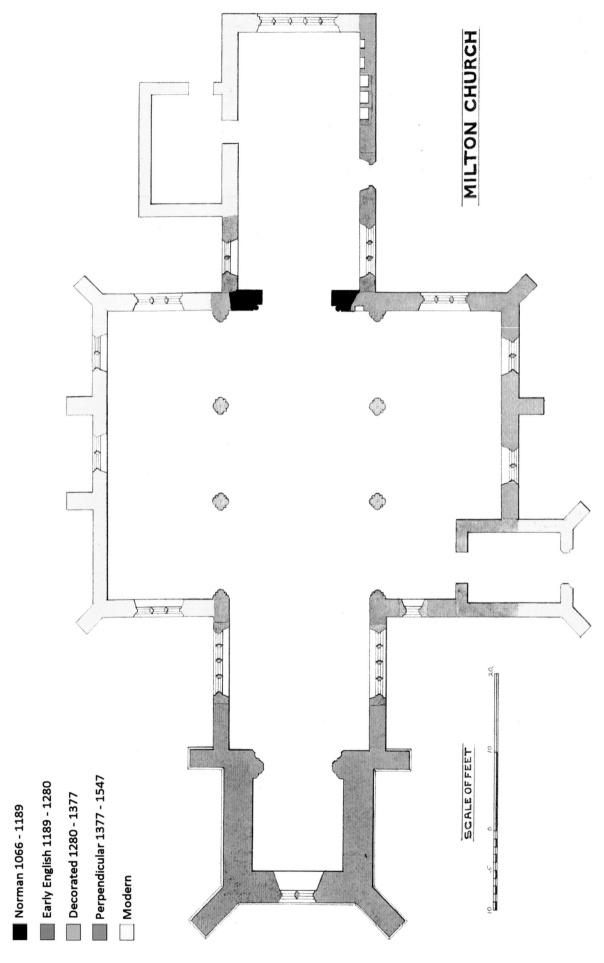

MILTON CHURCH

Norman 1066 - 1189
Early English 1189 - 1280
Decorated 1280 - 1377
Perpendicular 1377 - 1547
Modern

SCALE OF FEET

ALTAR RAILS

COFFIN SLAB

south a largish Nitch with traces of colour. In the south wall is a small Piscina with a crocketted label of Decorated date. It is divided inside about half way up by a stone shelf.

The Porch was formerly an unsightly structure, part of which remains with the inner door which is classical in character. In 1864 a gabled Gothic front was tacked on, the appearance of the whole is awkward.

The Tower is embattled of Decorated date and has a two-light West Window.

Bells. The Belfry has single-light windows of debased character. There are three bells none of Medieval date with inscriptions as follow.

1. Miles Graye made me 1665 (This must have been one of his last castings, he died 1666).

2. Thomas Newman made me 1717.

3. Non clamor sed Amor cantat in ore Dei 1601. This bell though having no makers name has been pronounced by competent authority to be the work of Toby Norris of Stamford (Clay 46).

Inscriptions.

On the floor of the Sanctuary on the north side of the Altar is a good brass but of rather late date. It formerly lay upon an altar tomb. It has the effigies of a judge and his wife, he wears his robes, his wife a loose dress with puffed and slashed sleeves. Over their heads is this coat elaborately mantelled. Per pale 3 wolves heads erased counterchanged. (Cole from the Layer M.S. gives them as tigers heads but they more resemble wolves.) Crest. Above an esquires helmet. A wolfs head erased per pale. There is a marginal hem with an inscription at the

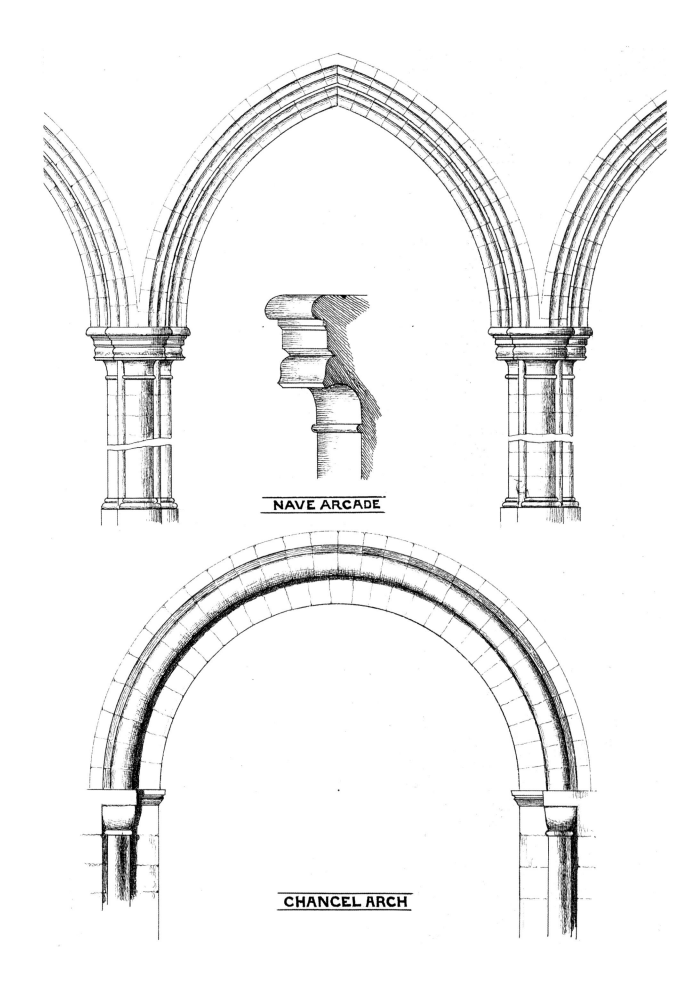

NAVE ARCADE

CHANCEL ARCH

(𝕺rate pro anima 𝕲ulielmi 𝕮oke)
Armigeri unius Justiciarum domini Regis de Comũ ni
Banco Qui obiit bicesimo Quarto die Augusti
Anno domini Millesimo Quingentesimir
Quinquagisimo Tetria, et pro bono Statu Aliciæ uxoris
ejus Quæ monumentiui fieri fecit.

corners of which are medallions with the symbols of the Evangelists. The inscription is perfect with the exception of the top which however is supplied by Cole as follows.

Beneath the brass of the man are two boys and above him a scroll with this 𝕻lebs sine lege ruit. Beneath that of the woman three girls and above her a scroll with this 𝕸ulier casta dos pulcherrima. Beneath the whole is a square plate with these lines.

Marmore sub duro 𝕲ulielmus 𝕮ocus humatur
Judex justitia notus ubique sua.
Ingenis 𝕳abuit, Doctrina Cognicione
Nec non et magno preditus eloquio.
𝕳ic bonus atque pius magna pietate coruscans,
Virtutum semper versus alumnus erat.
Nunc merito bita defunctum lugimus, eheu!
Hoc moriente biro nemo dolore caret.

Symbols for the four Evangelists
John (Eagle)   Matthew (Angel)
Mark (Winged Lion)   Luke (Winged Bull)

There is a black marble slab beneath the Piscina with a long inscription but now much obliterated and in some parts illegible. Transcribed from Clays History of Milton.

"Eliz. Johannis Lane A.M. hujus ecclesiæ Rectoris Uxor koupidia ac dilectissima ob. 9no die Nov. An. Sal. Humanæ 1743 æt. 27. Quem semper acerbum, semper honoratum (voluit sic numeri) habebo. Ostendunt terris hanc tantum Fata, neque ultra esse sinunt.

She was a wife, take her for all, in all I shall not look upon her like again.

MILTON CHURCH

SOUTH SIDE OF CHANCEL

SEDILIA

Fæmina ingenius orta parentibus jam tenebris in cunabulis orphana, educta libere: rei familiaris egregie perita. Just vero, quantasque serumnas durante brevissimo hujus vitæ curriculo, per malitiam clanculum in tenderis operantem, necnon apertem, audacem et impudentem, quinetiam per superbiam in altum evecti pseudo fratris unius saltem togati hominis causas nullus dubito sed non sine numine tam immaturæ mortis constanti animo pertulit. Summa Dies, cum corda universi hominum generis apertissima fuerint indicabit. Greek Διὰ τῶν ἀγνώστων σοῦ παθημάτων ἐλέησον ἡμᾶς Κύριε." *

On a marble tablet on the north wall.

Sub Altari Situm eſt
Quod Mortale fuit,
SARÆ
Uxoris, O. NAYLOR A.M.
Hujus Eccleſiæ Rectoris;
Illa,
In Maritum Amore,
In Liberos Pietate,
In Amicos Fidelitate,
Nulli Secunda,
Ôbiit
Sexto die Martii
MDCCLX
Ætatis ſuæ
LIV.

On a tablet on the south wall.

Marmor Hoc
Memoriæ ſacrum
OLIVERI NAYLOR, A.M.
Cujus juxta Uxorem, Reliquiæ
infra conduntur
olim Hujus Eccleſiæ Rectoris,
ſumma Pietate
Filii duo poſuerunt.

Variolis correptus,
ad Mercedem earum Virtutum
capiendam,
Quæ Eum deſideratum
Omnibus,
præcipue vero Propinquis ſuis
et amicis,
efficiunt,
abiit decimo octavo Die Febrii
Anno Dom. MDCCLXXV
Ætatis 71.

In the South Aisle on a brass plate on the east wall is the following inscription very rudely cut and surmounted with this coat:

Three crescents two and one (Harris) impaling. A bend engrailed between six martlets (Tempest).

HERE LYETH THE BODY OF
sonne of William Harris Esquier
IOHN HARRIS GENT. ⌃ BORNE THE
25 OF IUNE 1609 INTERRED THE
18 OF OCTOBER 1659 AND ALLSO
THE BODIES OF WILLIAM,
IAMES, GEORGE MICHALE
BRIGET, ANNE and BRIGET
THE YOUNGER SONNES &
DAUGHTERS OF THE SAID IOHN
HARRIS AND MARTHA HIS WIFE
DAUGHTER OF THOMAS TEMPEST OF
WHADDON ESQVIER, SHE HAD LIVING
THEN WHEN SHE ERECTED THIS 3
SONNES AND 7 DAVGHTERS Aᵒ. Dᵒ. 1660.

At the top of the tablet are the father and three sons and the mother and two daughters rudely incised.

On a white marble tablet on the respond of the Nave Arcade.

SACRED TO THE MEMORY OF
GEORGE NICHOLLS ESQᴿ.
OF CONNINGTON HOUSE CAMBRIDGESHIRE,
OB. APRIL 15. 1812, ÆT. 67.
ALSO OF
PHILIPPA, HIS WIDOW,
OB. OCTOBER 9. 1837. ÆT. 86,
AND OF
PHILIPPA, THEIR BELOVED AND ONLY CHILD,
OB. JUNE 21. 1795, ÆT. 15.

———

ALSO OF TWO SISTERS OF Mᴿˢ NICHOLLS.
JANE, WIDOW OF THE REVᴰ RICHᴰ FAYERMAN,
RECTOR OF OBY, NORFOLK,
OB. OCTOBER 16, 1821, ÆTt. 72.
AND ANNE SPELMAN
OB. JUNE 30, 1835 ÆT. 78.

———

On the south wall beginning from the east are the following marble tablets.

---

* Greek text:- Have pity on us, Lord, because of your unknown sufferings.

1 IN THE VAULT BENEATH ARE DEPOSITED
IN THE STEADFAST HOPE OF A JOYFUL
RESURRECTION
THE REMAINS OF THE REVEREND SAMUEL
KNIGHT M.A.
ONLY SON OF THE REVEREND SAMUEL
KNIGHT D.D. FORMERLY PREBENDARY OF ELY.
HE DEPARTED THIS LIFE ON THE VITH DAY OF
JANUARY MDCCXDC
IN THE LXXIID YEAR OF HIS AGE.

HIS ONLY SON ERECTS THIS IN MEMORY OF THE
BEST OF FATHERS.

HERE ALSO REST THE REMAINS OF SARAH
SPELMAN
ELDEST SISTER OF ELIZABETH WIFE OF
SAMUEL KNIGHT ESQ.
WHO DEPARTED THIS LIFE ON THE VITH DAY OF
SEPTEMBER MDCCCVI
IN THE LXIST YEAR OF HER AGE.

SHE DIED IN A MOMENT, IN A MOMENT WHICH
SHE THOUGHT NOT OF
YET NOT UNPREPARED.
READER, BE THOU LIKEWISE READY.

2. Between the windows is a tablet surmounted by a bas relief of Flaxman's Subject. The spirit of the deceased conveyed heavenward by an angel. Beneath is this inscription.

SACRED TO THE MEMORY OF
ELIZABETH,
WIFE OF SAMUEL KNIGHT ESQR OF THIS PLACE,
WHO AFTER A FEW HOURS ILLNESS ONLY,
EXCHANGED THIS LIFE FOR A BETTER ON THE
17TH OF JUNE 1800
IN THE 39TH YEAR OF HER AGE.

OF WOMEN O THOU LOVLIEST AND THOU BEST !
ENTER, ELIZA, ON THY PROMISED REST.
(MYSTERIOUS PROOF OF HEAVEN's TRANSCENDENT
LOVE)
ALL BUT TRANSLATED TO THE REALMS ABOVE !
THY HUSBAND PARDON FOR HIS GRIEF IMPLORES,
HE WEEPS IN FRAILTY, BUT IN FAITH ADORES.
THE CHRISTIAN FEELS THY GAIN : BUT MUST BEMOAN
AS MAN, HIS CHILDREN's LOSS : - YET MORE HIS OWN.
BRIGHT EXCELLENCE ! WITH EVERY VIRTUE FRAUGHT !
SUCH MAY WE BE ! BY THY EXAMPLE TAUGHT :
PURE IN THE EYE OF HEAVEN, LIKE THEE APPEAR
SHOULD WE THIS HOUR, DEATH's AWFUL SUMMONS
HEAR ;
LIKE THEE ALL OTHER CONFIDENCE DISOWN,
AND LOOKING TO THE CROSS OF CHRIST ALONE,
IN MEEKNESS TREAD THE PATH THY STEPS HAVE
TROD,
AND FIND, WITH THEE, ACCEPTANCE FROM
OUR GOD !

3. On a marble tablet beneath a pediment this.

SAMUEL KNIGHT
BORN JULY XITH. M.D.CC.LIV.
DIED JUNE VIITH. M.D.CCC.XXXV.
MY CHILDREN, FRIENDS, AND THOU BELOVED WIFE,
DEAR PIOUS PARTNER OF MY CLOSING LIFE!
WATCHING (AS DUTY PROMPTS) MY PARTING BREATH,
MOURN NOT AS VOID OF HOPE A CHRISTIAN'S DEATH,
CONTROL THE MOURNFUL, THE EMBITTER'D SIGH;
ON CHRIST, MY GOD AND SAVIOUR I RELY;
CHRIST STILL THE SAME (WHAT THOUGH IV'E LIVED
TO SEE
TOW'RDS ROME'S FELL POWER A SAD APOSTACY)
VILE AS I AM, WASH'D IN HIS BLOOD, I KNOW;
MY SCARLET SINS ARE MADE AS WHITE AS SNOW.
"INCREASE MY FAITH, I PRAYED; REPENTANCE GIVE,
"AND IN THY REST, O LORD, MY SOUL SHALL LIVE;
"CELESTIAL GIFT; THY HOLY SPIRIT SEND
"TO LEAD EACH THOUGHT TO GOOD, FROM ILL DEFEND;
"TILL I, BLEST INMATE OF THY PURE ABODE,
"THROUGH ALL ETERNITY BEHOLD MY GOD.

FRANCES KNIGHT, WIDOW OF THE ABOVE,
DIED DEC. 10TH A. D. 1844.

On the west wall of South Aisle is a white marble tablet by Chantry with this inscription.

SACRED TO THE MEMORY OF
SAMUEL KNIGHT JUNR
ONLY SON OF SAMUEL KNIGHT ESQRE OF MILTON,
WHO PEACEFULLY DEPARTED THIS LIFE
ON THE 2ND DAY OF JUNE 1829 IN THE 39TH YEAR
OF HIS AGE.
TRUSTING IN THE TENDER MERCIES OF HIS GOD,
THROUGH THE MEDIATION OF HIS REDEEMER.
HOW DEARLY LOVED, HOW DEEPLY MOURNED,
BY HER WHO CONSECRATES THIS STONE CAN
BE KNOWN ONLY TO HIM
UNTO WHOM ALL HEARTS ARE OPEN.

On a stone slab in the South Aisle is this.

Here lieth the
body of William
Kettle who dyed
the 30th day of June
1700 in ye 69
year of his age.
Catherine his wife
died 20th of August 1727
aged 86 years.

There is another slab but the inscription is worn away. Just inside the Porch door is a good sepulchral slab, probably of 13th century date, it is quite perfect and has a good foliated cross carved upon it. This was found in 1864

In the North Aisle on a small tablet is this.

IN MEMORY OF

ISAAC MARSH,

WHO DIED THE 5TH OF MARCH 1837;

AGED 65 YEARS.

Above the Porch door are the Royal Arms in a frame. These were transferred from Landbeach Church in 1826. Beneath a board with this.

The Incorporated Society for Building & Churches

GRANTED £25 A.D. 1864, TOWARDS ENLARGING AND RESTORING THIS CHURCH BY WHICH ADDITIONAL ACCOMODATION HAS BEEN OBTAINED FOR 86 PERSONS. THE ENTIRE AREA WILL ACCOMMODATE 300 AT THE LEAST. THE SITTINGS ARE ALL FREE, AND SUBJECT TO ANNUAL ASSIGNMENT BY THE CHURCH WARDENS, SUITABLE PROVISION BEING MADE FOR THE POORER INHABITANTS.

Stained Glass.

Of the old stained glass mentioned by Cole, there now remains but very little, and what coats of arms there are have been so ruthlessly "made up" that it is almost impossible to recognise them. In the East Window of the South Aisle are some quarterings. I made out the coat three lioness rampant and a chevron between three garbs mentioned by Cole. There is a shield of 22 quarters the tinctures being much decayed but the outlines well preserved. Among them are these. A fret - Three bars - A fret - A chevron between three billets - A bend, a chevron - A saltire and chief. The two south windows of this aisle have the tracery filled with a yellow pattern with the initials J.P.B (John Percy Baumgartner) 1855.

The small window by the Porch is by Constable of Cambridge. Subject, Jacobs dream. This is very poor.

The West Window of the Tower is filled with stamped quarries by Powell of London. This is vile.

The North Window of the Nave by Constable of Cambridge has subjects: Christ blessing little children and the Baptism of our Lord. This is very bad.

The East Window of the North Aisle has 3 medallions in bistre and yellow the drawing good. Subjects, the death of Annanias and Sapphira and figures of St. Catherine and St. Margaret. These were placed in the Church by Cole 1779. Here are also a figured quarry and two coats of the arms of Elizabeth brought from one of the side chapels of Kings College Chapel.

The South Window of the Chancel is of three lights. The subject is the Marriage at Cana by Hardman of Birmingham and is the least objectionable of all.

The East Window of the Chancel was filled with stained glass at the expense of the Rector, it consists of patterns by Bolton of London and is very poor.

Exterior.

On the exterior of the east wall of the Chancel is a fixed slab with this inscription.

Here Lies the body of
Th^s. Cannon, who died Iune 15th 1726: Aged17.
His Master & Mistress Erect this little
Monument to his Memory as an
Acknowledgem^t for his faithful Service
the four years He lived with them.
God grant that He and they may find
mercy in the Lord at that Day.

Additional Notes on the Church.

The South Aisle was repaired in 1855 by John Percy Baumgartner whose initials are introduced in the tracery of the windows. The east end formed the Manor Chapel, this however as at present existing and called until very recent times L'Estrange's Chapel did not include the whole of what is now thought to belong to the Lord of the Manor, viz. two out of three bays of the Aisle. Cole in 1744 says of it "Above half of the South Aisle is divided from the rest by a screen which is stalled round for a private Chapel or Oratory. On the north side near the old Altar stands a very old Altar Tomb of Purbeck marble with nothing on it as does another on the opposite side against the south wall. A little above the Piscina is an awkward kind of mural monument of stone and in it a brass plate (to Harris now at East end)." Blomefield mentions a very ancient Altar Tomb in the South Aisle with the inscription lost and says "by the arms of Le Strange in the East window and it being called Strange's Chapel, I make no doubt but that one of that ancient family is interred beneath." The floor of the whole Chapel, two bays in extent, is raised one step above the Aisle. The Nitch on the south was opened by the late Vicar Mr. Champneys and found to contain certain images, these through carelessness are now lost or destroyed.

The Jacobean woodwork in the Chancel seats and the door to the Vestry were brought from the old

Rectory house. The present Communion Rails belonged to Kings College Chapel.

The Church was restored in 1864 when the North Aisle was rebuilt, the whole interior of the Church was reseated and rearranged. At the same time a sum of £530 having been raised for all the above purposes by means of contributions of the Revd John Chapman and his friends, by whom the Pulpit and Reading Desk were given. The Lectern was an Easter offering made in 1865 by the Rev^d Dr Giles, then owner and occupier of the Manor House.

The Communion plate consists of two small silver cups and two plates also of silver. One of the cups is of some antiquity and is nicely ornamented round the bowl. A cup somewhat larger in size the gift of the Rector is that commonly used. The inside of the bowl is gilt and at the bottom, so as not to be visible without examination, is the following inscription. "Dedicated to the service of God by John Chapman M.A. Rector of Milton 1853." The larger of the two plates has the arms probably of the donor, ermine two boars passant. Crest. A boars head erect (the arms of Whichcote probably the gift of Benjamin Whichcoat, Rector 1661 - 1683). On the back of the smaller plate is "Milton Church the gift of the Revd L.C. Powys, Curate 1829."

Cole records that he glazed the new windows of the North Aisle and put in a great deal of painted glass, viz. a crucifix, St. Paul with Ananias and Sapphira and the arms of some Lords of the Manor. These probably relate to the quartered coats in the East Window South Aisle.

Blomefield mentions as hanging in the Chancel an achievement with the arms of Duncomb in memory of Mrs Stephens who was a member of that family. Per chevron engrailed sable and argent three talbots heads erased counterchanged, with Ulster badge. Impaling, Per chevron argent and gules in chief two cocks sable in a base a saltire humetty or. Moriendo vivo.

The Tower was and still continues to be regularly fitted up internally in the upper stage as a pigeon house by means of square holes cut in the four walls for the pigeons to build in. The Tower has a clock on its west face put up in 1848 at an expense of £53, the money came chiefly from the Directors of the Great Eastern Railway as compensation for Parish land required by them for their works.

Portions of an Altar Tomb in memory of Richard Stephens, Rector, who died 1727 remains in the churchyard beneath the East Window and bears an inscription to his widow above mentioned.

Diana Stephens, Filia Francisci Duncomb de Comitatu Surriæ Baronetti et Relicta Ricardi Stephens in summatabula hujus monumenti memorate, cum per decem menses marito superfuisset ob. 16° die Junii 1728 æt 65.

The Register commences in 1705.

A List of Rectors.

Peter de Woseri	Rector in	1279
Henry		
Ralph.	Rector at the beginning of the 14th century.	
P . . .	Rector in 1345	1345
John Scott. instituted 29th May 1349 on the presentation of Roger le Strange		1349
John Epurston	died	1395
Eubulo le Strange	died 1399, instituted	1395
Philip Seneschal	admitted 18th Sept	1399
Eudo la Zouch at the resignation of P.S. admitted 10 May		1402
Thomas Kirkebird, in exchange with E la Z. admitted 15 Nov.		1403
John Woodham	instituted 5 Nov.	1406
William Lavender, probably instituted in		1429
Thomas Spake	Resigned in	1449
John Pevey on the resignation of T.S.		
Walter Luyton (Ruyton?) said to have become Rector		1472
James Strathberell occurs as Rector 1488 and		1493
Richard Hownson	Rector in	1506
John Richard Harrison was Rector in 1516 died		1542
Richard Johnes his name occurs 1545,1551. presented		1542.3
John Moodyer on the resignation of R.J. instituted		1555
James Whytfeld	was Rector in	1565
John Taylor A.M. was Rector 1595 - 6 instituted, June		1568
Roger Goade, died 1610, instituted about		1600
Thomas Goade, died 1638, instituted Sept.		1610
Samuel Collins succeeded Tho. Goade. died		1651
Benjamin Whichcote, died 1683 instituted		1660
Samuel Thomas, died 1691, instituted		1683
Charles Roderick, died 1712, instituted		1692
Richard Stephens, died 1727, instituted Sept.		1712
Adam Elliott B.A. died 1735, instituted Jan.		1727.8
Willyam Willimot, died 1737, instituted		1735
John Lane succeeded, shot by highwaymen 1746, instituted		1737
Oliver Naylor succeeded, died 1775, instituted		1746
Graham Jepson, instituted July		1775

Samuel Knight,
    on resignation of G.J. inducted July 1776
Edward Reynolds   succeeded, died 1796   1790
Thomas Key   succeeded   1796
William George Freeman, succeeded,
    instituted 1812
John Chapman,   succeeded, instituted 1841

Vicars.
John de Borewell (Burwell), Vicar in Nov. 1348
Robert Rayson,   succeeded.
Roger Blase, resigned in favour of John Alvene 1394
John Alvene in exchange with Roger Blase.
John Hawforth . . .   died 1397
John Goodhyne   succeeded 28th April
    1397, resigned 1401
Richard Morys   instituted 23rd July 1401
    exchanged 1404
John Hawkere   in exchange with
    Richard Morys
John Grene . . .   resigned 1446
Eudo Quey   instituted 28 Sept. 1446
    was Vicar in 1472
Edward Why . . .   died 1489
William Haryest (or Hayhurst)
    instituted 6th April 1489, died 1493
John Wade,   instituted 4th July 1493
    resigned the same year. 1493
Richard Streytberell M.A.
    instituted 16th Dec. 1493
Henry Holland,   deprived apparently
    late in the year 1516
Richard Alanson (Alyson)
    instituted 10 Jan 1516.17 died 1529
John Crispe,   occurs as Vicar witnessing
    wills 1538 and 1544. 1544
Thomas Hyssam   signs as Vicar 4th August 1552
Henry Colly,   instituted 7th Oct. 1555
    resigned before 1557
William Kellam,   instituted 10th Nov.
    1604, buried 19th Oct. 1620
Thomas Barnham M.A.   succeeded.
Edward Johnson, Vicar in 1631.
    Ejected 7th Jan. 1644.5
John Radcliffe M.A.
    Fellow of Magdalen Col. Vicar in 1664
John Bilton,   Fellow of Magdalen B.A.
    appears to have been 1669 - 71

William Crosse,   Fellow of Sydney Sussex
    Col. apparently Vicar 1670
John Maulyverer,   Fellow of Magdalen,
    Vicar in 1672 and in 1683
James Bernard,   Fellow of Kings College
    probably succeeded.
Richard Stephens,
    probably Vicar 1686, certainly so in 1692
Samuel Noyes,   Fellow of Kings College
    Vicar in 1699
William Bond,   Fellow of Caius College,
    sequestrator in 1781
Samuel Vince,   of Caius College . . .
    sequestrator 1789 to 1813
James Slade,   Fellow of Emannuel College
    sequestrator 1813, res. 1817
William Sharpe,   of Trinity College
    succeeded, resigned 1821
Alldersey Dicken   of Sidney Sussex Col.
    succeeded, resigned 1837
Charles John Champnes of S. Albans Hall,
    Oxford succeeded, vacated his charge
    and put an end to the double tenure
    of the living in 1846

A List of Church Furniture,
This is from the Archdeacons Book, drawn up
c.1306.

"Ecclesia de Middletone non appropriata: est ibi
rector et vicarius, et taxatur ad XV marcas:
solvit pro synodalibus ijs. iiijd. procurationibus
xviijd: denariis sancti Petri ijs: Ornamenta sunt
hæc: duo missalia sufficientia: iiij gradalia:
(unum menubrum cristallinum:) duo troperia: j
antiphonarium: ij legende, quarum j bona et alia
in duobus voluminibus: j manuale: turribulum
bonum: tria paria vestimentorum cum
pertinentiis: j calix bonus et aluis debilis: iij
rochete: vij superpellicia: chrismatorium
bonum: (ij candelabra) iij phiole: pixis eburnea:
ij cruces cappachori: ij frontalia: ij turribula:
lanterna: j vexillum: velum templi: item unum
vestimentum cum casula alba: stola: crux
argentea: manipulum cum optimis paruris:
tunica dalmatica et capa chori: et unus pannus
de baldekyno de dono domini Rudulphi
rectoris."

OLD PLASTERWORK HOUSE

HOUSE OCCUPIED BY COLE

Cooke of Milton

Arms. Per pale argent and sable three wolves heads erased counterchanged.
Crest. A wolf's head erased per pale argent and sable.

. . . . Cooke of Chesterton Co. Cambs. ⊤ . . . . .

William Cooke. Justice of the Common Pleas ob. 25 Aug. 1553 ⊤ Alice.
bur. at Milton where his brass remains.

son.   Thomas Cooke of Milton living 1571 ⊤ Audrey . . . .   three daughters.

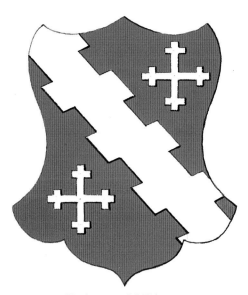

Pelsett of Milton

Arms. Gules a bend raguly between two crosses crosslet argent.

William Pelsett of ⊤ . . . . sister of Dr. Leeds Master   John Dolman of ⊤ Jane d. of Sabcotts
Itham, Co. Kent.   of Clare Hall, Cambs.   Newnham Co. Herts.   in Co. Lincs.

Gawen Pelsett of ⊤ Jane.   James.   Christopher.   Grace = William Turpin of
Itham Co. Kent.   Bassingbourn.

William Pelsett of = Anne d. of Roger Goade   Elizabeth ux.   Constance ux. Roger Gostwick
Milton in Co.   Doctor of Divinity Provost   Thom. Cage   p'son of Sandford Courtney Co.
Cambridge 1619.   of King's College, Cambs.   of Stow.   Devon. Willington Co. Beds.

MILTON CHURCH

— Stained Glass.

— Le Strange.

— Brass. William Cooke. 1553.

Scade.

— Stained Glass.

Harris.   Tempest.

— Brass. John Harris 1659. —

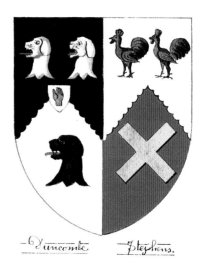

—Duncombe.   Stephens.

Achievement.

OAKINGTON

16 May 1883.

The Church.

The Church is dedicated to St. Andrew and consists of Chancel, Nave, North and South Aisles and West Tower. The interior is unrestored. The body of the Church is of 13th century work with later insertions.

The Chancel walls are Early English, the East Window is Perpendicular. On the south side are three lancets, a Priests Door, and a two-light window of early character with a plain circle in the head, probably coeval with the lancets. Beneath the westernmost lancet is a square low side window divided by a mullion now blocked up. On the north side are three lancets and a low side window similar to that on the south. All the lancets have slightly trefoiled heads. There is one step at the Chancel Arch and two to the Altar. The east wall inside is faced with alabaster to the height of the window sill, beneath which runs a string of the same material. There is a square Aumbry in the south wall. The floor is roughly paved with tiles and slabs. The roof is plain and poor. A pew of Jacobean date with good carved panels and original hinges to the door.

The Nave. The Arcade consists of five arches, simply chamfered resting on pillars, octagonal on the north side, circular on the south. The caps and bases are of Early English character. The Nave is filled with high deal pews and paved with broken bricks and stones. There is no Clerestory.

The South Aisle is Early English with later insertions of Perpendicular windows of poor character. The South Door is original and has shafts in the jambs and a double chamfered arch. By the West Window is a blocked up lancet or rather traces of one. There is a double Early English Piscina.

The North Aisle appears to have been rebuilt late in the 15th century. It has four windows and a door (now blocked) with square head and cusped spandrils to the north and similar windows to east and west, all with tracery of good character. On either side of the East Window is a Nitch with crocketted canopy and pinnacles. At the west end of this Aisle is an iron bound chest now used as a coal store. This end used as a general rubbish depository is screened off by the lower panels of what was probably the Chancel Screen. The panels are of excellent character, double cusped and have painted patterns in diaper, white on a vermilion ground, excellent examples of 15th or 16th century decoration. Standing against the north wall are four very good coffin slabs with foliated crosses in relief, two of which are of the same design. Three of these were dug up in the churchyard some years back.

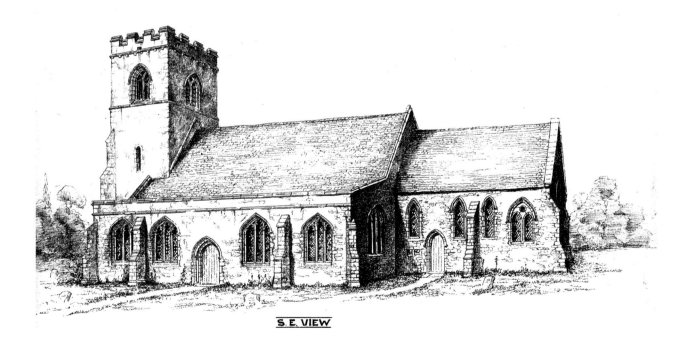

S.E. VIEW

211

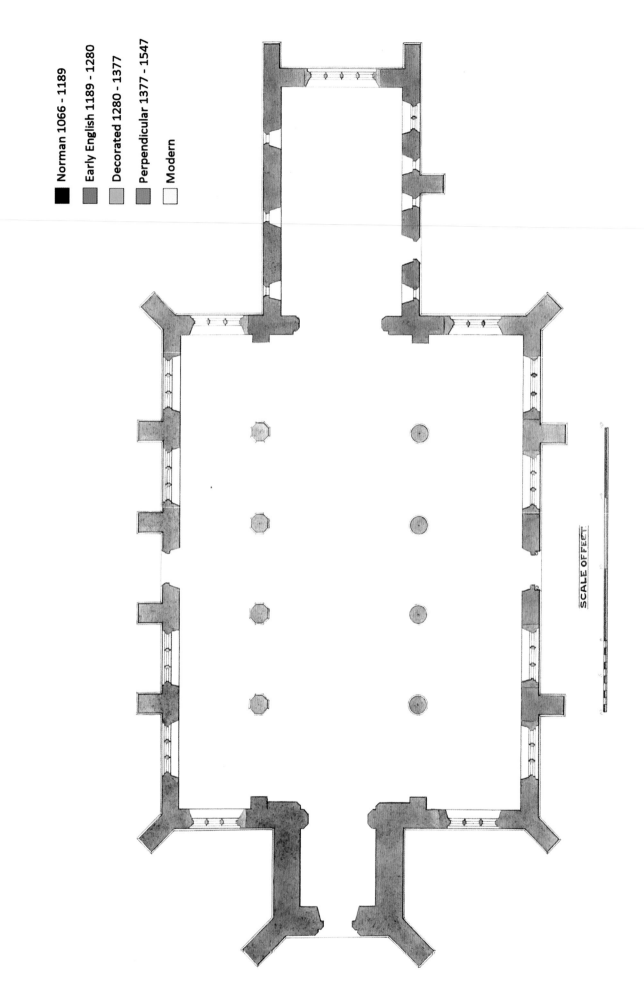

Norman 1066 - 1189
Early English 1189 - 1280
Decorated 1280 - 1377
Perpendicular 1377 - 1547
Modern

SCALE OF FEET

The Font is of late Norman date, the bowl is square with shallow round headed arcades rudely worked on the sides. It is finished below with a Perpendicular base mould resting on five octagonal shafts of the same character.

The Tower is bold and massive with angled buttresses to the height of the Belfry floor, of very early Decorated character, slightly later than the Chancel and Nave Arcades. The original corbel table remains but the parapet has been replaced by Perpendicular battlements. The Belfry windows are of two lights and have pierced heads. The West Door has a double chamfered arch, the window above is of Perpendicular date.

The Bells. In the Belfry are four bells with these inscriptions.
1 and 3. Miles Graye made me 1655.
2. Omnia fiant ad gloriam Dei.
   W. Hemington C.W. 1748.
4. Miles Graie made me 1656.
The second is by Joseph Eayre.
The weight of the tenor 7 Cwt.

Stained Glass. In the tracery of the two easternmost windows in the north wall of the North Aisle are fragments of stained glass about 100 years old. In the easternmost also are older portions, a good head, and remains of escutcheons, patterns &c.

Fragments of early glass in a North Aisle window

In the Chancel are the following windows filled with modern stained glass.

On the south.
1. Christ and the Woman of Samaria. In a circle above is this coat. Argent a chevron between 3 owls sable, impaling. Gules six crosses crosslet fitché or, and this inscription.

2. The glass in the second window is of diaper work.

3. Christ the Light of the World adapted from Holman Hunts picture. Beneath is this inscription.

On the north side is a stained glass window of The Good Shepherd. Beneath it is this.

Inscriptions.
In the Chancel.

Sindrey 1709. On a slab before the altar

> Sub hoc marmore
> sepultus jacet
> Guido Sindrey
> generosus
> qui obiit Junii XXII.
> Anno {Christi MDCCIX
>   {Ætatis XXXIX

213

N. SIDE

S. SIDE

CAPS AND BASES OF NAVE PIERS

S. DOORWAY

N. DOORWAY

CAP AND BASE

ARCH MOULDING

OAKINGTON CHURCH

DETAILS OF STONEWORK

Webster 1840.
On a stone slab

T.W. 1840. M.A.W. 1841

Above which on a tablet on the north wall.

TO THE MEMORY OF THE
REV^D THOMAS WEBSTER, B.D.
RECTOR OF ST BOTOLPHS, CAMBRIDGE, AND THIRTY
YEARS VICAR OF THIS PARISH
WHO DIED MAY THE 9TH 1840 AGED 60.

ERECTED IN GRATEFUL REMEMBRANCE BY HIS
AFFECTIONATE PARISHIONERS

Webster 1841.
On a second tablet.

IN MEMORY OF
MARY ANN
WIDOW OF THE LATE REV^D THO^S WEBSTER B.D.
WHO DEPARTED THIS LIFE
JANUARY 26TH 1841, AGED 59 YEARS.

Sindrey 1761 & 1771.
On a slab in the centre of the Chancel.

Guy Sindrey Esqre
departed this life
Ianr^y 26, 1761,
aged (6?)9 years.
Mrs Grace Sindrey
wife of Guy Sindrey Esqre
departed this life
October 13th 1771 aged 63 years.

A slab with a matrix of a brass inscription.

In the Nave.
By the Chancel Arch is a slab with inscription surmounted by this coat. On a bend a lure, an esquires helmet in the dexter chief in the sinister chief a mullet.

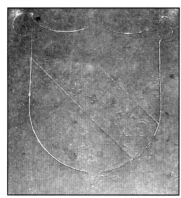

M. S.
Lente Viator in Æde Sacra si cœlum spiras
Oculos primum ad Terram hanc demitte ubi Iacet
Ornatissima in paucis Matrona
Anna Iohannis Buck nuper Uxor
Et Thomæ Brooke filia

Quædam Patre quam Marito armigero notabilis
Vivens cotidie moriebatur
Ut mortua viuciet
In Deum O. M. religione
Pietate in Parente
In Verum fide
Charitate in Liberos
In Pauperes munificentia
Et in omnes humanitate clara
Excessit 3° Idus Decemb.

Anno {Salutis 1657
       { Ætatis 56

With matrix of brass inscription much defaced.

Love piety and sacred knowledge lye
here all interred . . George Hatton second son
of Robert Hatton 16–0.

In the South Aisle on a black marble slab surmounted by this coat. On a bend between two eagles displayed a fret, a mullet in dexter chief. Crest. On a chapeau a wyvern.

Agnofcit Homo ignofcit Deus.
HEIC INNATUS EST ROBERTVS
AVDELY DE GRANSDON MAGNA
IN COMITATV VENANTODVNI ARMI=
GER QVI VIXIT ANN 65 MENS : 8 :
& DEVIXIT 2DO DIE NOVEMB : 1654.

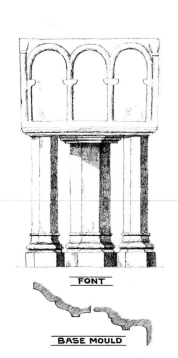

FONT

BASE MOULD

PAINTED PANEL OF SCREEN

E. END OF N. AISLE

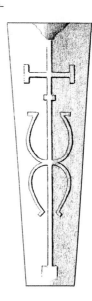

COFFIN LIDS

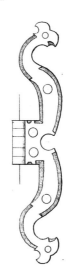

PANEL AND HINGE TO PEW IN CHANCEL.

Pedigree of Buck of Westwick Oakington

Thomas Buck of Oakley alias Ugley in Essex ⊤

Thomas Buck A.M. and one of the Esquires Beadles of the University of Cambridge ob. s.p. 4. May 1679 æt. circa 76. Married 1. Anne dau. of John Rowley of Barkway in Hertfordshire Esqre. 2. Elizabeth dau. of William Coppinger of Buckshall Suffolk Esqre. 3. Elizabeth dau. of . . . White D.D.	John Buck A.M. and one of the Esquire Beadles of the University of Cambridge. ob. 22 Oct. 1680 æt. 83.	Anne dau. of Thos. Brooke one of the Esquire Beadles of the University but descended out of Yorkshire	Thomas Buck of Ricards in the Parish of Ashton in Essex ⊤	Anne mar. Thomas Metcalfe of Bartlow in Essex.
			1. Thomas 2. Francis	

Mary dau. of John Johnson D.D. of Whitechapel Lond. Widow of Ralph Davenant of Whitechapel Rector 2. wife.	=	Thomas Buck of Westwick in Cambridgeshire æt. 56, 1684, one of His Majesty's Justices of the Peace for this County	⊤	Rebecca dau. of Thomas Lovering of Norwich 1 wife.	Samuel Buck of Grays Inn in Middlesex Esqre, 1684 æt. 53. Mar Anne dau. and coheir of . . . Rowley only son of John Rowley of Barkway Esqre. ⊤ Anne æt. 9. 1684	Anne Elizabeth died young

4. Hatton Buck æt. 11. 1684	3. Samuel Buck æt. 23. 1684	2. John Buck ob. cœlebs	1 Thomas Buck of Fen Ditton æt. 28. 1684 ⊤	Anne dau. of Thomas Allen of Goring in Oxfordshire Esqre	1. Elizabeth mar. Chr. Hatton of Triplow Cambridgeshire Esqre

Thomas æt. 11 months   Elizabeth æt 4.   Rebecca æt. 3.   2. Rebecca wife of Gilbert Wigmore of Little Shelford Esqre.

A patent granted by Sir John Borough Knt. Garter to Thomas and John Buck 2. Oct. 1639. 15 Car.

Pedigree of Shute

Arms. Per chevron sable and or in chief two eagles displayed of the last.

Crest. A griffin sejant or pierced through the breast with a broken spear sable headed argent ruled gules.

Note. The eagle shewn in base is an error.

Robert Shute a native of Gargrave Co. Yorks afterwards ⊤ Thomasine dau. of Christopher
of Oakington Co. Cambs. Justice of the King's Bench │ Burgoyne of Longstanton Co. Cambs.
8 Feb. 1585-6. Died April 1590.

| Bridget bap. | John bap. | Robert bap. 25 Feb. 1564-5 | George bur. | Thomas bap. |
| 3 Dec. 1562 | 29 Aug. 1563 | bur. 16 Nov. 1565-6 | 5 June 1567 | 11 Sept 1573 |

The above from the Parish Register of Oakington.

The Visitation of Cambridgeshire 1619 give the children of Robert Shute as follow.

Francis (afterwards of Upton   John. Christopher. Thomas. Jane (mar. John Hatton of
Leicestershire from whom the   Longstanton from whom
Viscounts Barrington.)   Viscounts Hatton. vide peerages.)
                                                                    (mar. Richard Holford of
                                                                 Longstanton. vide pedigree of
                                                                    Holford. Vis. Cambs 1619.)

The family appear to have resided at Oakington but a short time.

OVER

June 29 1883.

The Church.

The Church is dedicated to St. Mary the Virgin and consists of Chancel, Nave, North and South Aisles, South Porch, West Tower and Spire. This is one of the finest Churches in the County and architecturally of great interest.

<u>The Chancel</u> is of Decorated date with Perpendicular insertions but practically rebuilt in 1840 by Trinity College. There are three windows on the south and two on the north side. These have Decorated external mouldings but the inner moulding and tracery are Perpendicular insertions. The East Window is Perpendicular of five lights inserted in the jambs of an earlier Decorated window. There is one step at the Chancel Arch and three to the Altar. On the north and south sides are Priests Doors. Below the East Window is a broad band

of stonework sculptured with angels with extended wings and monogram I.H.S., this is modern. Projecting from the south wall is a Piscina of peculiar design, a square headed trefoil with an inner moulding of earlier character than the outer and finished with an embattled cornice. The outer portion was evidently reworked at the same period as the external mouldings of the windows. The Sedillia is formed by the sill of the easternmost window on the south side. There is a square Aumbry. The Chancel Arch is Decorated, the shafts probably cut away when the Screen was erected. The latter has good Perpendicular tracery

Over Church as it is today.

219

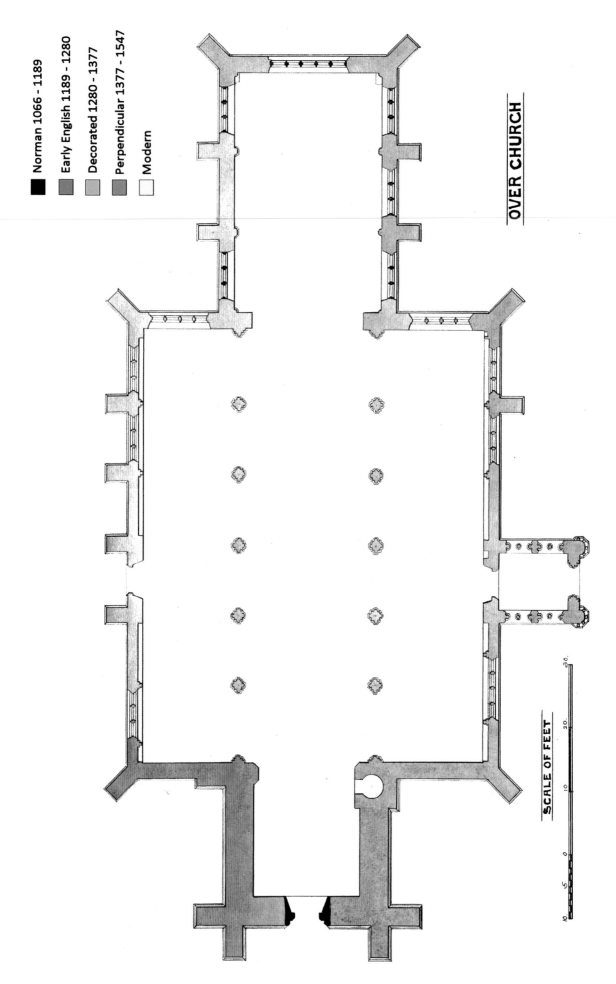

Norman 1066 - 1189
Early English 1189 - 1280
Decorated 1280 - 1377
Perpendicular 1377 - 1547
Modern

OVER CHURCH

SCALE OF FEET

and groined loft. A Decorated bell cot with Sanctus Bell remains. The roof is of flat pitch with tie beams and open rafters. The choir stalls are good, well moulded with carved elbows and misereries on which are carved these coats.

1. A chevron between three harts heads erased.

2. Three rams heads affronte (probably Ramsey Abbey).

3. Three crosses crosslet flory and escallop in chief.

These stalls are reported to have been brought from Ramsey Abbey.

The Nave consists of an arcade of six arches, the piers are well moulded with small octagonal shafts on each face, finished with carved and embattled caps. The arch mouldings are continuous with those of the pier. The Clerestory windows are of two lights and have alternately traceried and simply cusped heads. The roof is good with well moulded tie beams and king posts with curved and moulded ribs resting on stone canopied Nitches, each of which contains a figure and is supported by a grotesque corbel. The Arcade, although evidently coeval with the Decorated Aisles, gives the impression of a later character, especially is this noticeable in the design of the caps and bases and the free use of the battlement for decorative purposes. The Pulpit is Jacobean or later, elaborately carved and finished with a canopy. It rests on a pedestal of earlier date. The Font is good coeval with the earlier portions of the Church, octagonal with cusped panels, the mouldings enriched with the four leaved flower. Each panel contains blank shields, the shaft has crocketted ogee Nitches on each face. Angels with extended wings are sculptured at each angle beneath the bowl.

The Aisles are very fine and at a glance would seem to be of earlier date than the Nave Arcade. There are three good Decorated windows in the south wall with traceried heads beneath nearly flat segmental arches. A broad arcade runs along the

THE SOUTH AISLE

OUTSIDE

INSIDE

 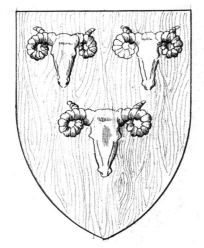 

Shields on the misereries of the Choir Stalls

 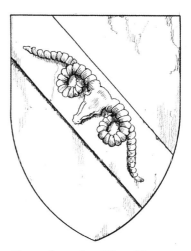

Slab to Sackville Wade 1676   Carved on the West Doorway

south wall inside with well moulded segmental arches enclosing the windows. These arches rest on circular shafts in plan (see sketch) finished with Decorated 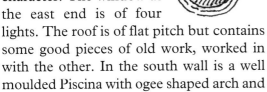 caps with bases of earlier character. The window at the east end is of four lights. The roof is of flat pitch but contains some good pieces of old work, worked in with the other. In the south wall is a well moulded Piscina with ogee shaped arch and label finished with a finial.

The North Aisle is similar to the south. The roof is modern framed in oak with moulded principals and purlins. There is no Piscina. At the west end stands a modern Lectern and an old parish chest. Externally the aisles have bold gabled buttresses with moulded angles and embattled parapet with a broad moulding below enriched with ball flower and leaf ornament. Fine grotesque gargoyles rest on the gables of the buttresses.

The South Porch is particularly fine, with a richly moulded archway and shafted jambs. The side windows are also well moulded and finished with shafts all similar in character with the arcade inside, the early form of the bases especially noticeable. The two side buttresses are formed by engaged shafts rising to the embattled parapet from which are octagonal shafted pinnacles, the parapet is of similar design to that of the aisle.

The Tower is of Decorated date finished with a broach Spire with two-light Belfry windows with quatrefoil in the head and transomed. The West Door and Window are Perpendicular insertions, the former square headed with canopies in the jambs. Above is a vesica shaped moulding with sculpture of the Virgin clothed with the Sun and standing on the Moon. On the doorway are also sculptured these coats.
1. Three crowns (Ely).
2. On a bend a rams head affronté.
The door and hinges are original.

223

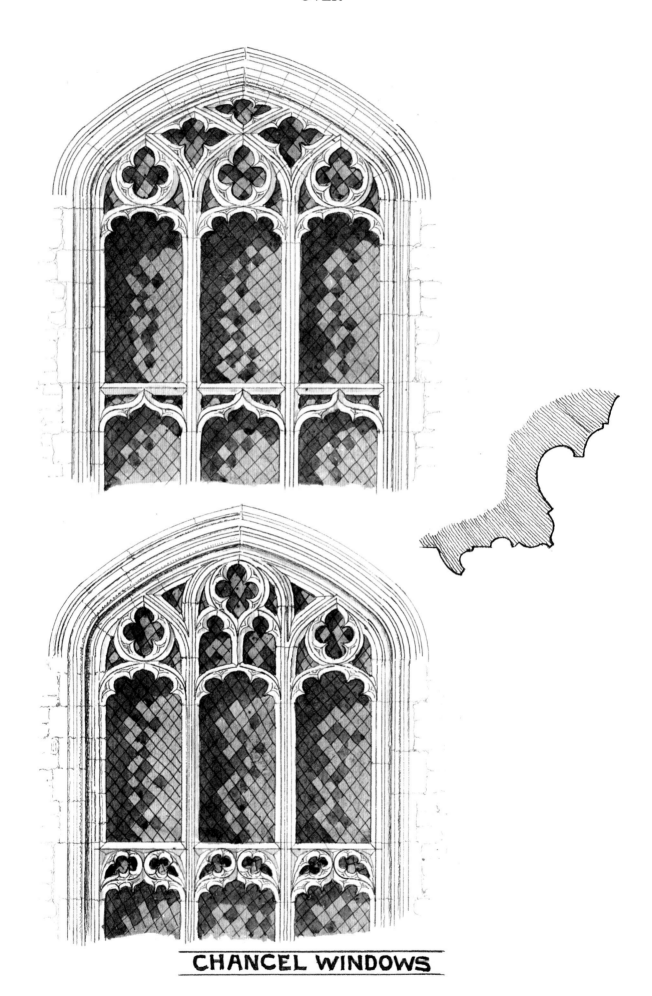

CHANCEL WINDOWS

Bells. The Belfry contains six bells and a Sanctus Bell with these inscriptions.
1. 1819.
2 & 3. Robt. Taylor and sons founders 1819.
4. Robert Adams Overseer 1819.
5. Robt. Taylor and Son St. Neots recast this peal May 28. 1819. Levitt Inglett and Ingle Robinson Churchwardens.
6. I to the Church the living call and to the grave I summons all.
Weight of Tenor 14cwt.

Notes.

This Church is peculiar on account of the early forms of mouldings exhibited in juxtaposition with others of later character. The whole was evidently built at one period, c.1330, notwithstanding, the bases of the Aisle Arcades are of pure Early English character. In the 15th century the church underwent some amount of restoration, the Chancel windows were renewed but some of the original mouldings were retained. This conservatism rarely found in the Middle Ages is also noticeable in the Piscina in the Chancel. There were formerly Chantries of The Holy Trinity, Blessed Virgin Mary, St. Catherine and St. Nicholas.

The South Porch, South Aisle window and buttress are engraved in Rickmans "Gothic Architecture" with the following, respectively assigned, c.1328, c.1350, c.1300. They are really contemporary, probably c.1330. The Font is engraved in Simpsons Fonts.

Inscriptions.

For so fine a Church the inscriptions are extremely meagre. In the Chancel on a slab on the north side surmounted by this coat. A saltire between four escallops (Wade) impaling. A fess ermine between three mullets.

HERE LIES INTERRED THE BODY'S OF SACKVIIIE WADE ESQVI^R LORD OF THIS MANNOVR WHO DIED ON THE FOVRTEEN DAY OF JANUARY 1676 AND ALSO OF MARGARET HIS WIFE WHO DIED ON THE SEAVENTH DAY OF THE SAME MONETH 1676.

On the south side on a slab.

HERE LYETH THE BODY
OF ROBERT WEST GENT
WHO DECEASED MARCH Y^e 11
& WAS BURIED Y^e 18th
Anno { Domini 1683
{ Ætat: Suæ 60

In the South Aisle.

Here Lieth the Body of
ANN Wife of
NEWMAN PEARSON Gent
who departed this life Oct
in the Year of our Lord 171(2?)
and in the . . . year of her age.

In the North Aisle.

Sacred to the memory of
Elizabeth
the beloved wife of
Willm̃ Ingle Robinson
who died Dec. 10th 1835
aged 48 years.

NAVE ARCADE

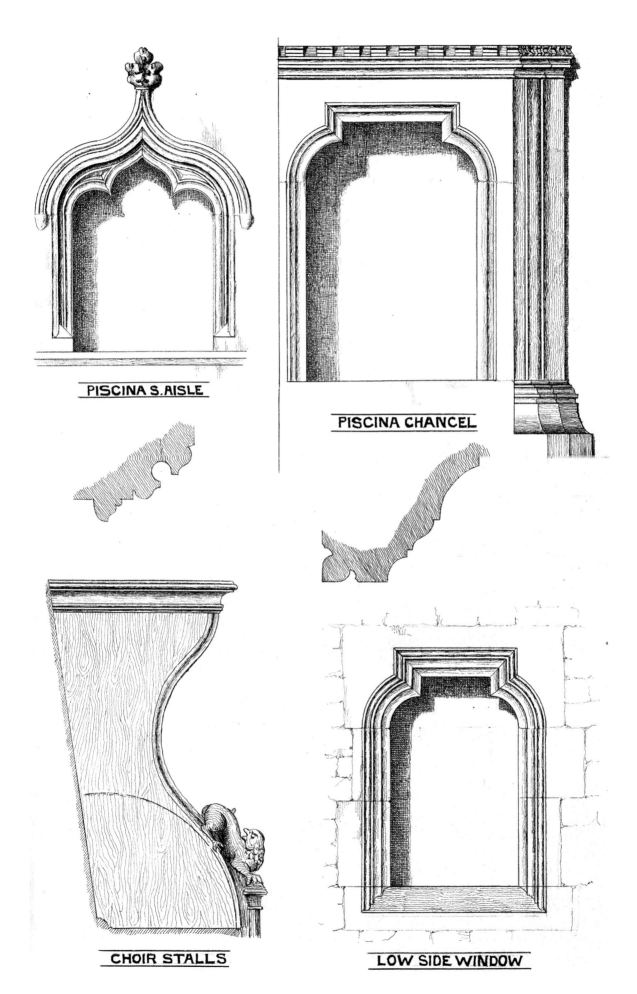

PISCINA S. AISLE

PISCINA CHANCEL

CHOIR STALLS

LOW SIDE WINDOW

OVER CHURCH

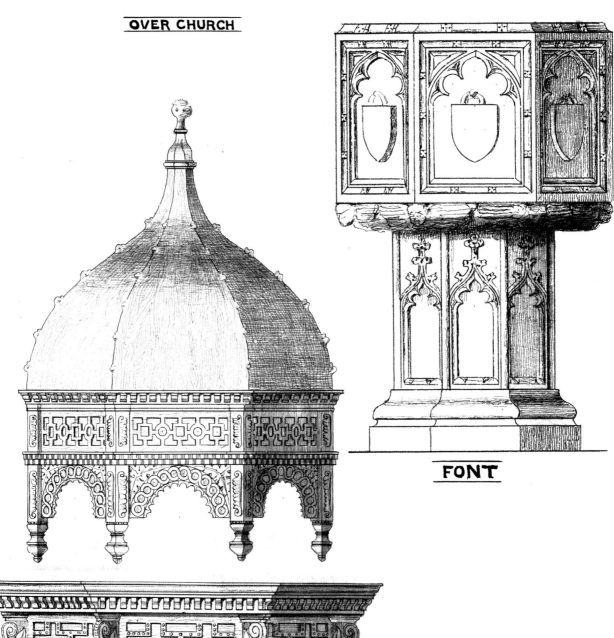

FONT

THE PULPIT

PAMPISFORD

The Church.

The Church is dedicated to St. John Baptist and consists of Chancel, Nave, North Aisle, South Porch and West Tower with a lead Spire.

The Church has been ruined by the restorer. On the exterior not an original stone remains saving perhaps some windows in the Chancel and with the exception of the Arcade but little within. The architect employed at the Restoration, was G. Goldie.

The Chancel is completely carpeted hiding whatever inscriptions there may be on the floor. There is one step at the Chancel Arch, and three to the Altar. The oldest portion of the Chancel is of the 13th century, a lancet on the north side. The East Window is Perpendicular of three lights; there are two square headed Perpendicular windows on the south and a Priests Door of Decorated date. The Sanctuary walls are lined with modern Gothic panelling and a cusped arcade above, also modern. The face of the walls inside is of rubble workpointed. In the south wall is a Piscina of Perpendicular date. The roof is plastered. Against the north wall is an old Perpendicular Altar Tomb with cusped panels and shields on the sides but the brass inscription has disappeared. The Sedilia is modern, made of oak of poor design. In the Sanctuary is an old chair the back of which is carved in relief, the carving is rude. It represents Abraham offering Isaac. The Chancel Arch is of Decorated date, above it is a corbel. The Screen is of late Perpendicular character of poor design, the opening to the Rood Loft is on the north side with a four centered archway.

Carved Tympanum over the South Doorway.

Pampisford Church as it is today.

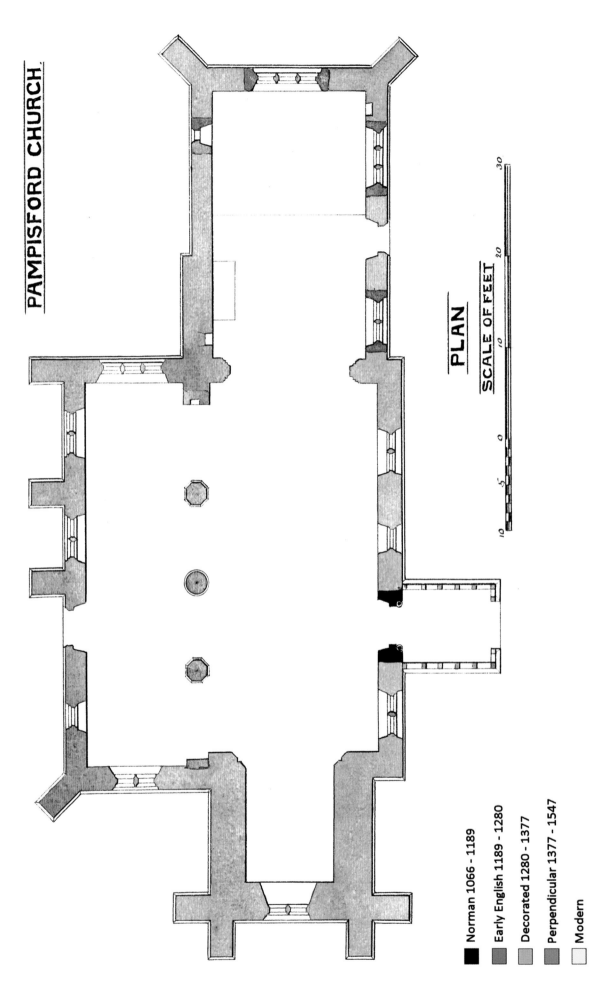

PAMPISFORD CHURCH.

PLAN

SCALE OF FEET

Norman 1066 - 1189

Early English 1189 - 1280

Decorated 1280 - 1377

Perpendicular 1377 - 1547

Modern

The Chancel as seen from the Nave.

The South Porch.

The Nave consists of four arches of late Norman or transitional date, pointed in form and without mouldings. Two of the piers are octagonal, the central one circular, the caps and bases are of the plainest description, in the east respond is a Nitch. There are three windows of Decorated character on the south, modern insertions, and a Norman doorway with sculptured tympanum. All the woodwork is modern of poor Gothic character. The roof is modern with arched braces and moulded collars with wall pieces resting on shafts with elaborately carved heads and corbels.

The Font has an octagonal bowl standing on a square pedestal, late Norman, probably coeval with the Nave Arcade. It is furnished with an elaborate modern cover of carved oak with crockets and finial representing the Baptism of our Lord.

The Porch is modern of timber with elaborately traceried sides.

Parkers Topography, 1848, gives the windows both of Nave and Aisles as Perpendicular.

The North Aisle has three Decorated windows and a door in the north wall, all modern insertions, a two-light Decorated window to the west and a three-light in the eastern wall. This is enclosed beneath a wide arch the width of the Aisle having Decorated caps and mouldings, formerly the entrance to a Chapel or Sacristy. This window is modern nor did there ever exist a Decorated window here as the blocked up arch plainly shews. The old window, if any, was in all probability a Perpendicular one inserted at the time the arch was blocked. The roof of this aisle is modern.

The Tower is of Decorated date with a wide Arch with well moulded caps and an opening above it. The West Window and Belfry windows are of two lights. The Tower is embattled and finished with a small lead Spire.

Bells. In the Belfry are four bells with these inscriptions.
1. and 2. Thomas Mears London fecit 1841.
3. C. & G. Mears founders London 1848.
4. J. Eayre Fecit 1743.
   I. H. S. Nazarenus Rex Judeorum.

Glass. The lancet in the Chancel is filled with modern stained glass. The easternmost window of the Nave is by Favell and Ellis of Cambridge and has this inscription.

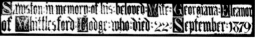

NAVE ARCADE

CHANCEL WINDOWS

FONT

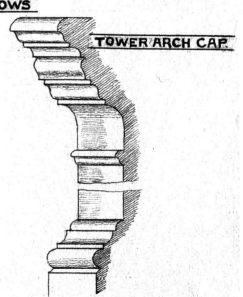

TOWER ARCH CAP.

Inscriptions.

There are no inscriptions visible in the Chancel. In the North Aisle is this tablet with a coat of arms. Quarterly 1 & 4. Per pale gules and azure three demi lions passant gardant or. (Hamond). 2 & 3 gules on a chevron argent three mullets sable (Carr) impaling. Ermine a chevron azure charged with three crosses flory or between three falcons ppr. (Maling).

SACRED
TO THE MEMORY OF
MARGARET,
THE LAMENTED WIFE OF
WILLIAM PARKER HAMOND ESQᴿᴱ
OF PAMPISFORD HALL,
AND YOUNGEST DAUGHTER OF THE LATE
JOHN MALING ESQᴿᴱ OF THE GRANGE, COUNTY
OF DURHAM;
WHO DEPARTED THIS LIFE
28ᵀᴴ JUNE 1845.

Over the East Window of the North Aisle this hatchment. Quarterly 1. Hamond. 2. Argent a stag passant gules on a canton azure a galley or (Parker). 3. Argent a mullet sable. (Ashton). 4. Carr, impaling Maling as above.

Above the North Door within a florid modern Gothic canopy.

+ SACRED
TO THE MEMORY
OF
WILLIAM PARKER HAMOND ESQᴿᴱ
OF HALING HOUSE SURRY
WHO DEPATED THIS LIFE
SEPTEMBER 4ᵀᴴ 1812, AGED 54 YEARS,
OF
MARY HIS WIFE,
DAUGHTER OF SIR ROBERT CARR, BART.
WHO DIED OCTᴿ 28ᵀᴴ 1850. AGED 82 YEARS.
AND OF
MARY ELIZABETH THEIR DAUGHTER
WHO DIED SEPᴿ. 21ˢᵀ 1794, AGED 3 YEARS.

Over the west window North Aisle.
SACRED TO THE MEMORY OF
CAROLINE,
THE BELOVED AND DEEPLY LAMENTED WIFE OF
RODERICK MACKENZIE, ESQᴿᴱ
OF FLOWERBURN, ROSS-SHIRE,
AND DAUGHTER OF Mᴿˢ PARKER HAMOND
OF PAMPISFORD ;
ON THE TWENTIETH OF OCTOBER, 1841,
AGED 22 YEARS.

On the south wall of the Chancel outside on a tablet.

Nearby beneath this tablet
are deposited the remains
of Richd Walter Nash
who departed August 26ᵗʰ 1806
aged 62 years.
A better friend and parent ne'er was man
his feelings from his manners smoothly ran
His pity gave e'er charity began
Also Martha Nash
daughter of the above
who departed July 15ᵗʰ 1790
aged 17 years
Mary Ann
daughter of William and Frances Nash
of Abington
who died March 10ᵗʰ 1822
aged 17 years
and the above named Frances Nash who
departed this life at Abington October 1ˢᵗ
1820 64 years of age.
The said William Nash
son of Richard Wallis Nash
departed this life at Tramore
County of Waterford Ireland June 3ʳᵈ 1847
78 years of age his remains deposited in
the Churchyard of that Parish.

Coat of Maling from Stained Glass window

233

Pedigree of Hamond of Pampisford Hall

Sir William Hamond Knt. of Carshalton ╤ Mary . . .
a South Sea Director ob. 1747 æt. 77.

Peter ob. 1753.   William 1 son ╤ Anne dau. of John Parker Citizen of London   John ob. 1759.
Turkey Merchant   she died 1736.

Cordwill 2 son   1 William of ╤ Elizabeth his cousin dau. of   3 Peter ob. 1794 ╤ Anne Jarman
drowned at   Carshalton   William Parker Esq. by   in Bloomsbury Sq.
Tooling 1760   ob. 1777.   Eliz. relict of Edward Sringer
Esq. of Haling and dau. of John   Anne = Somerset Davies Esq. of
Parker Esq. and Elizabeth Ashton.   Croft Castle Co. Hereford.

Edmond 2.   Peter Ashton 3. Rector   4. Francis Thomas Rector of Widford = Maria dau. of Col.
of Widford Herts &   and Quidenham Norf. ob. 1824   Lovelace of
S. Mimms, Middlesex   leaving a son and daughter.   Quidenham.
ob. 1806

1. William Parker of Haling ╤ mar. 1790 Mary dau. of Sir Robert Carr Bart &
niece of Sir William Carr of Etal Co. Northumb.

2. Robert Carr   3. Edmund Glyn   4. Peter General = Christina Mary   5. Francis b. 1790 Mib.
14th Dragoons   Rector of Widford   Madras Artillery,   dau. of Lieut.   drowned off Winchelsea.
ob. 1837.   Herts, ob. 1826.   ob. 1859   Col. Bird.
leaving issue.   6. George b. 1804 an officer
in India mar. & left issue.

7. Henry Rector of Widford mar. and left issue.   1. Isabella Jane mar.   2. Louisa Grace mar.

William Parker of Haling house Surrey and ╤ mar. 1824 Margaret dau. of John Maling Esqre
Pampisford Hall J.P. for Herts and J.P. and   of the Grange Durham and Relict of
D.L. for Cambs. High Sheriff 1852-3.   Robert Nicholson Esqre of Bradley.
born 24 Nov. 1793, died 1873.

William Parker b. 3 Aug. 1827, Barrister at Law.
J.P. and D.L. for Cambridge, died Nov. 1884 unmarried.

Arms. Per pale Gules and azure three demi lions passant gardant or.
Crest. A wolfs head erased quarterly or and azure. Vis fortibus arma.

Note. The pellets in the coat of Carr should be mullets.
The bezants in the coat of Maling should be crosses moline.

RAMPTON

The Church.

The Church is dedicated to All Saints and consists of Chancel, Nave, South Aisle, Porch and West Tower. The Church is small but has interesting features; the interior is unrestored and the exterior but slightly.

<u>The Chancel</u> is of 14th century date with two good traceried windows on each side. The original East Window is blocked and a Churchwarden Window with wooden mullions inserted. There are no steps at the Chancel Arch and but one to the Sanctuary. The floor is tiled, the ceiling plastered, the tie beams and wall plates visible are moulded. Below the south west window is a small low side opening. There is a good cusped and richly moulded Piscina on the south with two basins and on the north a square Aumbry fitted with a modern door. On the north side beneath a well moulded archway of ogee form with crocketted label lies an old stone effigy of a knight, the legs are crossed, the right hand clasps his sword partly drawn from the sheath. The sculpture is defaced and no bearings are decipherable on the shield. The figure is encased

in mail, the right elbow resting on foliage of graceful conventional character, the feet rest on a lion. Over the mail is a surcoat falling in folds over the legs, the head is encased in a coif de maille.

N.E. VIEW.

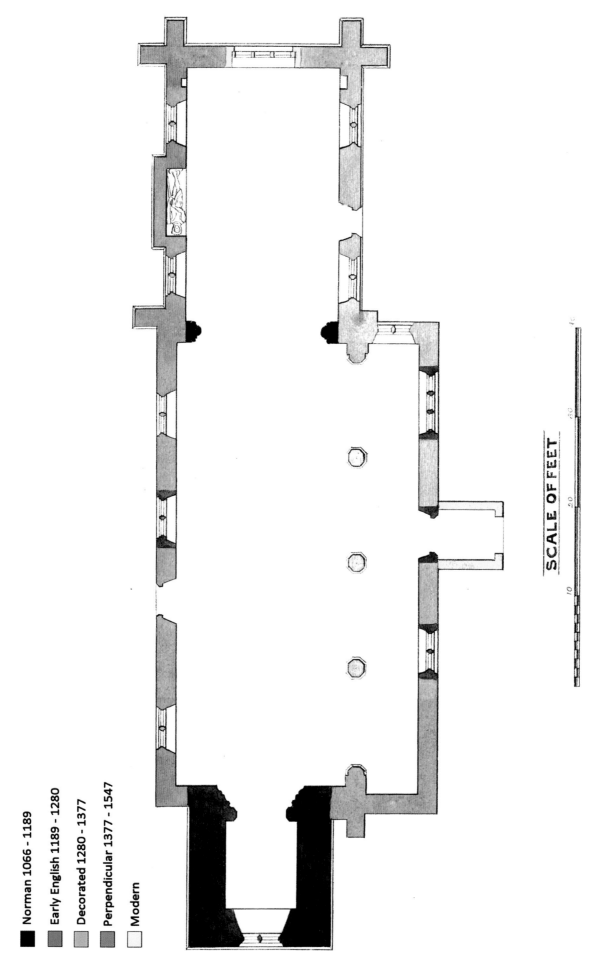

Norman 1066 - 1189

Early English 1189 - 1280

Decorated 1280 - 1377

Perpendicular 1377 - 1547

Modern

SCALE OF FEET

S.E. VIEW

Judging from the armour and the character of the sculptured foliage under the elbow, the figure is of earlier date than the canopy under which it lies, the latter being of mid 14th century date, c.1340. The effigy may possibly be that of Robert de Lisle who held Rampton, c.1260, (Cambridgeshire Fines). When the Chancel was rebuilt the effigy was taken from the earlier Chancel and placed in its present position. The original Chancel Arch still remains, pointed in form with scalloped caps of the late Norman period.

The Nave was originally Norman, portions of which doubtlessly still remain. In the 14th century when the Chancel was rebuilt, a South Aisle was added and windows inserted in the north wall. The Arcade consists of four arches on octagonal columns finished with well moulded caps. The arches display a double hollow moulding stopped above the capitals. The central window on the north side is of debased Perpendicular character, square headed,

the other two of 14th century date with good tracery. The easternmost has a small narrow Nitch in the eastern splay. There are some remains of original oak benches with square ends. The roof is Perpendicular framed with moulded tie beams and queen posts. The Pulpit with sounding board is of Jacobean date. The Font has a round bowl mounted on a small octagonal Perpendicular Font of clunch which serves for a base. The Nave roof is thatched with reed.

The South Aisle has two Perpendicular windows and a door, the latter with quatrefoils in the spandrils and a Nitch above. The East Window is of two lights of 14th century date. There is a small Perpendicular Piscina. The South Porch is of brick of 18th century date.

The Tower is unbuttressed, of Perpendicular date, of poor design and with a single-light Belfry window. It is embattled and finished with a diminutive Spire. The Tower Arch is well moulded.

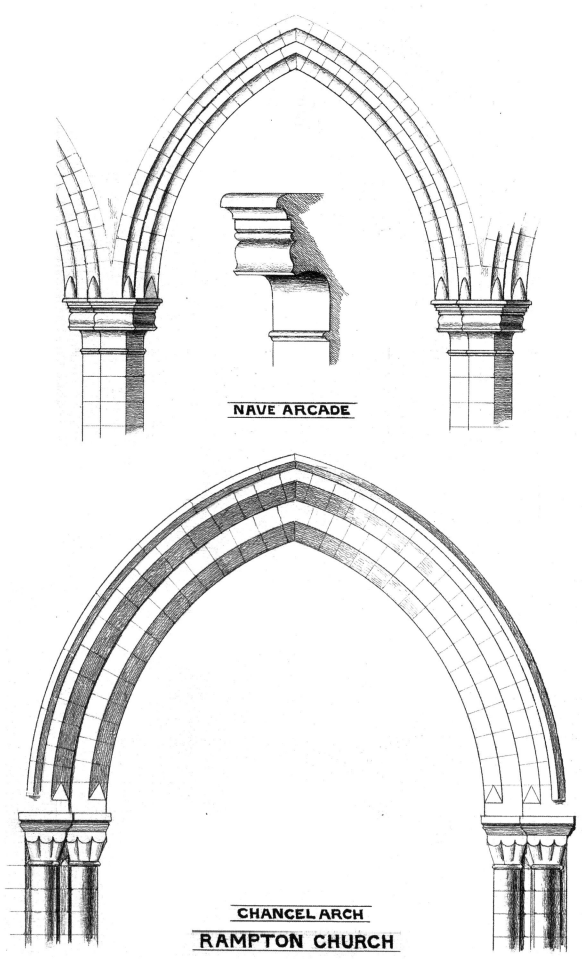

NAVE ARCADE

CHANCEL ARCH

RAMPTON CHURCH

Bells. In the Belfry are three bells with these inscriptions.
1. Thomas Newman made mee.
   J. Rule. J. Marshall C.W. 1713.
2. Sancte Oswalde ora pro nobis.
3. Sancta Maria ora pro nobis.

Two and three are in old English capitals and each have two stamps before the letters, one a pattern the other a bell on a shield between the letters T.B.

Glass. There are slight remains of old stained glass in the tracery of the eastern and westernmost windows of the Nave, in the former of debased character, perhaps early in the 19th century. The East Window of the South Aisle has some good 14th century glass including the Maria Monogram Crowned. This was inserted at the restoration in 1910. At the same time some of the tracery of the original five-light Decorated East Window was recovered together with fragments of Norman and later remains, now deposited in the Tower.

Inscriptions.

These are few.
In the Chancel are these slabs.

1.
> Here Lieth ÿ
> Body of ANN
> HOBBSON who died
> June ÿ 6th 1733.
> Here also was
> Interr'd ÿ body
> of ELIZABETH
> ÿ Daughter of
> JOHN and ALICE
> HOBBSON
> died Aug. ÿ 12. 1734.

2.
> Here also lies Interr'd
> DICKMAN HOBSON,
> who died May ÿ 18th
> 1747
> Aged 9 years.
> And also ÿ body of
> DICKMAN NEAVE
> Who died June ÿ 18th
> 1717.

3.
> In memory of
> JOHN HOBSON
> who died February ÿ 8th 1742.
> Aged 36 years
> and also of
> JOHN HOBSON
> his son
> who died April ÿ 8th 1773
> aged 37.

4.
> HERE LYETH INTERED THE
> BODY OF IOANE STVBBIN
> WIFE TO EDMUND STVBBIN
> LATE RECTOR OF THIS PARISH
> WHO DEPARTED THIS LIFE
> THE 21 OF IVLY IN THE YEARE
> ANNO-DOMINI 1661 AND IN
> THE 56 YEAR OF HER AGE.

5.
> HERE lie the Remains of
> FRANCES
> Late Wife of the Revd Mr MEADES,
> Rector of this Parish.
> She departed *this* Life,
> In a well-grounded Hope of a *better*
> On the *30th* of *July 1762*,
> And in the *55th* Year of her Age.
> *She was*
> *A truly excellent Woman.*
> Also
> of WILLIAM MEADES Clerk
> the diligent & faithfull Pastor of ÿ Church
> forty four Years
> Whose humane & benevolent Disposition
> gained him Respect whilst living,
> and occasioned his Death to be lamented.
> He died 2d of May 1780,
> Aged 80 Years.

6.
> Hic jacet Elizabetha
> Fleetwood Neville
> Hujus Ecclesiæ Rectoris
> Conjux Dilectissima
> Obijt Septembris 2o
> Anno {Dom: 1710
> {Ætatis 43o

7.
> Beneath this Stone
> Lies the Body of
> John Rulf
> Who departed this Life
> November ye 16
> 17..4.
> Aged 77 Years.

In the Nave is the matrix of a good Decorated cross with border inscription. "Notes on Cambridgeshire 1827" gives the following inscription in old Lombardic capitals, probably the inscription on the above mentioned border.

> Syre Nicholas de Hunting . . . e gist ici Dieu qel alme syt merci.

There is another slab in the Chancel with a matrix of a small brass.

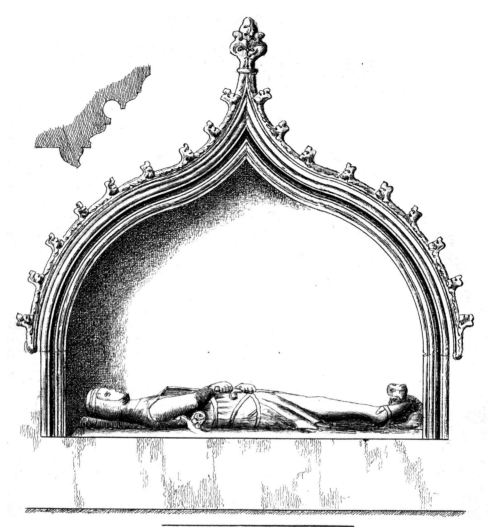

EFFIGY IN CHANCEL

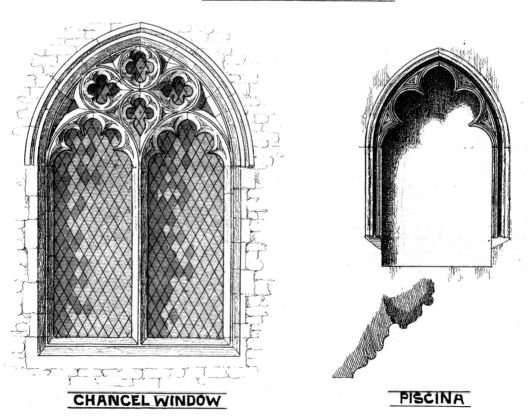

CHANCEL WINDOW   **PISCINA**

TEVERSHAM

March 1st 1883.

The Church.

The Church is dedicated to All Saints and consists of Chancel, Nave, North and South Aisles, South Porch and West Tower.

<u>The Exterior.</u> The Church was ruthlessly restored apparently in 1882 and again in 1888 - 1891. There was an earlier restoration in 1863. The south side of the Chancel has been restored but the stonework of the windows is original. There are three windows all of Decorated character, the easternmost square headed of two lights, the central of two lights with a quatrefoil in the head. The westernmost is a low side single light window with a cusped head, the lower portion is blocked. The east end is entirely modern, with a three-light window. On the north side are two windows and a Priests Door. Nave and Aisles originally Early English but with Decorated windows inserted. On the south are two two-light Decorated windows with plain cusped heads enclosed beneath segmental arches, these are much restored. The south inner door to the Porch is Early English with shafts in the jambs and carved caps but most of the work is modern. The East Window in the South Aisle is two-light Decorated. The North Aisle has two windows to the north, one of which is a small single light with cusped head, the sill being about 18 inches from the ground. The North Door is of earlier character. There are windows to east and west. There are no Clerestory windows. The South Porch is modern, of poor design with a simply chamfered doorway. There is no gable cross or side windows.

The Tower is Perpendicular finished with stepped battlements, the buttresses terminate at the Belfry stage. The Belfry windows are of two lights traceried, the West Window is of three lights. When the Tower was added to the Church the westernmost arcade of the Nave was demolished, thus curtailing the length of the Church westward.

<u>The Interior.</u> The Chancel was restored in 1863 at which time an arcade was built against the east wall. The roof is octagonal with moulded ribs and carved angels in the cornice. The choir stalls are modern with elbows of good design. The Sedilia and Piscina on the south side are very good, Perpendicular, but somewhat defaced. The former consists of three ogee arches of different design, crocketted and rising against a stone back of pierced tracery work. The design of the easternmost arch is richest but much defaced. At the back of the seats are the remains of colour, a dark red ground, semé of trefoils and **tȝc** in chocolate. This was discovered

Teversham Church as it is today.

241

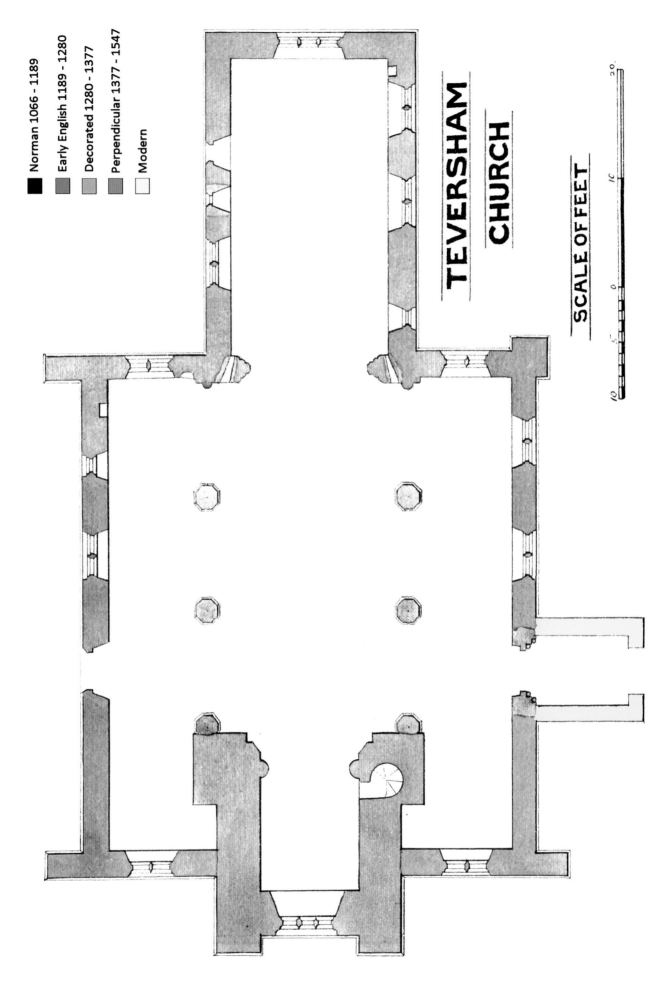

in 1882. The Screen between Chancel and Nave is good Perpendicular, the tracery work fairly perfect. The cornice however is poor and modern. The close panels below, on the south are Jacobean, those on the north original.

The Nave Arcade is good Early English, the arches moulded with a double hollow 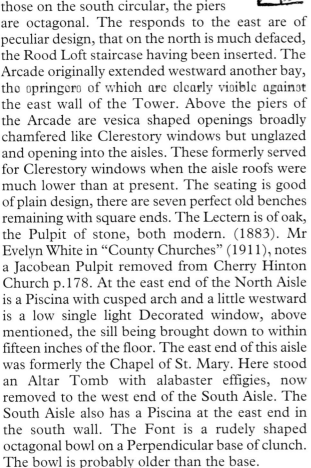 stopped above the capitals. These are carved with foliage. The abaci of those on the north are octagonal, of those on the south circular, the piers are octagonal. The responds to the east are of peculiar design, that on the north is much defaced, the Rood Loft staircase having been inserted. The Arcade originally extended westward another bay, the springers of which are clearly visible against the east wall of the Tower. Above the piers of the Arcade are vesica shaped openings broadly chamfered like Clerestory windows but unglazed and opening into the aisles. These formerly served for Clerestory windows when the aisle roofs were much lower than at present. The seating is good of plain design, there are seven perfect old benches remaining with square ends. The Lectern is of oak, the Pulpit of stone, both modern. (1883). Mr Evelyn White in "County Churches" (1911), notes a Jacobean Pulpit removed from Cherry Hinton Church p.178. At the east end of the North Aisle is a Piscina with cusped arch and a little westward is a low single light Decorated window, above mentioned, the sill being brought down to within fifteen inches of the floor. The east end of this aisle was formerly the Chapel of St. Mary. Here stood an Altar Tomb with alabaster effigies, now removed to the west end of the South Aisle. The South Aisle also has a Piscina at the east end in the south wall. The Font is a rudely shaped octagonal bowl on a Perpendicular base of clunch. The bowl is probably older than the base.

The only fragments of stained glass are to be seen in the West Window.

The Belfry contains one bell with this inscription, "Taylor St. Neots founder 1799."

In Blomefields time there were three bells of which two bore inscriptions in old English letters "Sancta Katerina ora pro nobis." and "Sancta Maria ora pro nobis."

Inscriptions.
The monumental inscriptions are few and with one exception of little interest.

In the Chancel are some slabs covered by choir stalls, one dated 1834. On a stone on the south side is this referring to the above.

THESE STONES IN MEMORY OF
CATHERINE, ELLEN AND ANNE ASHLEY

WERE REMOVED FROM THE EAST END
OF THIS CHANCEL, ON ITS
RESTORATION A. D. 1862
ANN ASHLEY
APRIL 3. 1852
AGED 68.

On the north wall of the Chancel is a tablet with this.

NEAR THIS PLACE
ARE DEPOSITED THE REMAINS OF THE
REV^D JOHN BROCKLEBANK, B.D.
RECTOR OF TEVERSHAM, AND OF WILLINGHAM,
BOTH IN THE COUNTY OF CAMBRIDGE.
HE SUFFERED FROM THE EFFECTS OF
PARALYSIS FOR SIXTEEN YEARS
AND DIED IN PIOUS RESIGNATION TO THE
DIVINE WILL,
THE 26TH DAY OF MAY A.D. 1843 ;
IN THE 76TH YEAR OF HIS AGE.

*Such as he was the Last Great
Day will tell.*

In the North Aisle is a slab, almost illegible, to Thomas Heyrick or Neyrick dated 1786 and 1800.

At the west end of the South Aisle is a fine monument with two recumbent figures in alabaster. The tomb is formed with different coloured marbles and on the sides are these coats.
1. A lion rampant.
2. Of fourteen quarterings.

1. A lion rampant debruised by a bend raguly (Stewart).
2. A fess chequy.
3. Three boars heads couped.
4. A lion rampant.
5. A chevron between three roundels.
6. A lion rampant gardant crowned.
7. A tower embattled.
8. An eagle displayed double headed.
9. A cross fleury between four martlets.
10. . . . .
11. Three lions passant paleways.
12. A lion rampant within a bordure engrailed.
13. A chevron between three lions faces.
14. A griffin segreant. Impaling . . . as above.

Note that these quarterings differ from those given in the Visitation of Cambridgeshire 1619.

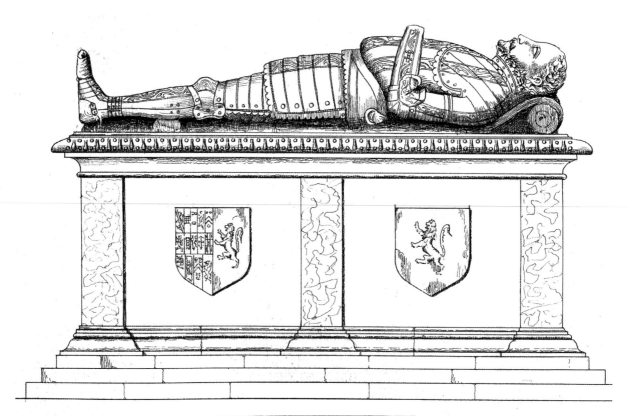

EDWARD STEWARD, 1596.

S. DOORWAY.

"Hoc memoriæ monumentum pietatis ergo
posuit Thomas Jermy."
"Hic jacet Edwardus cui magna ex stripe
Stywardus."
"Cognomen Scoticis majoribus armiger ortus."
"Convenere fides que pietas veneranda
sonectus."
"Certævere genus pietas prudentia juris."
"Tam bene transactæ vitæ laus et (f) ama
manebunt."
"Una hic Margeriæ conduntur conjugis assa."
"Fæmina chara bonis Kyrberi sanguinis hæres."
"Unanimes vixere decem ter tresque per annos."
"Natorumque trium tot natarumque parentes."
"Hæres patris erat, spes sola Johanna superstes."
"Sponsa Thomæ Jermy quem sternmatis ejus a
vita."
"Protulit amicerum sedes Suffolcica Brightwell."

In the middle of the Nave is a black marble slab
with this inscription and arms. Three lions
rampant gardant in a chief. Crest. A tiger sejant
ducally gorged. (Rant). Impaling. A lion rampant
gardant. Crest. A griffon statant with wings
displayed (Jermy). Note. The dexter side of the
shield is much worn and as it lies uncovered in the
passage of the Nave will soon be obliterated.

Rant   Jermy
Slab to John Rant 1696

For Remembrance of IOHN RANT
Efq & IOHAN his only wife,
She was daughter & Coheyrefs of
EDWARD 2ᵈ son of Sʳ THOMAS IERMY
Kᵗ of ẙ Bath & was born here in *TEVERSHAM*
May 29ᵗʰ 1636 & buried Oct: 22ᵈ 1663.
He was 2ᵈ son of ROGER RANT of
SWAFHAM-PRIORY in this County Esq.
Baptised Sept: 20ᵗʰ 1626.
He was Batchelor of Civill Lawes, Barifter
at comon Law & Iuftice of ẙ Peace.
He died Oct: 30ᵗʰ 1696 leaving behind
him 2 Children IOHN & ELIZABETH.

Glass fragments in West Window

WINDOW & PISCINA N. AISLE.

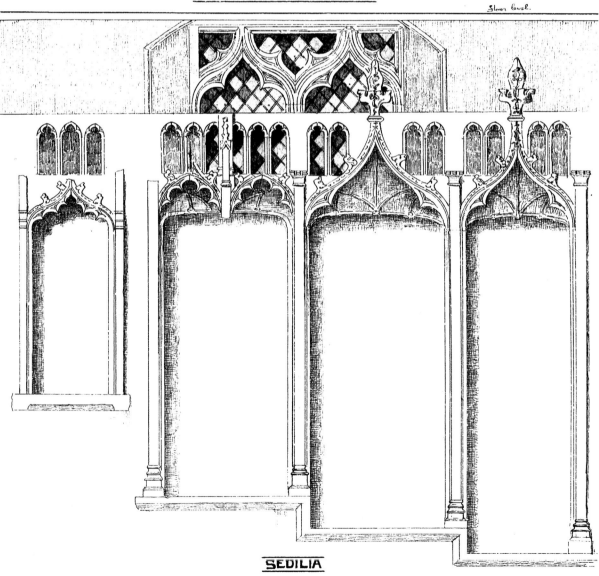

SEDILIA

Engaine of Teversham

Sir Robert Engaine Aº 10 Ric. I (1198-9) et 10 regis Johis (1208) ⊤

William Engaine temp. 8 Hen. III (1223) ⊤

Robert Engaine 53 Hen. III (1268) ⊤

William Engaine de Teversham in Co. Cantabr. ⊤

John de Engraine de Teversham in Co. Cambr. ob.37 Edward III (1362-3) ⊤ Joane dau. of . . . . .

Sir John Engraine Knt. ⊤ Margaret cozen and heir	Thomas.	Katherine mar.	Eliz. mar
36 Edwd. III (1361-2) fuit of John de la Hay.		Sir John	Grey of
æt. 24 anoru. ad mortem		Burgh Knt.	Wilton.
patris an. 37. Edw III.			

Joane dau. and coheir of Sir John Engaine   William Engaine.   Mary mar. Bliton.
4 Ric. II (1380), mar. Sir Baldwin St. George Knt.   11 Hen. IV (1409).
         4 Ric. II. ob 1425 (vide S. George).

Pedigree of Steward

Arms granted 1596. (Berry) The above coat from the monument of Edward Steward ob.1596.
1 and 2. Stewart.   3. Boreley.   4. Walkfare (elsewhere tinctures differ) 5. Baskerville.   6. Bestney.
7.   8.   9. Spenlow. 10.   11. Fitz Geffrey. 12. Beruen. 13. Blackney. 14.

Nicholas Styward de Well in Com. Norff. Armiger ⊤ Cicelia Baskerville.

Richard of Well   2. Nicholas ⊤ Elizabeth d. of   2. Robert Symon, ⊤ Johanna d. & heir of
  Co. Norf.   . . . Lucas.   Armiger.   Edward Bestney of Soame.

Sir William Steward ⊤ Catherin dau. of Tho.   2. Edward of Teversham ⊤ Margaret d & h. of
  of the Ile of Ely.   Panie of Castell Acre.   ob.1596 bur. Teversham.   Richard Kirby of
                                                    Cambridge Knt.

Catherin.   Sir Tho. Steward Knt. = Bridgett dau. of   Elianor. Elizabeth.   1 wife.
   High Sheriff of Cambridge   John Poole
     & Huntingdon.   of York.   1. Robert.

Thomas s.p.   Elizabeth ob. s.p.   Joane ob. s.p.   Mary ob. s.p.   Joane d. & h. uxor Thomas Jenny
  Edward s.p.   Francis ob. s.p.   Anne ob. s.p.   Knt. of the Bath.

3. Marcus Styward of Stuntney ⊤ Anne d & h of Rob. Hewick   4. Johannes Steward of Morshin ⊤
  in the Ile of Ely.   Doct. of Phissick to   Norff. mar . . . d & h of
               9. Elizabeth. bur. 4 April 1604.   Shouldham of Shouldham.

Sir Symon Steward of Stontney ⊤ Grace dau. of Edward St. Barbe of Ashington Co. Som.

Robert Steward Esq. ob 17 May 1634 ⊤ Mary d. of Sir Thom.   5 son. Thos. Steward of Cambridge
  bur. St. Clements Danes, London.   Reresby of Thriber   1619. mar. Peyton d. of Willm.
                  Co. York.   Allen of Cambridge =

Thomas.   Grace.

WATERBEACH

The Church is dedicated to St. John and consists of Chancel, Clerestoried Nave, Aisles, North Porch and an Embattled Tower with clock and five bells.

The Chancel.

Waterbeach Church as it is today.

WESTERNMOST ARCH NAVE ARCADE

CAP

ARCH MOULD

BASE

WINDOW JAMB

Six Corbels in the North Aisle showing Angels playing musical instruments.

Decorative Pulpit of 1879.

Mosaic Panels on the sides of the Pulpit. The Sermon on the Mount and The Preaching of St. Paul.

Pedigree of Robson

Mr. Robson exhibited a scocheon of these arms thus under written.

"The arms and crest of Thomas, Gyles and Robert Robson, the sons of James Robson late of Cambr. Gent. the which arms and crest I do ratify and confirm to them and their posteritie for ever bearing due differences. Dated this 3rd day of Mar. 1635. Ri. St. George Clarencieux king of arms. Note. This was but a copy and no original, as also that Mr. Robson who made the entry takes James Robson above mentioned to be brother to his grandfather by another mother." (vis. Cambs 1684)

John Robson of Lynn in Norf. ob. circa 1630 = Anne dau. of . . .

1. John Robson of Waterbeach = Mary dau. of William Knight
   ob. 1680 æt. 65.   of Gransden Parva in Cambridgesh.

John Robson of = Sarah dau. of   2. William   4. Yaxley   5. Jeremy of = Mary dau. of
Waterbeach   Nic Marriot of   æt. 36.   ob. inf.   Waterbeach   William Barrs
æt. 37.1684.   Branston Northants. 3. Yaxley   æt. 28. 1684. of Waterbeach.
                                   ob. inf.

2. Dorothy mar. William Knight   3. Mary.   4. Elizabeth.   1. Anne mar. Ric. Ballard
   of Wickin in Cambsh.   citizen of London.

2. Yaxley Robson of   3. James   4. Jeremie Robson = Rebecca dau. of Thomas   Johanna wife
Lynn now living in   Robson   of Waterbeach   Blaney of Barrington   of . . . Peck of
Scotland cœlebs.   ob. cœlebs. ob. 1683.   in Cambridgesh.   Waterbeach.

In the Chancel of Grantchester Church are two slabs with the above arms, one to
"Mrs Anne Robson, Second Daughter of Mr James Robson Alderman & Mayor of Cambridge.
She dyed July 15th 1731 aged 60 years."

The other to
"Mrs Mary Robson Daughter of Mr James Robson (Late Alderman of Cambridge)
died 23. Decemr. 1721 Aged 53 Years."

GREAT WILBRAHAM

The Church is dedicated to St. Nicholas and consists of Chancel, Nave, North and South Transepts, South Porch and Embattled West Tower with Pinnacles, a clock and five bells.

Church Interior.

Font.

CREAT WILBRAHAM CHURCH

S.ELEVATION
SCALE OF FEET.

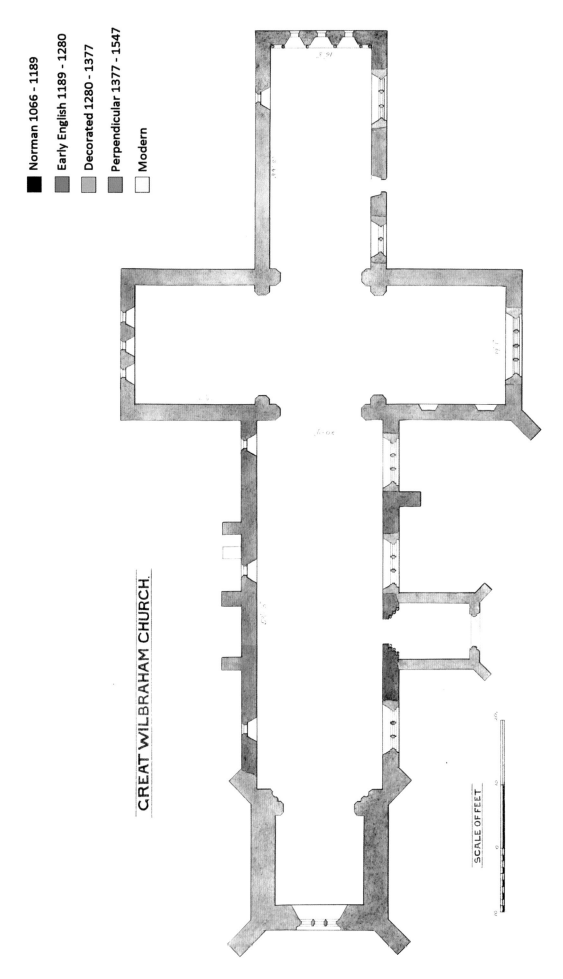

GREAT WILBRAHAM CHURCH.

Norman 1066 - 1189
Early English 1189 - 1280
Decorated 1280 - 1377
Perpendicular 1377 - 1547
Modern

SCALE OF FEET

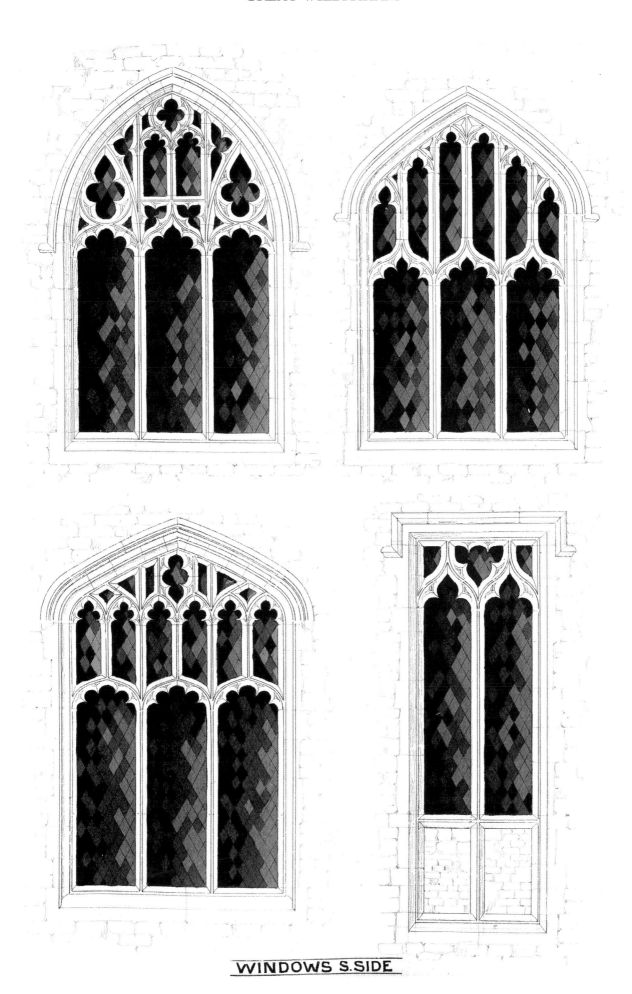

WINDOWS S.SIDE

Memorial and Crest of the Monument to Thomas-Watson Ward on the North wall of the Chancel.

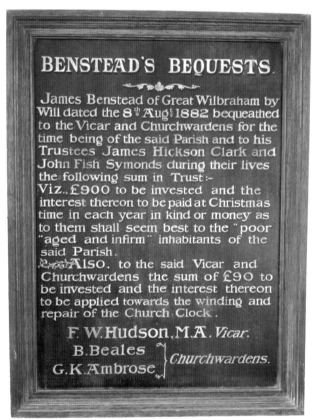

Board detailing the Bequests of James Benstead

Coat above the Memorial to Joannes Ward

INDEX

This Index does not include persons or items mentioned in lists of Fines, Rectors, Vicars or in Family Pedigrees.